ABOUT THIS PUBLICATION

FOR SERVICE ASSISTANCE

Customer Service
1.704.898.0770

North Carolina General Statues is published by The Muliti-Media Group of Greater Charlotte in Charlotte, North Carolina. Copyright 2015 by the Multi-Media Group of Greater Charlotte. This book or parts thereof may not be reproduced in any form, stored in a retrieval system, or transmitted in any form by any means—electronic, mechanical, photocopy, recording or otherwise—without prior written permission of the publisher, except as provided by United States of America copyright law.

The records required by U.S. Code 2257(a) through (c) and the pertinent regulations 28 C.F.R. Cli. 1, Part 75 with respect to this publication and all materials associated with such records are maintained by The Multi-Media Group of Greater Charlotte, Publisher and available for review by Attorney General.

www.visionbooks.org

Copyright © 2015 by MMGGC
All rights reserved!

TID: 5071824
ISBN (10) digit: 1502988380
ISBN (13) digit: 978-1502988386

123-4-56789-01239-Paperback
123-4-56789-01239-Hardback

First Edition

090520140547

Printed in the United States of America

2015 EDITION

North Carolina Criminal Law And Procedure-Pamphlet # 62

Printed In conjunction with the Administration of the Courts

North Carolina Criminal Law and Procedure
Pamphlet Reference Guide

Chapters	Pamphlet
Chapter 1 Civil Procedure	1
Chapter 1 Civil Procedure (Continue)	2
Chapter 1A Rules of Civil Procedure	2
Chapter 1B Contribution.	2
Chapter 1C Enforcement of Judgments.	2
Chapter 1D Punitive Damages.	2
Chapter 1E Eastern Band of Cherokee Indians.	2
Chapter 1F North Carolina Uniform Interstate Depositions and Discovery Act.	2
Chapter 2 - Clerk of Superior Court [Repealed and Transferred.]	3
Chapter 3 - Commissioners of Affidavits and Deeds [Repealed.]	3
Chapter 4 - Common Law	3
Chapter 5 - Contempt [Repealed.]	3
Chapter 5A - Contempt	3
Chapter 6 - Liability for Court Costs	3
Chapter 7 - Courts [Repealed and Transferred.]	3
Chapter 7A – Judicial Department	3
Chapter 7A – Continuation (Judicial Department)	4
Chapter 7A – Continuation (Judicial Department)	5
Chapter 7B - Juvenile Code	5
Chapter 8 - Evidence	6
Chapter 8A - Interpreters for Deaf Persons [Recodified.]	6
Chapter 8B - Interpreters for Deaf Persons	6
Chapter 8C - Evidence Code	6
Chapter 9 - Jurors	6
Chapter 10 - Notaries [Repealed.]	6
Chapter 10A - Notaries [Recodified.]	6
Chapter 10B - Notaries	6
Chapter 11 - Oaths	6
Chapter 12 - Statutory Construction	6
Chapter 13 - Citizenship Restored	6
Chapter 14 - Criminal Law	7
Chapter 14 –Criminal Law (Continuation)	8
Chapter 15 - Criminal Procedure	9
Chapter 15A - Criminal Procedure Act (Continuation)	10
Chapter 15A - Criminal Procedure Act (Continuation)	11
Chapter 15B - Victims Compensation	11
Chapter 15C - Address Confidentiality Program	11
Chapter 16 - Gaming Contracts and Futures	11
Chapter 17 - Habeas Corpus	11

Chapter 17A - Law-Enforcement Officers [Recodified.]	11
Chapter 17B - North Carolina Criminal Justice Education and Training System [Recodified.] Chapter 17C - North Carolina Criminal Justice Education and Training Standards Commission	11 11
Chapter 17D - North Carolina Justice Academy	11
Chapter 17E - North Carolina Sheriffs' Education and Training Standards Commission	11
Chapter 18 - Regulation of Intoxicating Liquors [Repealed.]	12
Chapter 18A - Regulation of Intoxicating Liquors [Repealed.]	12
Chapter 18B - Regulation of Alcoholic Beverages	12
Chapter 18C - North Carolina State Lottery	12
Chapter 19 - Offenses against Public Morals	12
Chapter 19A - Protection of Animals	12
Chapter 20 - Motor Vehicles	13
Chapter 20 - Motor Vehicles (Continuation)	14
Chapter 20 - Motor Vehicles (Continuation)	15
Chapter 20 - Motor Vehicles (Continuation)	16
Chapter 21 - Bills of Lading	17
Chapter 22 - Contracts Requiring Writing	17
Chapter 22A - Signatures	17
Chapter 22B - Contracts Against Public Policy	17
Chapter 22C - Payments to Subcontractors	17
Chapter 23 - Debtor and Creditor	17
Chapter 24 – Interest	17
Chapter 25 – Uniform Commercial Code	18
Chapter 25 – Uniform Commercial Code (Continuation)	19
Chapter 25A – Retail Installment Sales Act	20
Chapter 25B - Credit	20
Chapter 25C - Sales of Artwork	20
Chapter 26 - Suretyship	20
Chapter 27 - Warehouse Receipts [Repealed.]	20
Chapter 28 - Administration [Repealed.]	20
Chapter 28A - Administration of Decedents' Estates	20
Chapter 28B - Estates of Absentees in Military Service	20
Chapter 28C - Estates of Missing Persons	20
Chapter 29 - Intestate Succession	21
Chapter 30 - Surviving Spouses	21
Chapter 31 - Wills	21
Chapter 31A - Acts Barring Property Rights	21
Chapter 31B - Renunciation of Property and Renunciation of Fiduciary Powers Act	21
Chapter 31C - Uniform Disposition of Community Property Rights at Death Act	21
Chapter 32 - Fiduciaries	21
Chapter 32A - Powers of Attorney	21
Chapter 33 - Guardian and Ward [Repealed and Recodified.]	21

Chapter 33A - North Carolina Uniform Transfers to Minors Act	21
Chapter 33B - North Carolina Uniform Custodial Trust Act	21
Chapter 34 - Veterans' Guardianship Act	22
Chapter 35 - Sterilization Procedures	22
Chapter 35A - Incompetency and Guardianship	22
Chapter 36 - Trusts and Trustees [Repealed.]	22
Chapter 36A - Trusts and Trustees	22
Chapter 36B - Uniform Management of Institutional Funds Act [Repealed.]	22
Chapter 36C - North Carolina Uniform Trust Code	22
Chapter 36D - North Carolina Community Third Party Trusts, Pooled Trusts	23
Chapter 36E - Uniform Prudent Management of Institutional Funds Act	23
Chapter 37 - Allocation of Principal and Income [Repealed.]	23
Chapter 37A - Uniform Principal and Income Act	23
Chapter 38 - Boundaries	23
Chapter 38A - Landowner Liability	23
Chapter 39 - Conveyances	23
Chapter 39A - Transfer Fee Covenants Prohibited	23
Chapter 40 - Eminent Domain [Repealed.]	23
Chapter 40A - Eminent Domain	23
Chapter 41 - Estates	23
Chapter 41A - State Fair Housing Act	23
Chapter 42 - Landlord and Tenant	23
Chapter 42A - Vacation Rental Act	23
Chapter 43 - Land Registration	23
Chapter 44 - Liens	24
Chapter 44A - Statutory Liens and Charges	24
Chapter 45 - Mortgages and Deeds of Trust	24
Chapter 45A - Good Funds Settlement Act	24
Chapter 46 - Partition	24
Chapter 47 - Probate and Registration	25
Chapter 47A - Unit Ownership	25
Chapter 47B - Real Property Marketable Title Act	25
Chapter 47C - North Carolina Condominium Act	25
Chapter 47D - Notice of Settlement Act [Expired.]	25
Chapter 47E - Residential Property Disclosure Act	25
Chapter 47F - North Carolina Planned Community Act	25
Chapter 47G - Option to Purchase Contracts	25
Chapter 47H - Contracts for Deed	25
Chapter 48 - Adoptions +	26
Chapter 48A - Minors	26
Chapter 49 - Bastardy	26
Chapter 49A - Rights of Children	26
Chapter 50 - Divorce and Alimony	26
Chapter 50A - Uniform Child-Custody Jurisdiction and	

Enforcement Act	26
Chapter 50B - Domestic Violence	26
Chapter 50C - Civil No-Contact Orders	26
Chapter 51 - Marriage	26
Chapter 52 - Powers and Liabilities of Married Persons	27
Chapter 52A - Uniform Reciprocal Enforcement of Support Act [Repealed.]	27
Chapter 52B - Uniform Premarital Agreement Act	27
Chapter 52C - Uniform Interstate Family Support Act	27
Chapter 53 - Banks	27
Chapter 53A - Business Development Corporations and North Carolina Capital Resource Corporations	28
Chapter 53B - Financial Privacy Act	28
Chapter 54 - Cooperative Organizations	28
Chapter 54A - Capital Stock Savings and Loan Associations [Repealed.]	28
Chapter 54B - Savings and Loan Associations	29
Chapter 54C - Savings Banks	29
Chapter 55 - North Carolina Business Corporation Act	30
Chapter 55A - North Carolina Nonprofit Corporation Act	31
Chapter 55B - Professional Corporation Act	31
Chapter 55C - Foreign Trade Zones	31
Chapter 55D - Filings, Names, and Registered Agents for Corporations, Nonprofit Corporations, and Partnerships	31
Chapter 56 - Electric, Telegraph and Power Companies [Repealed.]	31
Chapter 57 - Hospital, Medical and Dental Service Corporations [Recodified.]	31
Chapter 57A - Health Maintenance Organization Act [Recodified.]	31
Chapter 57B - Health Maintenance Organization Act [Recodified.]	31
Chapter 57C - North Carolina Limited Liability Company Act.	31
Chapter 58 - Insurance.	32
Chapter 58 - Insurance (Continuation)	33
Chapter 58 - Insurance (Continuation)	34
Chapter 58 - Insurance (Continuation)	35
Chapter 58 - Insurance (Continuation)	36
Chapter 58 - Insurance (Continuation)	37
Chapter 58 - Insurance (Continuation)	38
Chapter 58A - North Carolina Health Insurance Trust Commission [Recodified.]	38
Chapter 59 - Partnership.	39
Chapter 59B - Uniform Unincorporated Nonprofit Association Act.	39
Chapter 60 - Railroads and Other Carriers [Repealed and Transferred.]	39
Chapter 61 - Religious Societies	39
Chapter 62 - Public Utilities	39

Chapter 62 - Public Utilities (Continuation)	40
Chapter 62A - Public Safety Telephone Service And Wireless Telephone Service	40
Chapter 63 - Aeronautics	40
Chapter 63A - North Carolina Global TransPark Authority	40
Chapter 64 - Aliens	40
Chapter 65 – Cemeteries	40
Chapter 66 - Commerce and Business	41
Chapter 67 - Dogs	41
Chapter 68 - Fences and Stock Law	41
Chapter 69 - Fire Protection	41
Chapter 70 - Indian Antiquities, Archaeological Resources and Unmarked Human Skeletal Remains Protection	42
Chapter 71 - Indians [Repealed.]	42
Chapter 71A - Indians	42
Chapter 72 - Inns, Hotels and Restaurants	42
Chapter 73 - Mills	42
Chapter 74 - Mines and Quarries	42
Chapter 74A - Company Police [Repealed.]	42
Chapter 74B - Private Protective Services Act [Repealed.]	42
Chapter 74C - Private Protective Services	42
Chapter 74D - Alarm Systems	42
Chapter 74E - Company Police Act	42
Chapter 74F - Locksmith Licensing Act	42
Chapter 74G - Campus Police Act	42
Chapter 75 - Monopolies, Trusts and Consumer Protection	42
Chapter 75A - Boating and Water Safety	43
Chapter 75B - Discrimination in Business	43
Chapter 75C - Motion Picture Fair Competition Act	43
Chapter 75D - Racketeer Influenced and Corrupt Organizations	43
Chapter 75E - Unlawful Activities in Connection With Certain Corporate Transactions	43
Chapter 76 - Navigation	43
Chapter 76A - Navigation and Pilotage Commissions	43
Chapter 77 - Rivers, Creeks, and Coastal Waters	43
Chapter 78 - Securities Law [Repealed.]	43
Chapter 78A - North Carolina Securities Act	43
Chapter 78B - Tender Offer Disclosure Act [Repealed.]	43
Chapter 78C - Investment Advisers	43
Chapter 78D - Commodities Act	43
Chapter 79 - Strays [Repealed.]	43
Chapter 80 - Trademarks, Brands, etc.	44
Chapter 81 - Weights and Measures [Recodified.]	44
Chapter 81A - Weights and Measures Act of 1975.	44
Chapter 82 - Wrecks [Repealed.]	44
Chapter 83 - Architects [Recodified.]	44

Chapter 83A - Architects	44
Chapter 84 - Attorneys-at-Law	44
Chapter 84A - Foreign Legal Consultants	44
Chapter 85 - Auctions and Auctioneers [Repealed.]	44
Chapter 85A - Bail Bondsmen and Runners [Recodified.]	44
Chapter 85B - Auctions and Auctioneers	44
Chapter 85C - Bail Bondsmen and Runners [Recodified.]	44
Chapter 86 - Barbers [Recodified.]	44
Chapter 86A - Barbers	44
Chapter 87 - Contractors	44
Chapter 88 - Cosmetic Art [Repealed.]	44
Chapter 88A - Electrolysis Practice Act	44
Chapter 88B - Cosmetic Art	45
Chapter 89 - Engineering and Land Surveying [Recodified.]	45
Chapter 89A - Landscape Architects	45
Chapter 89B - Foresters	45
Chapter 89C - Engineering and Land Surveying	45
Chapter 89D - Landscape Contractors	45
Chapter 89E - Geologists Licensing Act	45
Chapter 89F - North Carolina Soil Scientist Licensing Act	45
Chapter 89G - Irrigation Contractors	45
Chapter 90 - Medicine and Allied Occupations	45
Chapter 90 - Medicine and Allied Occupations (Continuation)	46
Chapter 90 - Medicine and Allied Occupations (Continuation)	47
Chapter 90 - Medicine and Allied Occupations (Continuation)	48
Chapter 90A - Sanitarians and Water and Wastewater Treatment Facility Operators	48
Chapter 90B - Social Worker Certification and Licensure Act	48
Chapter 90C - North Carolina Recreational Therapy Licensure Act	48
Chapter 90D - Interpreters and Transliterators	48
Chapter 91 - Pawnbrokers [Repealed.]	48
Chapter 91A - Pawnbrokers Modernization Act of 1989	48
Chapter 92 - Photographers [Deleted.]	48
Chapter 93 - Certified Public Accountants	48
Chapter 93A - Real Estate License Law	49
Chapter 93B - Occupational Licensing Boards	49
Chapter 93C - Watchmakers [Repealed.]	49
Chapter 93D - North Carolina State Hearing Aid Dealers and Fitters Board.	49
Chapter 93E - North Carolina Appraisers Act	49
Chapter 94 - Apprenticeship	49
Chapter 95 - Department of Labor and Labor Regulations	49
Chapter 95 - Department of Labor and Labor Regulations (Continuation)	50
Chapter 96 - Employment Security	50
Chapter 97 - Workers' Compensation Act	50
Chapter 97 - Workers' Compensation Act (Continuation)	51

Chapter 98 - Burnt and Lost Records	51
Chapter 99 - Libel and Slander	51
Chapter 99A - Civil Remedies for Criminal Actions	51
Chapter 99B - Products Liability	51
Chapter 99C - Actions Relating to Winter Sports Safety and Accidents	51
Chapter 99D - Civil Rights	51
Chapter 99E - Special Liability Provisions	51
Chapter 100 - Monuments, Memorials and Parks	51
Chapter 101 - Names of Persons	51
Chapter 102 - Official Survey Base	51
Chapter 103 - Sundays, Holidays and Special Days	51
Chapter 104 - United States Lands	51
Chapter 104A - Degrees of Kinship	51
Chapter 104B - Hurricanes or Other Acts of Nature	51
Chapter 104C - Atomic Energy, Radioactivity and Ionizing Radiation [Repealed and Recodified.]	51
Chapter 104D - Southern States Energy Compact	51
Chapter 104E - North Carolina Radiation Protection Act	51
Chapter 104F - Southeast Interstate Low-Level Radioactive Waste Management Compact [Repealed]	51
Chapter 104G - North Carolina Low-Level Radioactive Waste Management Authority Act of 1987 [Repealed]	51
Chapter 105 - Taxation	51
Chapter 105 - Taxation (Continuation)	52
Chapter 105 - Taxation (Continuation)	53
Chapter 105 - Taxation (Continuation)	54
Chapter 105A - Setoff Debt Collection Act	55
Chapter 105B - Defaulted Student Loan Recovery Act	55
Chapter 106 - Agriculture	55
Chapter 106 - Agriculture (Continue)	56
Chapter 106 - Agriculture (Continue)	57
Chapter 107 - Agricultural Development Districts [Repealed.]	57
Chapter 108 - Social Services [Repealed and Recodified.]	57
Chapter 108A - Social Services	57
Chapter 108B - Community Action Programs	58
Chapter 108C Medicaid and Health Choice Provider Requirements.	58
Chapter 108D Medicaid Managed Care for Behavioral Health Services.	58
Chapter 109 - Bonds [Recodified.]	58
Chapter 110 - Child Welfare	58
Chapter 111 - Aid to the Blind	58
Chapter 112 - Confederate Homes and Pensions [Repealed.]	58
Chapter 113 - Conservation and Development	58
Chapter 113 - Conservation and Development (Continuation)	59

Chapter 113A - Pollution Control and Environment	59
Chapter 113A - Pollution Control and Environment (Continuation)	60
Chapter 113B - North Carolina Energy Policy Act of 1975	60
Chapter 114 - Department of Justice	60
Chapter 115 - Elementary and Secondary Education [Repealed.]	60
Chapter 115A - Community Colleges, Technical Institutes, and Industrial Education Centers [Repealed.]	60
Chapter 115B - Tuition and Fee Waivers	60
Chapter 115C - Elementary and Secondary Education	60
Chapter 115C - Elementary and Secondary Education (Continuation)	61
Chapter 115C - Elementary and Secondary Education (Continuation)	62
Chapter 115C - Elementary and Secondary Education (Continuation)	63
Chapter 115D - Community Colleges	63
Chapter 115E - Private Educational Facilities Finance Act [Recodified]	63
Chapter 116 - Higher Education	63
Chapter 116 - Higher Education (Continuation)	63
Chapter 116A - Escheats and Abandoned Property [Repealed.]	64
Chapter 116B - Escheats and Abandoned Property	64
Chapter 116C - Continuum of Education Programs	64
Chapter 116D - Higher Education Bonds	64
Chapter 117 - Electrification	64
Chapter 118 - Firemen's and Rescue Squad Workers' Relief and Pension Funds [Recodified.]	64
Chapter 118A - Firemen's Death Benefit Act [Repealed.]	64
Chapter 118B - Members of a Rescue Squad Death Benefit Act [Repealed.]	64
Chapter 119 - Gasoline and Oil Inspection and Regulation	64
Chapter 120 - General Assembly	65
Chapter 120 - General Assembly (Continuation)	66
Chapter 120 - General Assembly (Continuation)	67
Chapter 120C - Lobbying	67
Chapter 121 - Archives and History	67
Chapter 122 - Hospitals for the Mentally Disordered [Repealed.]	67
Chapter 122A - North Carolina Housing Finance Agency	67
Chapter 122B - North Carolina Agricultural Facilities Finance Act [Repealed.]	67
Chapter 122C - Mental Health, Developmental Disabilities, and Substance Abuse Act of 1985	67
Chapter 122C - Mental Health, Developmental Disabilities, and Substance Abuse Act of 1985 (Continuation)	68
Chapter 122D - North Carolina Agricultural Finance Act	68

Chapter 122E - North Carolina Housing Trust and Oil Overcharge Act	68
Chapter 123 - Impeachment	69
Chapter 123A - Industrial Development [Repealed.]	69
Chapter 124 - Internal Improvements	69
Chapter 125 - Libraries	69
Chapter 126 - State Personnel System	69
Chapter 127 - Militia [Repealed.]	69
Chapter 127A - Militia	69
Chapter 127B - Military Affairs	69
Chapter 127C - Advisory Commission on Military Affairs	69
Chapter 128 - Offices and Public Officers	69
Chapter 128 - Offices and Public Officers (Continuation)	70
Chapter 129 - Public Buildings and Grounds	70
Chapter 130 - Public Health [Repealed.]	70
Chapter 130A - Public Health	70
Chapter 130A - Public Health (Continuation)	71
Chapter 130A - Public Health (Continuation)	72
Chapter 130B - Hazardous Waste Management Commission [Repealed.]	72
Chapter 131 - Public Hospitals [Repealed.]	72
Chapter 131A - Health Care Facilities Finance Act	72
Chapter 131B - Licensing of Ambulatory Surgical Facilities [Repealed.]	72
Chapter 131C - Charitable Solicitation Licensure Act [Repealed.]	72
Chapter 131D - Inspection and Licensing of Facilities	72
Chapter 131E - Health Care Facilities and Services	72
Chapter 131E - Health Care Facilities and Services (Continuation)	73
Chapter 131F - Solicitation of Contributions	73
Chapter 132 - Public Records	73
Chapter 133 - Public Works	74
Chapter 134 - Youth Development [Recodified.]	74
Chapter 134A - Youth Services [Repealed.]	74
Chapter 135 - Retirement System for Teachers and State Employees; Social Security; Health Insurance Program for Children	74
Chapter 135 - Retirement System for Teachers and State Employees; Social Security; Health Insurance Program for Children	75
Chapter 136 - Transportation	75
Chapter 136 - Transportation (Continuation)	76
Chapter 137 - Rural Rehabilitation [Repealed.]	76
Chapter 138 - Salaries, Fees and Allowances	76
Chapter 138A - State Government Ethics Act	76
Chapter 139 - Soil and Water Conservation Districts	76

Chapter 140 - State Art Museum; Symphony and Art Societies	76
Chapter 140A - State Awards System	76
Chapter 141 - State Boundaries	76
Chapter 142 - State Debt	76
Chapter 143 - State Departments, Institutions, and Commissions	77
Chapter 143 - State Departments, Institutions, and Commissions (Continuation)	78
Chapter 143 - State Departments, Institutions, and Commissions (Continuation)	79
Chapter 143 - State Departments, Institutions, and Commissions (Continuation)	80
Chapter 143A - State Government Reorganization	80
Chapter 143B - Executive Organization Act of 1973	80
Chapter 143B - Executive Organization Act of 1973 (Continuation)	81
Chapter 143B - Executive Organization Act of 1973 (Continuation)	82
Chapter 143C - State Budget Act	83
Chapter 143D - The State Governmental Accountability and Internal Control Act	83
Chapter 144 - State Flag, Official Governmental Flags, Motto, and Colors	83
Chapter 145 - State Symbols and Other Official Adoptions.	83
Chapter 146 - State Lands	83
Chapter 147 - State Officers	83
Chapter 148 - State Prison System	84
Chapter 149 - State Song and Toast	84
Chapter 150 - Uniform Revocation of Licenses [Repealed.]	84
Chapter 150A - Administrative Procedure Act [Recodified.]	84
Chapter 150B - Administrative Procedure Act	84
Chapter 151 - Constables [Repealed.]	84
Chapter 152 - Coroners	84
Chapter 152A - County Medical Examiner [Repealed.]	84
Chapter 152A - County Medical Examiner [Repealed.] (Continuation)	85
Chapter 153 - Counties and County Commissioners [Repealed.]	85
Chapter 153A - Counties	85
Chapter 153B - Mountain Resources Planning Act	85
Chapter 153C - Uwharrie Regional Resources Act	85
Chapter 154 - County Surveyor [Repealed.]	85
Chapter 155 - County Treasurer [Repealed.]	85
Chapter 156 - Drainage	85
Chapter 156 – Drainage (Continuation)	86

Chapter 157 - Housing Authorities and Projects	86
Chapter 157A - Historic Properties Commissions [Transferred.]	86
Chapter 158 - Local Development	86
Chapter 159 - Local Government Finance	86
Chapter 159 - Local Government Finance (Continuation)	87
Chapter 159A - Pollution Abatement and Industrial Facilities Financing Act [Unconstitutional.]	87
Chapter 159B - Joint Municipal Electric Power and Energy Act	87
Chapter 159C - Industrial and Pollution Control Facilities Financing Act	87
Chapter 159D - The North Carolina Capital Facilities Financing Act	87
Chapter 159E - Registered Public Obligations Act	87
Chapter 159F - North Carolina Energy Development Authority [Repealed.]	87
Chapter 159G - Water Infrastructure	87
Chapter 159H - [Reserved.]	87
Chapter 159I - Solid Waste Management Loan Program and Local Government Special Obligation Bonds	87
Chapter 160 - Municipal Corporations [Repealed And Transferred.]	87
Chapter 160A - Cities and Towns	88
Chapter 160A - Cities and Towns (Continuation)	89
Chapter 160B - Consolidated City-County Act	89
Chapter 160C - Baseball Park Districts [Repealed.]	90
Chapter 161 - Register of Deeds	90
Chapter 162 - Sheriff	90
Chapter 162A - Water and Sewer Systems	90
Chapter 162B Continuity of Local Government in Emergency.	90
Chapter 163 Elections and Election Laws.	90
Chapter 163 Elections and Election Laws. (Continuation)	91
Chapter 164 Concerning the General Statutes of North Carolina.	92
Chapter 165 Veterans.	92
Chapter 166 Civil Preparedness Agencies [Repealed.]	92
Chapter 166A North Carolina Emergency Management Act.	92
Chapter 167 State Civil Air Patrol [Repealed.]	92
Chapter 168 Persons with Disabilities.	92
Chapter 168A Persons With Disabilities Protection Act.	92

§ 115C-287.1. (Applicable to employees employed on or after July 1, 2014) Method of employment of principals, assistant principals, supervisors, and directors.

(a)   (1) All persons employed as school administrators shall be employed pursuant to this section.

(2)   Repealed by Session Laws 2013-360, s. 9.6(d), effective July 1, 2014.

(3)   For purposes of this section, school administrator means a:

a.   Principal;

b.   Assistant principal;

c.   Supervisor; or

d.   Director,

whose major function includes the direct or indirect supervision of teaching or of any other part of the instructional program.

(4)   Repealed by Session Laws 2013-360, s. 9.6(d), effective July 1, 2014.

(b)   Local boards of education shall employ school administrators upon the recommendation of the superintendent. The initial contract between a school administrator and a local board of education shall be for two to four years, ending on June 30 of the final 12 months of the contract. In the case of a subsequent contract between a principal or assistant principal and a local board of education, the contract shall be for a term of four years. In the case of an initial contract between a school administrator and a local board of education, the first year of the contract may be for a period of less than 12 months provided the contract becomes effective on or before September 1. A local board of education may, with the written consent of the school administrator, extend, renew, or offer a new school administrator's contract at any time after the first 12 months of the contract so long as the term of the new, renewed, or extended contract does not exceed four years. Rolling annual contract renewals are not allowed. Nothing in this section shall be construed to prohibit the filling of an administrative position on an interim or temporary basis.

(c) The term of employment shall be stated in a written contract that shall be entered into between the local board of education and the school administrator. The school administrator shall not be dismissed or demoted during the term of the contract except for the grounds and by the procedure by which a teacher may be dismissed or demoted for cause as set forth in G.S. 115C-325.4.

(d) If a superintendent intends to recommend to the local board of education that the school administrator be offered a new, renewed, or extended contract, the superintendent shall submit the recommendation to the local board for action. The local board may approve the superintendent's recommendation or decide not to offer the school administrator a new, renewed, or extended school administrator's contract.

If a superintendent decides not to recommend that the local board of education offer a new, renewed, or extended school administrator's contract to the school administrator, the superintendent shall give the school administrator written notice of his or her decision no later than May 1 of the final year of the contract. The superintendent's reasons may not be arbitrary, capricious, discriminatory, personal, political, or prohibited by State or federal law. No action by the local board or further notice to the school administrator shall be necessary unless the school administrator files with the superintendent a written request, within 10 days of receipt of the superintendent's decision, for a hearing before the local board. Failure to file a timely request for a hearing shall result in a waiver of the right to appeal the superintendent's decision. If a school administrator files a timely request for a hearing, the local board shall conduct a hearing pursuant to the provisions of G.S. 115C-45(c) and make a final decision on whether to offer the school administrator a new, renewed, or extended school administrator's contract.

If the local board decides not to offer the school administrator a new, renewed, or extended school administrator's contract, the local board shall notify the school administrator of its decision by June 1 of the final year of the contract. A decision not to offer the school administrator a new, renewed, or extended contract may be for any cause that is not arbitrary, capricious, discriminatory, personal, political, or prohibited by State or federal law.

(e) Repealed by Session Laws 1995, c. 369, s. 1.

(f) If the superintendent or the local board of education fails to notify a school administrator by June 1 of the final year of the contract that the school administrator will not be offered a new school administrator's contract, the school administrator shall be entitled to 30 days of additional employment or severance pay beyond the date the school administrator receives written notice that a new contract will not be offered.

(g) Repealed by Session Laws 2013-360, s. 9.6(d), effective July 1, 2014.

(h) An individual who holds a provisional assistant principal's license and who is employed as an assistant principal under G.S. 115C-284(c) shall be considered a school administrator for purposes of this section. Notwithstanding subsection (b) of this section, a local board may enter into one-year contracts with a school administrator who holds a provisional assistant principal's license. Nothing in this subsection or G.S. 115C-284(c) shall be construed to require a local board to extend or renew the contract of a school administrator who holds a provisional assistant principal's license. (1993, c. 210, s. 6; 1993 (Reg. Sess., 1994), c. 677, s. 16(a); 1995, c. 369, s. 1; 1998-220, s. 16; 1999-30, s. 3; 2003-291, s. 1; 2013-360, s. 9.6(d).)

§ 115C-288. Powers and duties of principal.

(a) To Grade and Classify Pupils. - The principal shall have authority to grade and classify pupils, except as provided in G.S. 115C-83.7(a). In determining the appropriate grade for a pupil who is already attending a public school, the principal shall consider the pupil's classroom work and grades, the pupil's scores on standardized tests, and the best educational interests of the pupil. The principal shall not make the decision solely on the basis of standardized test scores. If a principal's decision to retain a child in the same grade is partially based on the pupil's scores on standardized tests, those test scores shall be verified as accurate.

A principal shall not require additional testing of a student entering a public school from a school governed under Article 39 of this Chapter if test scores from a nationally standardized test or nationally standardized equivalent measure that are adequate to determine the appropriate placement of the child are available.

(b) To Make Accurate Reports to the Superintendent and to the Local Board. - The principal shall make all reports to the superintendent. Every principal of a public school shall make such reports as are required by the boards of education, and the superintendent shall not approve the vouchers for the pay of principals until the required monthly and annual reports are made: Provided, that the superintendents may require teachers to make reports to the principals and principals to make reports to the superintendent: Provided further, that any principal or supervisor who knowingly and willfully makes or procures another to make any false report or records, requisitions, or payrolls, respecting daily attendance of pupils in the public schools, payroll data sheets, or other reports required to be made to any board or officer in the performance of his duties, shall be guilty of a Class 1 misdemeanor and the certificate of such person to teach in the public schools of North Carolina shall be revoked by the Superintendent of Public Instruction.

(c)   To Improve Instruction and Community Spirit. - The principal shall give suggestions to teachers for the improvement of instruction.

(d)   To Conduct Fire Drills and Inspect for Fire Hazards. - It shall be the duty of the principal to conduct a fire drill during the first week after the opening of school and thereafter at least one fire drill each school month, in each building in his charge, where children are assembled. Fire drills shall include all pupils and school employees, and the use of various ways of egress to simulate evacuation of said buildings under various conditions, and such other regulations as shall be prescribed for fire safety by the Commissioner of Insurance, the Superintendent of Public Instruction and the State Board of Education. A copy of such regulations shall be kept posted on the bulletin board in each building.

It shall be the duty of each principal to inspect each of the buildings in his charge at least twice each month during the regular school session. This inspection shall include cafeterias, gymnasiums, boiler rooms, storage rooms, auditoriums and stage areas as well as all classrooms. This inspection shall be for the purpose of keeping the buildings safe from the accumulation of trash and other fire hazards.

It shall be the duty of the principal to file two copies of a written report once each month during the regular school session with the superintendent of his local school administrative unit, one copy of which shall be transmitted by the superintendent to the chairman of the local board of education. This report shall state the date the last fire drill was held, the time consumed in evacuating each building, that the inspection has been made as prescribed by law and such other information as is deemed necessary for fire safety by the Commissioner of

Insurance, the Superintendent of Public Instruction and the State Board of Education.

It shall be the duty of the principal to minimize fire hazards pursuant to the provisions of G.S. 115C-525.

(e)   To Discipline Students and to Assign Duties to Teachers with Regard to the Discipline, General Well-being, and Medical Care of Students. -

The principal shall have authority to exercise discipline over the pupils of the school under policies adopted by the local board of education in accordance with G.S. 115C-390.1 through G.S. 115C-390.12. The principal may use reasonable force pursuant to G.S. 115C-390.3 and may suspend students pursuant to G.S. 115C-390.5. The principal shall assign duties to teachers with regard to the general well-being and the medical care of students under G.S. 115C-307 and Article 26A of this Chapter.

(f)   To Protect School Property. - The principal shall protect school property as provided in G.S. 115C-523.

(g)   To Report Certain Acts to Law Enforcement and the Superintendent. - When the principal has personal knowledge or actual notice from school personnel that an act has occurred on school property involving assault resulting in serious personal injury, sexual assault, sexual offense, rape, kidnapping, indecent liberties with a minor, assault involving the use of a weapon, possession of a firearm in violation of the law, possession of a weapon in violation of the law, or possession of a controlled substance in violation of the law, the principal shall immediately report the act to the appropriate local law enforcement agency.

Notwithstanding any other provision of law, the State Board of Education shall not require the principal to report to law enforcement acts in addition to those required to be reported by law.

For purposes of this subsection, "school property" shall include any public school building, bus, public school campus, grounds, recreational area, or athletic field, in the charge of the principal.

The principal or the principal's designee shall notify the superintendent or the superintendent's designee in writing or by electronic mail regarding any report made to law enforcement under this subsection. This notification shall occur by the end of the workday in which the incident occurred when reasonably possible but not later than the end of the following workday. The superintendent shall provide the information to the local board of education.

Nothing in this subsection shall be interpreted to interfere with the due process rights of school employees or the privacy rights of students.

(h) To Make Available School Budgets and School Improvement Plans. - The principal shall maintain a copy of the school's current budget and school improvement plan, including any amendments to the plan, and shall allow parents of children in the school and other interested persons to review and obtain such documents in accordance with Chapter 132 of the General Statutes.

(i) To Evaluate Licensed Employees and Develop Mandatory Improvement Plans. - Each school year, the principal assigned to a low-performing school that has not received an assistance team shall provide for the evaluation of all licensed employees assigned to the school. The principal also shall develop mandatory improvement plans as provided under G.S. 115C-333(b) and G.S. 115C-333.1(b) and shall monitor an employee's progress under a mandatory improvement plan.

(j) To Transfer Student Records. - The principal shall not withhold the transfer of student records, except as is provided in G.S. 115C-403(b).

(k) To Sign Driving Eligibility Certificates and to Notify the Division of Motor Vehicles. - In accordance with rules adopted by the State Board of Education, the principal or the principal's designee shall do all of the following:

(1) Sign driving eligibility certificates that meet the conditions established in G.S. 20-11.

(2) Obtain the necessary written, irrevocable consent from parents, guardians, or emancipated juveniles, as appropriate, in order to disclose information to the Division of Motor Vehicles.

(3) Notify the Division of Motor Vehicles when a student who holds a driving eligibility certificate no longer meets its conditions.

(l) To Establish School Improvement Teams. - Each school year, the principal shall ensure that a school improvement team is established under G.S.

115C-105.27 for the purpose of developing, reviewing, and revising a school improvement plan.

(m) To Address the Unique Needs of Students With Immediate Family Members in the Military. - The principal shall develop a means for identifying and serving the unique needs of students who have immediate family members in the active or reserve components of the Armed Forces of the United States. (1955, c. 1372, art. 17, ss. 6, 8; 1957, c. 843; 1959, c. 573, s. 13; c. 1294; 1965, c. 584, s. 15; 1981, c. 423, s. 1; 1985 (Reg. Sess., 1986), c. 975, s. 4; 1987, c. 572, s. 3; 1993, c. 327, s. 1; c. 539, s. 883; 1994, Ex. Sess., c. 24, s. 14(c); 1995 (Reg. Sess., 1996), c. 716, s. 7.1; 1996, 2nd Ex. Sess., c. 18, s. 18.27; 1997-443, s. 8.29(t); 1998-5, s. 7; 1998-220, s. 13; 1999-243, s. 7; 1999-373, s. 2; 2001-424, s. 28.17(b); 2005-22, s. 5; 2009-410, s. 1; 2011-145, s. 7.13(s), (t); 2011-248, s. 1; 2011-282, s. 11; 2011-348, s. 5; 2011-391, s. 14(b); 2012-142, s. 7A.1(g); 2012-149, s. 7; 2012-194, s. 55(c).)

§ 115C-289. Assignment of principal's duties to assistant or acting principal; duties of State-funded assistant principals.

(a) Any duty or responsibility assigned to a principal by statute, State Board of Education regulation, or by the superintendent may, with the approval of the local board of education, be assigned by the principal to an assistant principal designated by the local board of education or to an acting principal designated by a principal.

(b) All persons employed as assistant principals in State-allotted positions, or as assistant principals in full-time positions regardless of funding source, in the public schools of the State or in schools receiving public funds, shall, in addition to other applicable requirements, be required either to hold or be qualified to hold a principal's certificate or a provisional assistant principal's certificate in compliance with applicable law and in accordance with the regulations of the State Board of Education. It shall be unlawful for any board of education to employ or keep in service any assistant principal who neither holds nor is qualified to hold a principal's certificate or a provisional assistant principal's certificate in compliance with applicable law and in accordance with the regulations of the State Board of Education. Persons who hold a provisional assistant principal's certificate and who are employed as assistant principals shall be employed under G.S. 115C-287.1(h).

(c) Repealed by Session Laws 1991, c. 689, s. 200(b).

(d) Assistant principals paid from State funds shall not have regularly assigned teaching duties. (1977, c. 539; 1981, c. 423, s. 1; 1987, c. 328; c. 830, s. 89(c); 1991, c. 689, s. 200(b); 1999-30, s. 2.)

§ 115C-289.1. Supervisor duty to report; intimidation of school employee.

(a) When a supervisor of a school employee has actual notice that the school employee has been the victim of an assault by a student in violation of G.S. 14-33(c)(6) resulting in physical injury, as that term is defined in G.S. 14-34.7, the supervisor shall immediately report to the principal the assault against the school employee. For the purpose of this subsection, the term "supervisor of a school employee" does not include the principal or superintendent.

(b) A principal, superintendent, or supervisor of a school employee shall not, by threats or in any other manner, intimidate or attempt to intimidate that school employee from reporting to law enforcement an assault by a student under G.S. 14-33(c)(6).

(c) Nothing in this section shall be interpreted to interfere with the due process rights of school employees or the privacy rights of students. (2012-149, s. 8.)

§ 115C-290. Reserved for future codification purposes.

Article 19A.

Standards Board for Public School Administration.

§§ 115C-290.1 through 115C-290.9: Repealed by Session Laws 2006-264, s. 56, effective August 27, 2006.

§ 115C-291: Reserved for future codification purposes.

§ 115C-292: Reserved for future codification purposes.

§ 115C-293: Reserved for future codification purposes.

§ 115C-294: Reserved for future codification purposes.

Article 20.

Teachers.

§ 115C-295. Minimum age and certificate prerequisites.

(a) All teachers employed in the public schools of the State or in schools receiving public funds, shall be required either to hold or be qualified to hold a certificate in compliance with the provision of the law or in accordance with the regulations of the State Board of Education: Provided, that nothing herein shall prevent the employment of temporary personnel under such rules as the State Board of Education may prescribe: Provided further, that no person shall be employed to teach who is under 18 years of age.

(b) It shall be unlawful for any board of education to employ or keep in service any teacher who neither holds nor is qualified to hold a certificate in compliance with the provision of the law or in accordance with the regulations of the State Board of Education. (1955, c. 1372, art. 18, ss. 1, 4; 1975, c. 437, s. 7; c. 731, ss. 1, 2; 1981, c. 423, s. 1; 1985 (Reg. Sess., 1986), c. 975, s. 16.)

§ 115C-295.1: Repealed by Session Laws 2011-145, s. 7.32, as added by Session Laws 2011-391, s. 17, effective July 1, 2011 and by Session Laws 2011-266, s. 1.39, effective July 1, 2011.

§ 115C-295.2: Repealed by Session Laws 2011-145, s. 7.32, as added by Session Laws 2011-391, s. 17, effective July 1, 2011, and by Session Laws 2011-266, s. 1.39, effective July 1, 2011.

§ 115C-295.3. Repealed by Session Laws 1999-96, s. 6.

§ 115C-296. Board sets licensure requirements; reports; lateral entry and mentor programs.

(a) (Applicable to school years before the 2014-2015 school year - see note.) The State Board of Education shall have entire control of licensing all applicants for teaching positions in all public elementary and high schools of North Carolina; and it shall prescribe the rules and regulations for the renewal and extension of all licenses and shall determine and fix the salary for each grade and type of license which it authorizes.

The State Board of Education may require an applicant for an initial degree certificate or graduate degree certificate to demonstrate the applicant's academic and professional preparation by achieving a prescribed minimum score on a standard examination appropriate and adequate for that purpose. The State Board of Education shall permit an applicant to fulfill any such testing requirement before or during the applicant's second year of teaching provided the applicant took the examination at least once during the first year of teaching. The State Board of Education shall make any required standard initial licensure exam sufficiently rigorous and raise the prescribed minimum score as necessary to ensure that each applicant has adequate academic and professional preparation to teach.

(a) (Applicable beginning with the 2014-2015 school year - see note.) The State Board of Education shall have entire control of licensing all applicants for teaching positions in all public schools of North Carolina; and it shall prescribe the rules and regulations for the renewal and extension of all licenses and shall determine and fix the salary for each grade and type of license which it authorizes.

The State Board of Education shall require an applicant for an initial bachelors degree license or graduate degree license to demonstrate the applicant's academic and professional preparation by achieving a prescribed minimum score on a standard examination appropriate and adequate for that purpose. Elementary education (K-6) and special education general curriculum teachers shall also achieve a prescribed minimum score on subtests or standard examinations specific to teaching reading and mathematics. The State Board of Education shall permit an applicant to fulfill any such testing requirement before or during the applicant's second year of teaching provided the applicant took the examination at least once during the first year of teaching. The State Board of Education shall make any required standard initial licensure exam rigorous and raise the prescribed minimum score as necessary to ensure that each applicant has received high-quality academic and professional preparation to teach effectively.

(a1) The State Board shall adopt policies that establish the minimum scores for any required standard examinations and other measures necessary to assess the qualifications of professional personnel as required under subsection (a) of this section. For purposes of this subsection, the State Board shall not be subject to Article 2A of Chapter 150B of the General Statutes. At least 30 days prior to changing any policy adopted under this subsection, the State Board shall provide written notice to all North Carolina schools of education and to all local boards of education. The written notice shall include the proposed revised policy.

(a2) The State Board of Education shall establish a schedule of fees for teacher licensure and administrative changes. The fees established under this subsection shall not exceed the actual cost of providing the service. The schedule may include fees for any of the following services:

(1) Application for demographic or administrative changes to a license.

(2) Application for a duplicate license or for copies of documents in the licensure files.

(3) Application for a renewal, extension, addition, upgrade, reinstatement, and variation to a license.

(4) Initial application for a New, In-State Approved Program Graduate.

(5) Initial application for an Out-of-State license.

(6) All other applications.

An applicant must pay any nonrefundable service fees at the time an application is submitted.

(a3) The State Board of Education shall report to the Joint Legislative Education Oversight Committee by March 15 in any year that the amount of fees in the fee schedule established under subsection (a2) of this section has been modified during the previous 12 months. The report shall include the number of personnel paid from licensure receipts, any change in personnel paid from receipts, other related costs covered by the receipts, and the estimated unexpended receipts as of June 30 of the year reported.

(b) (Applicable beginning with the 2013-2014 school year until the 2014-2015 school year - see note.) It is the policy of the State of North Carolina to maintain the highest quality teacher education programs and school administrator programs in order to enhance the competence of professional personnel licensed in North Carolina. To the end that teacher preparation programs are upgraded to reflect a more rigorous course of study, the State Board of Education, as lead agency in coordination and cooperation with the University Board of Governors, the Board of Community Colleges and such other public and private agencies as are necessary, shall continue to refine the several licensure requirements, standards for approval of institutions of teacher education, standards for institution based innovative and experimental programs, standards for implementing consortium based teacher education, and standards for improved efficiencies in the administration of the approved programs [, as follows]:

(1) Licensure standards. -

a. The licensure program shall provide for initial licensure after completion of preservice training, continuing licensure after three years of teaching experience, and license renewal every five years thereafter, until the retirement of the teacher. The last license renewal received prior to retirement shall remain in effect for five years after retirement. The licensure program shall also provide for lifetime licensure after 50 years of teaching.

b. The State Board of Education, in consultation with the Board of Governors of The University of North Carolina, shall evaluate and develop enhanced requirements for continuing licensure. The new requirements shall reflect more rigorous standards for continuing licensure and shall be aligned with high-quality professional development programs that reflect State priorities for improving student achievement. Standards for continuing licensure shall include at least eight continuing education credits with at least three credits required in a teacher's academic subject area.

c. The State Board of Education, in consultation with local boards of education and the Board of Governors of The University of North Carolina, shall (i) reevaluate and enhance the requirements for renewal of teacher licenses and (ii) consider modifications in the license renewal achievement and to make it a mechanism for teachers to renew continually their knowledge and professional skills.

(2) Teacher education programs.

a. The State Board of Education, as lead agency in coordination with the Board of Governors of The University of North Carolina, the North Carolina Independent Colleges and Universities, and any other public and private agencies as necessary, shall continue to raise standards for entry into teacher education programs.

b. Reserved for future codification.

c. To further ensure that teacher preparation programs remain current and reflect a rigorous course of study that is aligned to State and national standards, the State Board of Education, in consultation with the Board of Governors of The University of North Carolina, shall do all of the following to ensure that students are prepared to teach in elementary schools:

1. Provide students with adequate coursework in the teaching of reading and mathematics.

2. Assess students prior to licensure to determine that they possess the requisite knowledge in scientifically based reading and mathematics instruction that is aligned with the State Board's expectations.

3. Continue to provide students with preparation in applying formative and summative assessments within the school and classroom setting through technology-based assessment systems available in North Carolina schools that measure and predict expected student improvement.

4. Prepare students to integrate the arts across the curriculum.

d. The State Board of Education, in consultation with local boards of education and the Board of Governors of The University of North Carolina, shall evaluate and modify, as necessary, the academic requirements of teacher preparation programs for students preparing to teach science in middle and high schools to ensure that there is adequate preparation in issues related to science laboratory safety.

e.　The standards for approval of institutions of teacher education shall require that teacher education programs for all students include demonstrated competencies in (i) the identification and education of children with disabilities and (ii) positive management of student behavior and effective communication techniques for defusing and deescalating disruptive or dangerous behavior.

f.　The State Board of Education shall incorporate the criteria developed in accordance with G.S. 116-74.21 for assessing proposals under the School Administrator Training Program into its school administrator program approval standards.

(b)　(Applicable beginning with the 2014-2015 school year until the 2017-2018 school year - see note.) It is the policy of the State of North Carolina to maintain the highest quality teacher education programs and school administrator programs in order to enhance the competence of professional personnel licensed in North Carolina. To the end that teacher preparation programs are upgraded to reflect a more rigorous course of study, the State Board of Education, as lead agency in coordination and cooperation with the University Board of Governors, the Board of Community Colleges and such other public and private agencies as are necessary, shall continue to refine the several licensure requirements, standards for approval of institutions of teacher education, standards for institution based innovative and experimental programs, standards for implementing consortium based teacher education, and standards for improved efficiencies in the administration of the approved programs [, as follows]:

(1)　Licensure standards.

a.　The licensure program shall provide for initial licensure after completion of preservice training, continuing licensure after three years of teaching experience, and license renewal every five years thereafter, until the retirement of the teacher. The last license renewal received prior to retirement shall remain in effect for five years after retirement. The licensure program shall also provide for lifetime licensure after 50 years of teaching.

b.　The State Board of Education, in consultation with the Board of Governors of The University of North Carolina, shall evaluate and develop enhanced requirements for continuing licensure. The new requirements shall reflect more rigorous standards for continuing licensure and shall be aligned with high-quality professional development programs that reflect State priorities for improving student achievement. Standards for continuing licensure shall include at least eight continuing education credits with at least three credits required in a teacher's academic subject area. Standards for continuing licensure for elementary and middle school teachers shall include at least three continuing education credits related to literacy. Literacy renewal credits shall include evidence-based assessment, diagnosis, and intervention strategies for students not demonstrating reading proficiency. Oral language, phonemic and phonological awareness, phonics, vocabulary, fluency, and comprehension shall be addressed in literacy-related activities leading to license renewal for elementary school teachers.

c. The State Board of Education, in consultation with local boards of education and the Board of Governors of The University of North Carolina, shall (i) reevaluate and enhance the requirements for renewal of teacher licenses and (ii) consider modifications in the license renewal achievement and to make it a mechanism for teachers to renew continually their knowledge and professional skills.

(2) Teacher education programs.

a. The State Board of Education, as lead agency in coordination with the Board of Governors of The University of North Carolina, the North Carolina Independent Colleges and Universities, and any other public and private agencies as necessary, shall continue to raise standards for entry into teacher education programs.

b. Reserved for future codification.

c. To further ensure that teacher preparation programs remain current and reflect a rigorous course of study that is aligned to State and national standards, the State Board of Education, in consultation with the Board of Governors of The University of North Carolina, shall do all of the following to ensure that students are prepared to teach in elementary schools:

1. Provide students with adequate coursework in the teaching of reading and mathematics.

2. Assess students prior to licensure to determine that they possess the requisite knowledge in scientifically based reading and mathematics instruction that is aligned with the State Board's expectations.

3. Continue to provide students with preparation in applying formative and summative assessments within the school and classroom setting through technology-based assessment systems available in North Carolina schools that measure and predict expected student improvement.

4. Prepare students to integrate the arts education across the curriculum.

d. The State Board of Education, in consultation with local boards of education and the Board of Governors of The University of North Carolina, shall evaluate and modify, as necessary, the academic requirements of teacher preparation programs for students preparing to teach science in middle and high schools to ensure that there is adequate preparation in issues related to science laboratory safety.

e. The standards for approval of institutions of teacher education shall require that teacher education programs for all students include the following demonstrated competencies:

1. All teacher education programs. -

I. The identification and education of children with disabilities.

II. Positive management of student behavior and effective communication techniques for defusing and deescalating disruptive or dangerous behavior.

2. Elementary and special education general curriculum teacher education programs. -

I. Teaching of reading, including a substantive understanding of reading as a process involving oral language, phonological and phonemic awareness, phonics, fluency, vocabulary, and comprehension.

II. Evidence-based assessment and diagnosis of specific areas of difficulty with reading development and of reading deficiencies.

III. Appropriate application of instructional supports and services and reading interventions to ensure reading proficiency for all students.

f. The State Board of Education shall incorporate the criteria developed in accordance with G.S. 116-74.21 for assessing proposals under the School

Administrator Training Program into its school administrator program approval standards.

(b) (Applicable beginning with the 2017-2018 school year - see note.) It is the policy of the State of North Carolina to maintain the highest quality teacher education programs and school administrator programs in order to enhance the competence of professional personnel licensed in North Carolina. To the end that teacher preparation programs are upgraded to reflect a more rigorous course of study, the State Board of Education, as lead agency in coordination and cooperation with the University Board of Governors, the Board of Community Colleges and such other public and private agencies as are necessary, shall continue to refine the several licensure requirements, standards for approval of institutions of teacher education, standards for institution based innovative and experimental programs, standards for implementing consortium based teacher education, and standards for improved efficiencies in the administration of the approved programs. [, as follows]:

(1) Licensure standards.

a. The licensure program shall provide for initial licensure after completion of preservice training, continuing licensure after three years of teaching experience, and license renewal every five years thereafter, until the retirement of the teacher. The last license renewal received prior to retirement shall remain in effect for five years after retirement. The licensure program shall also provide for lifetime licensure after 50 years of teaching.

b. The State Board of Education, in consultation with the Board of Governors of The University of North Carolina, shall evaluate and develop enhanced requirements for continuing licensure. The new requirements shall reflect more rigorous standards for continuing licensure and shall be aligned with high-quality professional development programs that reflect State priorities for improving student achievement. Standards for continuing licensure shall include at least eight continuing education credits with at least three credits required in a teacher's academic subject area. Standards for continuing licensure for elementary and middle school teachers shall include at least three continuing education credits related to literacy. Literacy renewal credits shall include evidence-based assessment, diagnosis, and intervention strategies for students not demonstrating reading proficiency. Oral language, phonemic and phonological awareness, phonics, vocabulary, fluency, and comprehension shall be addressed in literacy-related activities leading to license renewal for elementary school teachers.

c. The State Board of Education, in consultation with local boards of education and the Board of Governors of The University of North Carolina, shall (i) reevaluate and enhance the requirements for renewal of teacher licenses, and (ii) consider modifications in the license renewal achievement and to make it a mechanism for teachers to renew continually their knowledge and professional skills, and (iii) integrate digital teaching and learning into the requirements for licensure renewal.

(2) Teacher education programs.

a. The State Board of Education, as lead agency in coordination with the Board of Governors of The University of North Carolina, the North Carolina Independent Colleges and Universities, and any other public and private agencies as necessary, shall continue to raise standards for entry into teacher education programs.

b. The State Board of Education, in consultation with the Board of Governors of The University of North Carolina, shall require that all students preparing to teach demonstrate competencies in using digital and other instructional technologies to provide high-quality, integrated digital teaching and learning to all students.

c. To further ensure that teacher preparation programs remain current and reflect a rigorous course of study that is aligned to State and national standards, the State Board of Education, in consultation with the Board of Governors of The University of North Carolina, shall do all of the following to ensure that students are prepared to teach in elementary schools:

1. Provide students with adequate coursework in the teaching of reading and mathematics.

2. Assess students prior to licensure to determine that they possess the requisite knowledge in scientifically based reading and mathematics instruction that is aligned with the State Board's expectations.

3. Continue to provide students with preparation in applying formative and summative assessments within the school and classroom setting through technology based assessment systems available in North Carolina schools that measure and predict expected student improvement.

4. Prepare students to integrate the arts across the curriculum.

d. The State Board of Education, in consultation with local boards of education and the Board of Governors of The University of North Carolina, shall evaluate and modify, as necessary, the academic requirements of teacher preparation programs for students preparing to teach science in middle and high schools to ensure that there is adequate preparation in issues related to science laboratory safety.

e. The standards for approval of institutions of teacher education shall require that teacher education programs for all students include the following demonstrated competencies:

1. All teacher education programs. -

I. The identification and education of children with disabilities.

II. Positive management of student behavior and effective communication techniques for defusing and deescalating disruptive or dangerous behavior.

2. Elementary and special education general curriculum teacher education programs. -

I. Teaching of reading, including a substantive understanding of reading as a process involving oral language, phonological and phonemic awareness, phonics, fluency, vocabulary, and comprehension.

II. Evidence-based assessment and diagnosis of specific areas of difficulty with reading development and of reading deficiencies.

III. Appropriate application of instructional supports and services and reading interventions to ensure reading proficiency for all students.

f. The State Board of Education shall incorporate the criteria developed in accordance with G.S. 116-74.21 for assessing proposals under the School Administrator Training Program into its school administrator program approval standards.

(b1) The State Board of Education shall require teacher education programs, master's degree programs in education, and master's degree programs in school administration to submit annual performance reports. The performance reports shall provide the State Board of Education with a focused review of the programs and the current process of accrediting these programs in order to ensure that the programs produce graduates that are well prepared to teach [, as follows]:

(1) Report contents. - The performance report for each teacher education program and master's degree program in education and school administration in North Carolina shall follow a common format and include at least the following elements:

a. Quality of students entering the schools of education, including the average grade point average and average score on preprofessional skills tests that assess reading, writing, math and other competencies.

b. Graduation rates.

c. Time-to-graduation rates.

d. Average scores of graduates on professional and content area examination for the purpose of licensure.

e. Percentage of graduates receiving initial licenses.

f. Percentage of graduates hired as teachers.

g. Percentage of graduates remaining in teaching for four years.

h. Graduate satisfaction based on a common survey.

i. Employer satisfaction based on a common survey.

j. Effectiveness of teacher education program graduates.

(2) Submission of annual performance reports. - Performance reports shall be provided annually to the Board of Governors of The University of North Carolina, the State Board of Education, and the boards of trustees of the independent colleges. The State Board of Education shall review the schools of education performance reports and the performance reports for masters degree programs in education and school administration each year the performance reports are submitted.

(3) Educator preparation program report card. - The State Board shall create a higher education educator preparation program report card reflecting

the information collected in the annual performance reports for each North Carolina institution offering teacher education programs and master of education programs. The report cards shall, at a minimum, summarize information reported on all of the performance indicators for the performance reports required by subdivision (1) of this subsection.

(4) Annual State Board of Education report. - The educator preparation program report cards shall be submitted to the Joint Legislative Education Oversight Committee on an annual basis by October 1.

(5) State Board of Education action based on performance. - The State Board of Education shall reward and sanction approved teacher education programs and master of education programs and revoke approval of those programs based on the performance reports and other criteria established by the State Board of Education.

(b2) An undergraduate student seeking a degree in teacher education must attain passing scores on a preprofessional skills test prior to admission to an approved teacher education program in a North Carolina college or university. The State Board of Education shall permit students to fulfill this requirement by achieving the prescribed minimum scores set by the State Board of Education for the Praxis I tests or by achieving the appropriate required score, as determined by the State Board of Education, on the verbal and mathematics portions of the SAT or ACT. The minimum combined verbal and mathematics score set by the State Board of Education for the SAT shall be 1,100 or greater. The minimum composite score set by the State Board of Education for the ACT shall be 24 or greater.

(c) It is the policy of the State of North Carolina to encourage lateral entry into the profession of teaching by skilled individuals from the private sector. To this end, before the 1985-86 school year begins, the State Board of Education shall develop criteria and procedures to accomplish the employment of such individuals as classroom teachers. Beginning with the 2006-2007 school year, the criteria and procedures shall include preservice training in (i) the identification and education of children with disabilities and (ii) positive management of student behavior, effective communication for defusing and deescalating disruptive or dangerous behavior, and safe and appropriate use of seclusion and restraint. Skilled individuals who choose to enter the profession of teaching laterally may be granted a lateral entry teaching license for no more than three years and shall be required to obtain licensure before contracting for a fourth year of service with any local administrative unit in this State.

(c1) The State Board of Community Colleges may provide a program of study for lateral entry teachers to complete the coursework necessary to earn a teaching license. To this end, the State Board of Education, in consultation with the State Board of Community Colleges, shall establish a competency based program of study for lateral entry teachers to be implemented within the Community College System no later than May 1, 2006. This program must meet standards set by the State Board of Education. To ensure that programs of study for lateral entry remain current and reflect a rigorous course of study that is aligned to State and national standards, the State Board of Education shall do all of the following to ensure that lateral entry personnel are prepared to teach:

(1) Provide adequate coursework in the teaching of reading and mathematics is available for lateral entry teachers seeking certification in elementary education.

(2) Assess lateral entry teachers are assessed prior to certification to determine that they possess the requisite knowledge in scientifically based reading and mathematics instruction that is aligned with the State Board's expectations.

(3) Prepare all lateral entry teachers to apply formative and summative assessments within the school and classroom setting through technology-based assessment systems available in North Carolina schools that measure and predict expected student improvement.

(4) (Applicable beginning with the 2017-2018 school year - see note.) Require that lateral entry teachers demonstrate competencies in using digital and other instructional technologies to provide high-quality, integrated digital teaching and learning to all students.

The State Board of Community Colleges and the State Board of Education shall jointly identify the community college courses and the teacher education program courses that are necessary and appropriate for inclusion in the community college program of study for lateral entry teachers. To the extent possible, any courses that must be completed through an approved teacher education program shall be taught on a community college campus or shall be available through distance learning.

In order to participate in the community college program of study for lateral entry teachers, an individual must hold at least a bachelors degree from a regionally accredited institution of higher education.

An individual who successfully completes this program of study and meets all other requirements of licensure set by the State Board of Education shall be recommended for a North Carolina teaching license.

(c2) It is further the policy of the State of North Carolina to ensure that local boards of education can provide the strongest possible leadership for schools based upon the identified and changing needs of individual schools. To this end, before the 1994-95 school year begins, the State Board of Education shall carefully consider a lateral entry program for school administrators to ensure that local boards of education will have sufficient flexibility to attract able candidates.

(d) The State Board shall adopt rules to establish the reasons and procedures for the suspension and revocation of licenses. The State Board shall revoke the license of a teacher or school administrator if the State Board receives notification from a local board or the Secretary of Health and Human Services that a teacher or school administrator has received a rating on any standard that was identified as an area of concern on the mandatory improvement plan that was below proficient or otherwise represented unsatisfactory or below standard performance under G.S. 115C-333(d) and G.S. 115C-333.1(f). In addition, the State Board may revoke or refuse to renew a teacher's license when:

(1) The Board identifies the school in which the teacher is employed as low-performing under G.S. 115C-105.37 or G.S. 143B-146.5; and

(2) The State Board shall automatically revoke the license of a teacher or school administrator without the right to a hearing upon receiving verification of the identity of the teacher or school administrator together with a certified copy of a criminal record showing that the teacher or school administrator has entered a plea of guilty or nolo contendere to or has been finally convicted of any of the following crimes: Murder in the first or second degree, G.S. 14-17; Conspiracy or solicitation to commit murder, G.S. 14-18.1; Rape or sexual offense as defined in Article 7A of Chapter 14 of the General Statutes. Felonious assault with deadly weapon with intent to kill or inflicting serious injury, G.S. 14-32; Kidnapping, G.S. 14-39; Abduction of children, G.S. 14-41; Crime against nature, G.S. 14-177; Incest, G.S. 14-178 or G.S. 14-179;

Employing or permitting minor to assist in offense against public morality and decency, G.S. 14-190.6; Dissemination to minors under the age of 16 years, G.S. 14-190.7; Dissemination to minors under the age of 13 years, G.S. 14-190.8; Displaying material harmful to minors, G.S. 14-190.14; Disseminating harmful material to minors, G.S. 14-190.15; First degree sexual exploitation of a minor, G.S. 14-190.16; Second degree sexual exploitation of a minor, G.S. 14-190.17; Third degree sexual exploitation of a minor, G.S. 14-190.17A; Taking indecent liberties with children, G.S. 14-202.1; Solicitation of child by computer to commit an unlawful sex act, G.S. 14-202.3; Taking indecent liberties with a student, G.S. 14-202.4; Prostitution, G.S. 14-204; Patronizing a prostitute who is a minor or a mentally disabled person, G.S. 14-205.2(c) or (d); Promoting prostitution of a minor or a mentally disabled person, G.S. 14-205.3(b); and child abuse under G.S. 14-318.4. The Board shall mail notice of its intent to act pursuant to this subdivision by certified mail, return receipt requested, directed to the teacher or school administrator at their last known address. The notice shall inform the teacher or school administrator that it will revoke the person's license unless the teacher or school administrator notifies the Board in writing within 10 days after receipt of the notice that the defendant identified in the criminal record is not the same person as the teacher or school administrator. If the teacher or school administrator provides this written notice to the Board, the Board shall not revoke the license unless it can establish as a fact that the defendant and the teacher or school administrator are the same person.

(3)   In addition, the State Board may revoke or refuse to renew a teacher's license when:

a.   The Board identifies the school in which the teacher is employed as low-performing under G.S. 115C-105.37 or G.S. 143B-146.5; and

b.   The assistance team assigned to that school makes the recommendation to revoke or refuse to renew the teacher's license for one or more reasons established by the State Board in its rules for license suspension or revocation.

The State Board may issue subpoenas for the purpose of obtaining documents or the testimony of witnesses in connection with proceedings to suspend or revoke licenses. In addition, the Board shall have the authority to contract with individuals who are qualified to conduct investigations in order to obtain all information needed to assist the Board in the proper disposition of allegations of misconduct by licensed persons.

(e) The State Board of Education shall develop a mentor program to provide ongoing support for teachers entering the profession. In developing the mentor program, the State Board shall conduct a comprehensive study of the needs of new teachers and how those needs can be met through an orientation and mentor support program. For the purpose of helping local boards to support new teachers, the State Board shall develop and distribute guidelines which address optimum teaching load, extracurricular duties, student assignment, and other working condition considerations. These guidelines shall provide that initially licensed teachers not be assigned extracurricular activities unless they request the assignments in writing and that other noninstructional duties of these teachers be minimized. The State Board shall develop and coordinate a mentor teacher training program. The State Board shall develop criteria for selecting excellent, experienced, and qualified teachers to be participants in the mentor teacher training program.

(e1) The State Board of Education shall allot funds for mentoring services to local school administrative units based on the highest number of employees in the preceding three school years who (i) are paid with State, federal, or local funds and (ii) are either teachers paid on the first or second steps of the teacher salary schedule or instructional support personnel paid on the first step of the instructional support personnel salary schedule.

Local school administrative units shall use these funds to provide mentoring support to eligible employees in accordance with a plan approved by the State Board of Education. The plan shall include information on how all mentors in the local school administrative unit will be adequately trained to provide mentoring support.

(f) The State Board of Education, after consultation with the Board of Governors of The University of North Carolina, shall develop a new category of teacher licensure known as the "Masters/Advanced Competencies" license. To receive this license, an applicant shall successfully complete a masters degree program that includes rigorous academic preparation in the subject area which the applicant will teach and in the skills and knowledge expected of a master teacher or the applicant shall demonstrate to the satisfaction of the State Board that the candidate has acquired the skills and knowledge expected of a master teacher.

Persons who qualify for a "G" certificate prior to September 1, 2000, shall be awarded a "Masters/Advanced Competencies" certificate without meeting additional requirements. On and after September 1, 2000, no additional "G" certificates shall be awarded. (1955, c. 1372, art. 18, s. 2; 1965, c. 584, s. 20.1; 1973, c. 236; 1975, c. 686, s. 1; 1981, c. 423, s. 1; 1983 (Reg. Sess., 1984), c. 1103, s. 6; 1987 (Reg. Sess., 1988), c. 1086, s. 96; 1989, c. 752, s. 66(a); 1993, c. 166, s. 1; c. 199, s. 4; 1995 (Reg. Sess., 1996), c. 716, s. 7; 1997-221, ss. 4(a), (b), 5, 7(a), 8, 9, 14, 17(a), (c); 1997-325, s. 1; 1997-383, s. 1; 1998-5, s. 5; 1998-131, s. 8; 1998-167, s. 1; 1999-96, s. 8; 2000-67, s. 9.2(a); 2001-129, s. 1; 2002-126, s. 7.39; 2003-284, s. 7.20(e); 2003-408, s. 1; 2004-124, s. 7.19(a); 2005-198, ss. 1, 2; 2005-205, s. 3; 2005-419, s. 1; 2007-166, s. 1; 2007-478, s. 1; 2007-484, s. 35; 2008-107, s. 7.8; 2009-59, s. 2; 2009-305, s. 1(b); 2011-348, s. 6; 2012-77, s. 1; 2013-11, s. 1; 2013-226, ss. 3, 5(a)-(c); 2013-360, s. 9.3(a)-(c); 2013-368, s. 22; 2013-410, s. 20(a).)

§ 115C-296.1. Expired.

§ 115C-296.2. National Board for Professional Teaching Standards Certification.

(a) State Policy. - It is the goal of the State to provide opportunities and incentives for good teachers to become excellent teachers and to retain them in the teaching profession; to attain this goal, the State shall support the efforts of teachers to achieve national certification by providing approved paid leave time for teachers participating in the process, lending teachers the participation fee, and paying a significant salary differential to teachers who attain national certification from the National Board for Professional Teaching Standards (NBPTS).

The National Board for Professional Teaching Standards (NBPTS) was established in 1987 as an independent, nonprofit organization to establish high standards for teachers' knowledge and performance and for development and operation of a national voluntary system to assess and certify teachers who meet those standards. Participation in the program gives teachers the time and the opportunity to analyze in a systematic way their professional development as teachers, successful teaching strategies, and the substantive areas in which they teach. Participation also gives teachers an opportunity to demonstrate superior ability and to be compensated as superior teachers. To receive NBPTS certification, a teacher must successfully (i) complete a process of developing a portfolio of student work and videotapes of teaching and learning activities and

(ii) participate in NBPTS assessment center simulation exercises, including performance-based activities and a content knowledge examination.

(b) Definitions. - As used in this subsection:

(1) A "North Carolina public school" is a school operated by a local board of education, the Department of Health and Human Services, the Division of Adult Correction of the Department of Public Safety, the Division of Juvenile Justice of the Department of Public Safety or The University of North Carolina; a school affiliated with The University of North Carolina; or a charter school approved by the State Board of Education.

(2) A "teacher" is a person who:

a. Either:

1. Is certified to teach in North Carolina; or

2. Holds a certificate or license issued by the State Board of Education that meets the professional license requirement for NBPTS certification;

b. Is a State-paid employee of a North Carolina public school;

c. Is paid on the teacher salary schedule; and

d. Spends at least seventy percent (70%) of his or her work time:

1. In classroom instruction, if the employee is employed as a teacher. Most of the teacher's remaining time shall be spent in one or more of the following: mentoring teachers, doing demonstration lessons for teachers, writing curricula, developing and leading staff development programs for teachers; or

2. In work within the employee's area of certification or licensure, if the employee is employed in an area of NBPTS certification other than direct classroom instruction.

(c) Payment of the NBPTS Participation Fee Paid Leave. - The State shall lend teachers the participation fee and shall provide up to three days of approved paid leave to all teachers participating in the NBPTS program who:

(1) Have completed three full years of teaching in a North Carolina public school; and

(2) Have (i) not previously received State funds for participating in any certification area in the NBPTS program, (ii) repaid any State funds previously received for the NBPTS certification process, or (iii) received a waiver of repayment from the State Board of Education.

Teachers participating in the program shall take paid leave only with the approval of their supervisors.

(d) Repealed by Session Laws 2009-451, s. 7.30(b), effective July 1, 2010, and applicable beginning with the 2010-2011 school year.

(d1) Repayment of the Application Fee. - A teacher shall repay the application fee to the State Education Assistance Authority within three years. The commencement of cash repayment shall begin 12 months following the disbursement of the loan funds. The State Education Assistance Authority may forgive the loan upon the death of the teacher or upon an injury deemed to leave the teacher totally and permanently disabled.

All funds appropriated to, or otherwise received by, the Authority to provide loans to teachers pursuant to this section, all funds received as repayment of loans, and all interest earned on these funds shall be placed in a trust fund. This fund shall be used only for loans made pursuant to this section and administrative costs of the Authority.

(e) Repealed by Session Laws 2009-451, s. 7.30(b), effective July 1, 2010, and applicable beginning with the 2010-2011 school year.

(e1) Repealed by Session Laws 2009-451, s. 7.41(a), effective June 30, 2011.

(f) Rules. - The State Education Assistance Authority shall adopt rules and guidelines regarding the loan and repayment of the NBPTS application fee. The State Board shall adopt policies and guidelines to implement the remainder of this section. (2000-67, s. 8.16; 2000-137, s. 3; 2008-86, s. 1; 2009-451, ss. 7.30(b), 7.41(a); 2009-575, s. 3H; 2010-31, s. 7.11(a); 2011-145, s. 19.1(h), (l).)

§ 115C-296.3: Expired June 30, 2004, by operation of Session Laws 2003-284, s. 7.20(h).

§ 115C-296.4: Repealed by Session Laws 2011-145, s. 7.31(a), as added by Session Laws 2011-391, s. 17, effective July 1, 2011, and by Session Laws 2011-266, s. 1.37(a), effective July 1, 2011.

§ 115C-296.5. North Carolina Center for the Advancement of Teaching; powers and duties of trustees; reporting requirement.

(a)   The North Carolina Center for the Advancement of Teaching (hereinafter called "NCCAT"), through itself or agencies with which it may contract, shall:

(1)   Provide career teachers with opportunities to study advanced topics in the sciences, arts, and humanities and to engage in informed discourse, assisted by able mentors and outstanding leaders from all walks of life; and

(2)   Offer opportunities for teachers to engage in scholarly pursuits through a center dedicated exclusively to the advancement of teaching as an art and as a profession.

(b)   Priority for admission to NCCAT opportunities shall be given to teachers with teaching experience of 15 years or less.

(c)   NCCAT may also provide training and support for beginning teachers to enhance their skills and in support of the State's effort to recruit and retain beginning teachers.

(d)   The Board of Trustees of the North Carolina Center for the Advancement of Teaching shall hold all the powers and duties necessary or appropriate for the effective discharge of the functions of NCCAT.

(e)   The Executive Director shall submit a copy of the NCCAT annual report to the Chair of the State Board of Education at the time of issuance. (1985, c. 479, s. 74; 2006-66, s. 9.15(a); 2009-451, ss. 9.13(b), (c).)

§ 115C-296.6. Composition of board of trustees; terms; officers.

(a) The NCCAT Board of Trustees shall be composed of the following membership:

(1) Two ex officio members: the Chairman of the State Board of Education and the State Superintendent of Public Instruction or their designees;

(2) Two members appointed by the General Assembly upon the recommendation of the President Pro Tempore of the Senate;

(3) Two members appointed by the General Assembly upon the recommendation of the Speaker of the House of Representatives; and

(4) Eight members appointed by the Governor, one from each of the eight educational regions.

The appointing authorities shall give consideration to assuring, through Board membership, the statewide mission of NCCAT.

(b) Members of the NCCAT Board of Trustees shall serve four-year terms. Members may serve two consecutive four-year terms. The Board shall elect a new chair every two years from its membership. The chair may serve two consecutive two-year terms as chair.

(c) The chief administrative officer of NCCAT shall be an executive director who shall be appointed by the NCCAT Board of Trustees. (1985, c. 479, s. 74; 1995, c. 490, s. 2; 2006-66, s. 9.15(b); 2009-451, s. 9.13(d), (e).)

§ 115C-296.7. North Carolina Teacher Corps.

(a) There is established the North Carolina Teacher Corps (NC Teacher Corps) to recruit and place recent graduates of colleges and universities and mid-career professionals as teachers in high needs public schools.

(b) The State Board of Education, in consultation with the Board of Governors of The University of North Carolina and the North Carolina Independent Colleges and Universities, shall develop and administer the NC Teacher Corps. In the development of the NC Teacher Corps, the State Board of Education shall consider examples of other successful teacher recruitment models used nationally and in other states.

(c) Applications shall be received annually for admission to the NC Teacher Corps. The State Board of Education shall establish application criteria, including, at a minimum, an award of a bachelor's degree from an accredited college or university. The State Board of Education may establish a committee to annually evaluate and select candidates for admission to the NC Teacher Corps.

(d) The State Board of Education shall identify local school administrative units with unmet recruitment needs, especially for career and technical education teachers, and high needs schools and shall coordinate placement of NC Teacher Corps members in those schools.

(e) The State Board of Education, in coordination with the Board of Governors, shall develop an intensive summer training institute for NC Teacher Corps members to provide coursework and training on essential teaching frameworks, curricula, and lesson-planning skills, as well as identification and education of students with disabilities, positive management of student behavior, effective communication for defusing and deescalating disruptive and dangerous behavior, and safe and appropriate use of seclusion and restraint. The intensive summer training institute also shall address identification of difficulty with reading development and of reading deficiencies and the provision of reading instruction, intervention, and remediation strategies.

(f) The State Board of Education, in coordination with the Board of Governors, shall provide ongoing support to NC Teaching Corps members through coaching, mentoring, and continued professional development.

(g) NC Teaching Corps members shall be granted lateral entry teaching licenses pursuant to G.S. 115C-296(c).

(h) (Effective July 1, 2014) The State Board of Education is authorized to contract for the administration of the NC Teacher Corps. (2012-142, s. 7A.7(a); 2013-1, s. 2(a); 2013-360, s. 8.21(c).)

§ 115C-297: Repealed by Session Laws 1989, c. 385, s. 2.

§ 115C-298: Repealed by Session Laws 1997-18, s. 9.

§ 115C-299. Hiring of teachers.

(a)   In the city administrative units, teachers shall be elected by the board of education of such administrative unit upon the recommendation of the superintendent of city schools.

Teachers shall be elected by the county and city boards of education upon the recommendation of the superintendent, in accordance with the provisions of G.S. 115C-276(j).

(b)   No person otherwise qualified shall be denied the right to receive credentials from the State Board of Education, to receive training for the purpose of becoming a teacher, or to engage in practice teaching in any school on the grounds that such person is totally or partially blind; nor shall any local board of education refuse to employ such a person on such grounds. (1955, c. 1372, art. 5, s. 4; 1971, c. 949; 1981, c. 423, s. 1; 1985 (Reg. Sess., 1986), c. 975, s. 5.)

§ 115C-300. In-service training.

Local boards of education are authorized to provide for the professional growth of teachers while in service and to pass rules and regulations requiring teachers to cooperate with their superintendent for the improvement of instruction in the classroom and for promoting community improvement. (1955, c. 1372, art. 5, s. 29; 1981, c. 423, s. 1.)

§ 115C-301. Allocation of teachers; class size.

(a)   Request for Funds. - The State Board of Education, based upon the reports of local boards of education and such other information as the State Board may require from local boards, shall determine for each local school administrative unit the number of teachers and other instructional personnel to be included in the State budget request.

(b) Allocation of Positions. - The State Board of Education is authorized to adopt rules to allot instructional personnel and teachers, within funds appropriated.

(c) Maximum Class Size for Kindergarten Through Third Grade. - The average class size for kindergarten through third grade in a local school administrative unit shall at no time exceed the funded allotment ratio of teachers to students in kindergarten through third grade. At the end of the second school month and for the remainder of the school year, the size of an individual class in kindergarten through third grade shall not exceed the allotment ratio by more than three students. In grades four through 12, local school administrative units shall have the maximum flexibility to use allotted teacher positions to maximize student achievement.

(d), (e) Repealed by Session Laws 2013-363, s. 3.3(a), effective July 1, 2013.

(f) Second Month Reports. - At the end of the second month of each school year, each local board of education, through the superintendent, shall file a report for each school within the school unit with the State Board of Education. The report shall be filed in a format prescribed by the State Board of Education and shall include the organization for each school, the duties of each teacher, the size of each class, and such other information as the State Board may require. As of February 1 each year, local boards of education, through the superintendent, shall report all exceptions to individual class size maximums in kindergarten through third grade that occur at that time.

(g) Waivers and Allotment Adjustments. - Local boards of education shall report exceptions to the class size requirements set out for kindergarten through third grade and significant increases in class size at other grade levels to the State Board and shall request allotment adjustments at any grade level, waivers from the requirements for kindergarten through third grade, or both. Within 45 days of receipt of reports, the State Board of Education, within funds available, may grant waivers for the excess class size in kindergarten through third grade.

(h) State Board Rules. - The State Board of Education shall adopt rules necessary for the implementation of this section.

(i) Repealed by Session Laws 2013-363, s. 3.3(a), effective July 1, 2013. (1955, c. 1372, art. 6, s. 6; 1963, c. 688, s. 3; 1965, c. 584, s. 6; 1969, c. 539; 1973, c. 770, ss. 1, 2; 1975, c. 965, s. 3; 1977, c. 1088, s. 4; 1981, c. 423, s. 1;

1983 (Reg. Sess., 1984), c. 1034, ss. 12, 13; 1985, c. 479, s. 55(b)(3)b; 1987, c. 738, s. 181; 1987 (Reg. Sess., 1988), c. 1025, s. 15; c. 1086, s. 89(a); 2010-31, s. 7.22(a); 2013-363, s. 3.3(a).)

§ 115C-301.1. Duty-free instructional planning time.

All full-time assigned classroom teachers shall be provided duty-free instructional planning time during regular student contact hours. The duty-free instructional planning time shall be provided to the maximum extent that (i) the safety and proper supervision of children may allow during regular student contact hours and (ii) insofar as funds are provided for this purpose by the General Assembly. If the safety and supervision of children does not allow duty-free instructional planning time during regular student contact hours for a given teacher, the funds provided by the General Assembly for the duty-free instructional planning time for that teacher shall revert to the general fund. Principals shall not unfairly burden a given teacher by making that teacher give up his or her duty-free instructional planning time on an ongoing, regular basis without the consent of the teacher. (1983, c. 761, s. 88; 1999-163, s. 1; 2006-153, s. 3.)

§ 115C-302: Repealed by Session Laws 1997-443, s. 8.38(d).

§ 115C-302.1. Salary.

(a) Prompt Payment. - Teachers shall be paid promptly when their salaries are due provided the legal requirements for their employment and service have been met. All teachers employed by any local school administrative unit who are to be paid from local funds shall be paid promptly as provided by law and as State-allotted teachers are paid.

(b) Salary Payments. - State-allotted teachers shall be paid for a term of 10 months. State-allotted months of employment for vocational education to local boards shall be used for the employment of teachers of vocational and technical education for a term of employment to be determined by the local boards of education. However, local boards shall not reduce the term of employment for any vocational agriculture teacher personnel position that was 12 calendar months for the 1982-83 school year for any school year thereafter. In addition, local boards shall not reduce the term of employment for any vocational agriculture teacher personnel position that was 12 calendar months for the 2003-2004 school year for any school year thereafter.

Each local board of education shall establish a set date on which monthly salary payments to State-allotted teachers shall be made. This set pay date may differ from the end of the month of service. The daily rate of pay for teachers shall equal midway between one twenty-first and one twenty-second of the monthly rate of pay. Except for teachers employed in a year-round school or paid in accordance with a year-round calendar, or both, the initial pay date for teachers shall be no later than August 31 and shall include a full monthly payment. Subsequent pay dates shall be spaced no more than one month apart and shall include a full monthly payment.

Teachers may be prepaid on the monthly pay date for days not yet worked. A teacher who fails to attend scheduled workdays or who has not worked the number of days for which the teacher has been paid and who resigns, is dismissed, or whose contract is not renewed shall repay to the local board any salary payments received for days not yet worked. A teacher who has been prepaid and continues to be employed by a local board but fails to attend scheduled workdays may be subject to dismissal under G.S. 115C-325 or other appropriate discipline.

Any individual teacher who is not employed in a year-round school may be paid in 12 monthly installments if the teacher so requests on or before the first day of the school year. The request shall be filed in the local school administrative unit which employs the teacher. The payment of the annual salary in 12 installments instead of 10 shall not increase or decrease the teacher's annual salary nor in any other way alter the contract made between the teacher and the local school administrative unit. Teachers employed for a period of less than 10 months shall not receive their salaries in 12 installments.

Notwithstanding this subsection, the term "daily rate of pay" for the purpose of G.S. 115C-12(8) or for any other law or policy governing pay or benefits based on the teacher salary schedule shall not exceed one twenty-second of a teacher's monthly rate of pay.

(b1)   The State Board of Education shall maintain the same policies related to masters pay for teachers that were in effect for the 2008-2009 fiscal year.

(c) Vacation. - Included within the 10-month term shall be annual vacation leave at the same rate provided for State employees, computed at one-twelfth of the annual rate for State employees for each month of employment. Local boards shall provide at least 10 days of annual vacation leave at a time when students are not scheduled to be in regular attendance. However, instructional personnel who do not require a substitute may use annual vacation leave on days that students are in attendance. Vocational and technical education teachers who are employed for 11 or 12 months may, with prior approval of the principal, work on annual vacation leave days designated in the school calendar and may use those annual vacation leave days during the eleventh or twelfth month of employment. Local boards of education may adopt policies permitting instructional personnel employed for 11 or 12 months in year-round schools to, with the approval of the principal, take vacation leave at a time when students are in attendance; local funds shall be used to cover the cost of substitute teachers.

On a day that pupils are not required to attend school due to inclement weather, but employees are required to report for a workday, a teacher may elect not to report due to hazardous travel conditions and to take an annual vacation day or to make up the day at a time agreed upon by the teacher and the teacher's immediate supervisor or principal. On a day that school is closed to employees and pupils due to inclement weather, a teacher shall work on the scheduled makeup day.

All vacation leave taken by the teacher will be upon the authorization of the teacher's immediate supervisor and under policies established by the local board of education. Annual vacation leave shall not be used to extend the term of employment.

Notwithstanding any provisions of this subsection to the contrary, no person shall be entitled to pay for any vacation day not earned by that person.

(c1), (c2) Repealed by Session Laws 2002-126, s. 7.11(a), effective July 1, 2002, and applicable only to leave days accruing after September 30, 2002.

(c3) Teachers may accumulate annual vacation leave days without any applicable maximum until June 30 of each year. In order that only 30 days of annual vacation leave carry forward to July 1, on June 30 of each year any teacher or other personnel paid on the teacher salary schedule who has accumulated more than 30 days of annual vacation leave shall convert to sick leave the remaining excess accumulation.

Upon separation from service due to service retirement, resignation, dismissal, reduction in force, or death, an employee shall be paid in a lump sum for accumulated annual leave not to exceed a maximum of 30 days. In addition to the maximum of 30 days pay for accumulated annual leave, upon separation from service due to service retirement, any teacher or other personnel paid on the teacher salary schedule with more than 30 days of accumulated annual vacation leave may convert some or all of the excess accumulation to sick leave for creditable service towards retirement. Employees going onto term disability may exhaust annual leave rather than be paid in a lump sum.

(d)   Personal Leave. - Teachers earn personal leave at the rate of .20 days for each full month of employment not to exceed two days per year. Personal leave may be accumulated without any applicable maximum until June 30 of each year. A teacher may carry forward to July 1 a maximum of five days of personal leave; the remainder of the teacher's personal leave shall be converted to sick leave on June 30. At the time of retirement, a teacher may also convert accumulated personal leave to sick leave for creditable service towards retirement.

Personal leave may be used only upon the authorization of the teacher's immediate supervisor. A teacher shall not take personal leave on the first day the teacher is required to report for the school year, on a required teacher workday, on days scheduled for State testing, or on the day before or the day after a holiday or scheduled vacation day, unless the request is approved by the principal. On all other days, if the request is made at least five days in advance, the request shall be automatically granted subject to the availability of a substitute teacher, and the teacher cannot be required to provide a reason for the request. Teachers may transfer personal leave days between local school administrative units. The local school administrative unit shall credit a teacher who has separated from service and is reemployed within 60 months from the date of separation with all personal leave accumulated at the time of separation. Local school administrative units shall not advance personal leave. Teachers using personal leave on teacher workdays shall receive full salary. Teachers using personal leave on other days shall receive full salary less the required substitute deduction. If, however, no substitute is hired for a teacher, the substitute reduction shall be refunded to that teacher.

(e) Teachers in Year-Round Schools. - Compensation for teachers employed in year-round schools shall be the same as teachers paid for a 10-month term, but those days may be scheduled over 12 calendar months. Annual leave, sick leave, workdays, holidays, salary, and longevity for teachers who are employed at year-round schools shall be equivalent to those of other teachers employed for the same number of months, respectively. Teachers paid for a term of 10 months in year-round schools shall receive their salary in 12 equal installments.

(f) Overpayment. - Each local board of education shall sustain any loss by reason of an overpayment to any teacher paid from State funds.

(g) Service in Armed Forces. - The State Board of Education, in fixing the State standard salary schedule of teachers as authorized by law, shall provide that teachers who entered the Armed Forces or auxiliary forces of the United States after September 16, 1940, and who left their positions for such service shall be allowed experience increments for the period of such service as though the same had not been interrupted thereby, in the event such persons return to the position of teachers, principals, and superintendents in the public schools of the State after having been honorably discharged from the Armed Forces or auxiliary forces of the United States.

(g1) Payment During Military Duty. - The State Board of Education shall adopt rules relating to leaves of absence, without loss of pay or time, for periods of military training and for State or federal military duty or for special emergency management service. The rules shall apply to all public school employees, including, but not limited to, school teachers, administrators, guidance counselors, speech language pathologists, nurses, and custodians employed by local boards of education or by charter schools. The rules shall provide that (i) the State pays any salary differential to all public school employees in State-funded positions, (ii) the employing local board of education pays any pay differential to all public school employees in locally funded positions, (iii) the employing charter school pays any pay differential to all public school employees in the charter school, and (iv) the employing local board of education pays the local supplement.

(h) Teachers Paid From Other Funds. - Every local board of education may adopt, as to teachers not paid out of State funds, a salary schedule similar to the State salary schedule, but it likewise shall recognize a difference in salaries based on different duties, training, experience, professional fitness, and continued service in the same school system. If a local board of education does not adopt a local salary schedule, the State salary schedule shall apply. No teacher shall receive a salary higher than that provided in the salary schedule, unless by action of the board of education a higher salary is allowed for special fitness, special duties, or under extraordinary circumstances.

When a higher salary is allowed, the minutes of the board shall show what salary is allowed and the reason. A board of education may authorize the superintendent to supplement the salaries of all teachers from local funds, and the minutes of the board shall show what increase is allowed each teacher.

(i) Longevity Pay. - Longevity pay shall be based on the annual salary on the employee's anniversary date.

(j) Parental Leave. - A teacher may use annual leave, personal leave, or leave without pay to care for a newborn child or for a child placed with the teacher for adoption or foster care. A teacher may also use up to 30 days of sick leave to care for a child placed with the teacher for adoption. The leave may be for consecutive workdays during the first 12 months after the date of birth or placement of the child, unless the teacher and local board of education agree otherwise. (1997-443, s. 8.38(e); 1999-237, s. 28.26(a), (b); 2002-126, s. 7.11(a); 2002-159, s. 37.5(a); 2003-301, s. 1; 2004-124, s. 7.20; 2004-180, s. 2; 2007-378, s. 1; 2008-107, s. 26.21(a); 2008-187, s. 45.5; 2008-209, ss. 1(a), 2; 2009-451, s. 7.35; 2011-183, s. 78; 2011-379, s. 5; 2012-13, s. 1; 2012-142, s. 7.14(a); 2013-240, s. 1.)

§ 115C-302.2: Repealed by Session Laws 2003-358, s. 1, effective January 1, 2004.

§ 115C-302.3. Salary credit for service in the Armed Forces.

(a) The State Board of Education shall establish rules for awarding credit for salary purposes to principals, assistant principals, and teachers who served in the Armed Forces of the United States and who have retired or who have received an Honorable Discharge. The rules shall include the following provisions:

(1) One full year of experience credit shall be awarded for each year of full-time relevant nonteaching work experience completed (i) while on active military duty in the Armed Forces of the United States and (ii) after earning a bachelor's degree.

(2) One full year of experience credit shall be awarded for each two years of full-time relevant nonteaching work experience completed (i) while on active duty in the Armed Forces of the United States and (ii) before earning a bachelor's degree.

(3) One full year of experience credit shall be awarded for every two years of full-time instructional or leadership duties while on active military duty in the Armed Forces of the United States, regardless of academic degree held while in instruction or leadership roles.

(b) The State Board of Education shall establish specific criteria within the rules for determining the relevance of nonteaching work experience earned while on active military duty that shall be credited toward an individual's total licensure experience rating for salary purposes. The criteria shall include the following components:

(1) A clearly defined process to explore, identify, recognize, and quantify the breadth and depth of career experiences, formal professional military education, and pertinent credentials of military veterans.

(2) A transparent and timely decision-making process for awarding complete credit for pertinent experience and education.

(3) A process for reviewing and accepting military transcripts and corresponding American Council on Education (ACE) recommendations for awarding academic and experiential credit.

(c) The State Board shall have continuing authority to cap nonteaching experience credit for Junior Reserve Officer Training Corps instructors as their pay formula includes both a State and federal funding component. (2013-268, ss. 1-3.)

§ 115C-303. Withholding of salary.

(a) No teacher shall be placed on the payroll of a local school administrative unit unless he holds a certificate as required by law, and unless a copy of the teacher's contract has been filed with the superintendent. No teacher may be paid more than he is due under the local school salary schedule in force in the local school administrative unit. Substitute and interim teachers shall be paid under rules of the State Board of Education.

(b) The board of education may withhold the salary of any teacher who delays or refuses to render such reports as are required by law, but when the reports are delivered in accordance with law, the salary shall be paid forthwith. (1955, c. 1372, art. 6, ss. 11, 13; 1975, c. 437, ss. 8, 9; 1981, c. 423, s. 1; 1985 (Reg. Sess., 1986), c. 975, s. 19.)

§ 115C-304. (Repealed effective July 1, 2014) Teacher tenure.

Tenure of teachers shall be determined in accordance with the provisions of G.S. 115C-325. (1981, c. 423, s. 1; 2013-360, s. 9.7(h).)

§ 115C-305: Repealed by Session Laws 2001-260, s. 2.

§ 115C-306: Repealed by Session Laws 1983, c. 770, s. 16.

§ 115C-307. Duties of teachers.

(a) To Maintain Order and Discipline. - It shall be the duty of all teachers, including student teachers, substitute teachers, voluntary teachers, and teacher assistants when given authority over some part of the school program by the principal or supervising teacher, to maintain good order and discipline in their respective schools. A teacher, student teacher, substitute teacher, voluntary teacher, or teacher assistant shall report to the principal acts of violence in school and students suspended or expelled from school as required to be reported in accordance with State Board policies.

(b) To Provide for General Well-Being of Students. - It shall be the duty of all teachers, including student teachers, substitute teachers, voluntary teachers, and teacher assistants when given authority over some part of the school program by the principal or supervising teacher, to encourage temperance, morality, industry, and neatness; to promote the health of all pupils, especially of children in the first three grades, by providing frequent periods of recreation, to supervise the play activities during recess, and to encourage wholesome exercises for all children.

(c)   To Provide Some Medical Care to Students. - It is within the scope of duty of teachers, including substitute teachers, teacher assistants, student teachers or any other public school employee when given such authority by the board of education or its designee to provide medical care to students as provided in G.S. 115C-375.1.

(d)   To Teach the Students. - It shall be the duty of all teachers, including student teachers, substitute teachers, voluntary teachers, and teacher assistants when given authority over some part of the school program by the principal or supervising teacher, to teach as thoroughly as they are able all branches which they are required to teach; to provide for singing in the school, and so far as possible to give instruction in the public school music.

(e)   To Enter into the Superintendent's Plans for Professional Growth. - It shall be the duty of all teachers, including student teachers, substitute teachers, voluntary teachers, and teacher assistants when given authority over some part of the school program by the principal or supervising teacher, to enter actively into the plans of the superintendent for the professional growth of the teachers.

(f)   To Discourage Nonattendance. - Teachers shall cooperate with the principal in ascertaining the cause of nonattendance of pupils that he may report all violators of the compulsory attendance law to the school social worker in accordance with rules promulgated by the State Board of Education.

(g)   To Make Required Reports. - A teacher shall make all reports required by the local board of education. The superintendent shall not approve the voucher for a teacher's pay until the required monthly and annual reports are made.

The superintendent may require a teacher to make reports to the principal.

A teacher shall be given access to the information in the student information management system to expedite the process of preparing reports or otherwise providing information. A teacher shall not be required by the local board, the superintendent, or the principal to (i) provide information that is already available on the student information management system; (ii) provide the same written information more than once during a school year unless the information has changed during the ensuing period; or (iii) complete forms, for children with disabilities, that are not necessary to ensure compliance with the federal Individuals with Disabilities Education Act (IDEA). Notwithstanding the forgoing, a local board may require information available on its student information management system or require the same information twice if the superintendent determines that there is (i) a compelling need and (ii) no more expeditious manner of providing the information to the local board. A school improvement team may request that the superintendent consider the elimination of a redundant reporting requirement for the teachers at its school if it identifies in its school improvement plan a more expeditious manner of providing the information to the local board. The superintendent shall recommend to the local board whether the reporting requirement should be eliminated for that school. If the superintendent does not recommend elimination of the reporting requirement, the school improvement team may request a hearing by the local board as provided in G.S. 115C-45(c).

Any teacher who knowingly and willfully makes or procures another to make any false report or records, requisitions, or payrolls, respecting daily attendance of pupils in the public schools, payroll data sheets, or other reports required to be made to any board or officer in the performance of their duties, shall be guilty of a Class 1 misdemeanor and the certificate of such person to teach in the public schools of North Carolina shall be revoked by the Superintendent of Public Instruction.

(h) To Take Care of School Buildings. - It shall be the duty of every teacher to instruct children in proper care of property and to exercise due care in the protection of school property, in accordance with the provisions of G.S. 115C-523. (1955, c. 1372, art. 17, ss. 4, 6; 1959, cc. 1016, 1294; 1969, c. 638, ss. 2, 3; 1971, c. 434; 1981, c. 423, s. 1; 1985, c. 642; c. 686, s. 2; 1989, c. 585, s. 4; 1993, c. 539, s. 884; 1994, Ex. Sess., c. 24, s. 14(c); 1997-443, s. 8.29(k); 2000-67, s. 8.18(a); 2005-22, s. 2(a); 2013-226, s. 11(b).)

§ 115C-308. Rules for teacher's conduct.

The conduct of teachers, the kind of reports they shall make, and their duties in the care of school property are subject to the rules and regulations of the local board, as provided in G.S. 115C-47(18). (1981, c. 423, s. 1.)

§ 115C-309. Student teachers.

(a) Student Teacher and Student Teaching Defined. - A "student teacher" is any student enrolled in an institution of higher education approved by the State Board of Education for the preparation of teachers who is jointly assigned by that institution and a local board of education to student teach under the direction and supervision of a regularly employed certified teacher.

"Student teaching" may include those duties granted to a teacher by G.S. 115C-307 and any other part of the school program for which either the supervising teacher or the principal is responsible.

(b) Legal Protection. - A student teacher under the supervision of a certified teacher or principal shall have the protection of the laws accorded the certified teacher.

(c) Assignment of Duties. - It shall be the responsibility of a supervising teacher, in cooperation with the principal and the representative of the teacher-preparation institution, to assign to the student teacher responsibilities and duties that will provide adequate preparation for teaching. (1969, c. 638, s. 1; 1981, c. 423, s. 1; 2012-194, s. 49.)

§ 115C-310. Teacher assistants engaged in student teaching.

The State Board of Education shall adopt a program to facilitate the process by which teacher assistants may become teachers.

Teacher assistants who participate in this program:

(1) Shall be enrolled in an approved teacher education program in a North Carolina institution of higher education; and

(2) Shall be employed in a North Carolina public school.

Local school administrative units are encouraged to assign teacher assistants to a different classroom during student teaching than the classroom they are assigned to as a teacher assistant. To the extent possible, they may be assigned to another school within the same local school administrative unit.

At the discretion of the local school administrative unit, teacher assistants may continue to receive their salary and benefits while student teaching in the same local school administrative unit where they are employed as a teacher assistant.

The State Board of Education shall consult with the Board of Governors of The University of North Carolina and the North Carolina Independent Colleges and Universities in the development of the program. Each approved teacher education program and each local school administrative unit shall administer this program beginning with the 2005-2006 academic year. (2005-302, s. 1.)

§ 115C-311. Reserved for future codification purposes.

§ 115C-312. Reserved for future codification purposes.

§ 115C-313. Reserved for future codification purposes.

§ 115C-314. Reserved for future codification purposes.

Article 21.

Other Employees.

§ 115C-315. Hiring of school personnel.

(a) Janitors and Maids. - In the city administrative units, janitors and maids shall be appointed by the board of education of such local school administrative unit upon the recommendation of the superintendent.

(b) Election by Local Boards. - School personnel shall be elected by the local board of education upon the recommendation of the superintendent, in accordance with the provisions of G.S. 115C-276(j).

It is the policy of the State of North Carolina to encourage and provide for the most efficient and cost-effective method of meeting the needs of local school administrative units for noncertified support personnel. To this end, the State Board of Education shall recommend to the General Assembly by November 1, 1984, a system using factors and formulas to determine the total number of noncertified support personnel allotted to local school administrative units. The recommended system for allotting noncertified support personnel shall include the proposed State's funding obligation for these positions and shall be developed in consultation with school-based support personnel or their representatives.

(c) Prerequisites for Employment. - All professional personnel employed in the public schools of the State or in schools receiving public funds shall be required either to hold or be qualified to hold a certificate in compliance with the provision of the law or in accordance with the regulations of the State Board of Education: Provided, that nothing herein shall prevent the employment of temporary personnel under such rules as the State Board of Education may prescribe.

(d) Certification for Professional Positions. - The State Board of Education shall have entire control of certifying all applicants for professional positions in all public elementary and high schools of North Carolina; and it shall prescribe the rules and regulations for the renewal and extension of all certificates and shall determine and fix the salary for each grade and type of certificate which it authorizes: Provided, that the State Board of Education shall require each applicant for an initial certificate or graduate certificate to demonstrate his or her academic and professional preparation by achieving a prescribed minimum score at least equivalent to that required by the Board on November 30, 1972, on a standard examination appropriate and adequate for that purpose: Provided, further, that in the event the Board shall specify the National Teachers Examination for this purpose, the required minimum score shall not be lower than that which the Board required on November 30, 1972.

(d1) Certification for School Nurses. - Notwithstanding any other provision of law or rule, school nurses employed in the public schools prior to July 1, 1998, shall not be required to be nationally certified to continue employment. School nurses not certified by the American Nurses' Association or the National Association of School Nurses shall continue to be paid based on the noncertified nurse salary range as established by the State Board of Education.

(e) Repealed by Session Laws 1989, c. 385, s. 3.

(f) Employing Persons Not Holding Nor Qualified to Hold Certificate. - It shall be unlawful for any board of education to employ or keep in service any professional person who neither holds nor is qualified to hold a certificate in compliance with the provisions of the law or in accordance with the regulations of the State Board of Education. (1955, c. 1372, art. 5, s. 4; art. 18, ss. 1-4; 1965, c. 584, s. 20.1; 1973, c. 236; 1975, c. 437, s. 7; c. 686, s. 1; c. 731, ss. 1,

2; 1981, c. 423, s. 1; 1983 (Reg. Sess., 1984), c. 1103, s. 9; 1985 (Reg. Sess., 1986), c. 975, s. 16; 1989, c. 385, s. 3; 2002-126, s. 7.41(a).)

§ 115C-316. Salary and vacation.

(a) School officials and other employees shall be paid promptly when their salaries are due provided the legal requirements for their employment and service have been met. All school officials and other employees employed by any local school administrative unit who are to be paid from local funds shall be paid promptly as provided by law and as state-allotted school officials and other employees are paid.

Public school employees paid from State funds shall be paid as follows:

(1) Employees Other than Superintendents, Supervisors and Classified Principals on an Annual Basis. - Each local board of education shall establish a set date on which monthly salary payments to employees other than superintendents, supervisors, and classified principals employed on an annual basis, shall be made. This set pay date may differ from the end of the calendar month of service. Employees may be prepaid on the monthly pay date for days not yet worked. An employee who fails to attend scheduled workdays or who has not worked the number of days for which the employee has been paid and who resigns or is dismissed shall repay to the local board any salary payments received for days not yet worked. An employee who has been prepaid and who continues to be employed by a local board but fails to attend scheduled workdays may be subject to dismissal or other appropriate discipline. The daily rate of pay shall equal the number of weekdays in the pay period. Included within their term of employment shall be annual vacation leave at the same rate provided for State employees, computed at one-twelfth (1/12) of the annual rate for state employees for each calendar month of employment. On a day that employees are required to report for a workday but pupils are not required to attend school due to inclement weather, an employee may elect not to report due to hazardous travel conditions and to take one of the employee's annual vacation days or to make up the day at a time agreed upon by the employee and the employee's immediate supervisor or principal. On a day that school is closed to employees and pupils due to inclement weather, an employee shall work on the scheduled makeup day. Included within their term of employment each local board of education shall designate the same or an equivalent number

of legal holidays as those designated by the State Human Resources Commission for State employees.

(2) School Employees Paid on an Hourly or Other Basis. - Salary payments to employees other than those covered in G.S. 115C-272(b)(1), 115C-285(a)(1) and (2), 115C-302.1(b) and 115C-316(a)(1) shall be made at a time determined by each local board of education. Expenditures for the salary of these employees from State funds shall be within allocations made by the State Board of Education and in accordance with rules and regulations approved by the State Board of Education concerning allocations of State funds: Provided, that school employees employed for a term of 10 calendar months in year-round schools shall be paid in 12 equal installments: Provided further, that any individual school employee employed for a term of 10 calendar months who is not employed in a year-round school may be paid in 12 monthly installments if the employee so requests on or before the first day of the school year. Such request shall be filed in the administrative unit which employs the employee. The payment of the annual salary in 12 installments instead of 10 shall not increase or decrease said annual salary nor in any other way alter the contract between the employee and the said administrative unit. Employees may be prepaid on the set pay date for days not yet worked. An employee who fails to attend scheduled workdays or who has not worked the number of days for which the employee has been paid and who resigns or is dismissed shall repay to the local board any salary payments received for days not yet worked. An employee who has been prepaid and who continues to be employed by a local board but fails to attend scheduled workdays may be subject to dismissal or other appropriate discipline. The daily rate of pay shall equal the number of weekdays in the pay period. Included within the term of employment shall be provided for full-time employees annual vacation leave at the same rate provided for State employees, computed at one-twelfth (1/12) of the annual rate for State employees for each calendar month of employment, to be taken under policies determined by each local board of education. On a day that employees are required to report for a workday but pupils are not required to attend school due to inclement weather, an employee may elect not to report due to hazardous travel conditions and to take one of his annual vacation days or to make up the day at a time agreed upon by the employee and his immediate supervisor or principal. On a day that school is closed to employees and pupils due to inclement weather, the employee shall work on the scheduled makeup day. Included within their term of employment, each local board of education shall designate the same or an equivalent number of legal holidays occurring within the period of employment as those designated by the State Human Resources Commission for State employees.

(3) Notwithstanding any provisions of this section to the contrary no person shall be entitled to pay for any vacation day not earned by that person. The first 10 days of annual leave earned by a 10- or 11-month employee during any fiscal year period shall be scheduled to be used in the school calendar adopted by the respective local boards of education. Vacation days shall not be used for extending the term of employment of individuals. Ten- or 11-month employees may accumulate annual vacation leave days as follows: annual leave may be accumulated without any applicable maximum until June 30 of each year. On June 30 of each year, any of these employees with more than 30 days of accumulated leave shall have the excess accumulation converted to sick leave so that only 30 days are carried forward to July 1 of the same year. All vacation leave taken by these employees shall be upon the authorization of their immediate supervisor and under policies established by the local board of education. The policies may permit teacher assistants who require a substitute and are employed for 11 or 12 months in year-round schools to take vacation leave at a time when students are in attendance; local funds shall be used to cover the cost of substitutes. Vacation leave for instructional personnel who do not require a substitute shall not be restricted to days that students are not in attendance. An employee shall be paid in a lump sum for accumulated annual leave not to exceed a maximum of 240 hours or 30 days when separated from service due to resignation, dismissal, reduction in force, death or service retirement. Upon separation from service due to service retirement, any annual vacation leave over 30 days will convert to sick leave and may be used for creditable service at retirement in accordance with G.S. 135-4(e). If the last day of terminal leave falls on the last workday in the month, payment shall be made for the remaining nonworkdays in that month. Employees retiring on disability retirement may exhaust annual leave rather than be paid in a lump sum. The provisions of this subdivision shall be accomplished without additional State and local funds being appropriated for this purpose. The State Board of Education shall adopt rules and regulations for the administration of this subdivision.

(4) Twelve-month school employees other than superintendents, supervisors and classified principals paid on an hourly or other basis whether paid from State or from local funds may accumulate annual vacation leave days as follows: annual leave may be accumulated without any applicable maximum until June 30 of each year. On June 30 of each year, any employee with more than 30 days of accumulated leave shall have the excess accumulation converted to sick leave so that only 30 days are carried forward to July 1 of the same year. All vacation leave taken by the employee will be upon the authorization of his immediate supervisor and under policies established by the local board of education. An employee shall be paid in a lump sum for

accumulated annual leave not to exceed a maximum of 240 hours or 30 days when separated from service due to resignation, dismissal, reduction in force, death, or service retirement. Upon separation from service due to service retirement, any annual vacation leave over 30 days will convert to sick leave and may be used for creditable service at retirement in accordance with G.S. 135-4(e). If the last day of terminal leave falls on the last workday in the month, payment shall be made for the remaining nonworkdays in that month. Employees retiring on disability retirement may exhaust annual leave rather than be paid in a lump sum. The provisions of this subdivision shall be accomplished without additional State and local funds being appropriated for this purpose. The State Board of Education shall adopt rules and regulations for the administration of this subdivision.

(4a) Employees employed on a 10- or 11-month basis at year-round schools shall be employed for the same total number of days as employees employed for a period of 10 or 11 calendar months, respectively, but those days may be scheduled over 12 calendar months. Annual leave, sick leave, workdays, holidays, salary, and longevity, for employees who are employed on a 10- or 11-month basis at year-round schools, shall be equivalent to those of employees employed for 10 or 11 calendar months, respectively.

(5) All of the foregoing provisions of this section shall be subject to the requirement that at least fifty dollars ($50.00), or other minimum amount required by federal social security laws, of the compensation of each school employee covered by the Teachers' and State Employees' Retirement System or otherwise eligible for social security coverage shall be paid in each of the four quarters of the calendar year.

(6) Each local board of education shall sustain any loss by reason of an overpayment to any school official or other employee paid from State funds.

(b) Every local board of education may adopt, as to school officials other than superintendents, principals and supervisors not paid out of State funds, a salary schedule similar to the State salary schedule, but it likewise shall recognize a difference in salaries based on different duties, training, experience, professional fitness, and continued service in the same school system; but if any local board of education shall fail to adopt such a schedule, the State salary schedule shall be in force.

(c) Longevity pay for 10-month employees is based on their annual salary and the longevity percentage may not be reduced by prorating the longevity pay for 10-month employees over a 12-month period.

(d) Expired pursuant to Session Laws 1998-212, s. 28.24, effective October 1, 2007. (1955, c. 1372, art. 5, s. 32; art. 18, s. 6; 1961, c. 1085; 1965, c. 584, s. 3; 1971, c. 1052; 1973, c. 647, s. 1; 1975, cc. 383, 608; c. 834, ss. 1, 2; 1979, c. 600, ss. 1-5; 1981, c. 423, s. 1; c. 639, ss. 2, 3; c. 730, s. 1; c. 946, s. 3; c. 947, s. 2; 1983, c. 872, ss. 5-7; 1985, c. 757, s. 145(g), (h); 1985 (Reg. Sess., 1986), c. 975, s. 15; 1987, c. 414, ss. 8, 9; 1989, c. 386, s. 3; 1989 (Reg. Sess., 1990), c. 1066, s. 94; 1991, c. 689, s. 39.3(b); 1993, c. 98, s. 2; c. 321, s. 73(d), (e); c. 475, s. 2; 1995, c. 450, s. 21; 1997-443, s. 8.38(h), (i); 1998-212, s. 28.24(b); 1999-237, s. 28.26(e), (f); 2002-126, s. 28.10(a); 2004-124, s. 31.18A(a); 2005-144, s. 7A.1; 2007-145, s. 7(a); 2007-326, s. 3(a); 2012-142, s. 7.14(b); 2013-382, s. 9.1(c).)

§ 115C-316.1. Duties of school counselors.

(a) School counselors shall implement a comprehensive developmental school counseling program in their schools. Counselors shall spend at least eighty percent (80%) of their work time providing direct services to students. Direct services do not include the coordination of standardized testing. Direct services shall consist of:

(1) Delivering the school guidance curriculum through large group guidance, interdisciplinary curriculum development, group activities, and parent workshops.

(2) Guiding individual student planning through individual or small group assistance and individual or small group advisement.

(3) Providing responsive services through consultation with students, families, and staff; individual and small group counseling; crisis counseling; referrals; and peer facilitation.

(4) Performing other student services listed in the Department of Public Instruction school counselor job description that has been approved by the State Board of Education.

(b) During the remainder of their work time, counselors shall spend adequate time on school counseling program support activities that consist of professional development; consultation, collaboration, and training; and program management and operations. School counseling program support activities do not include the coordination of standardized testing. However, school counselors may assist other staff with the coordination of standardized testing. (2013-360, s. 8.35(a).)

§ 115C-317. Penalty for making false reports or records.

Any school employee of the public schools other than a superintendent, principal, or teacher, who knowingly and willfully makes or procures another to make any false report or records, requisitions, or payrolls, respecting daily attendance of pupils in the public schools, payroll data sheets, or other reports required to be made to any board or officer in the performance of his duties, shall be guilty of a Class 1 misdemeanor and the certificate of such person to teach in the public schools of North Carolina shall be revoked by the Superintendent of Public Instruction. (1955, c. 1372, art. 17, s. 6; 1959, c. 1294; 1981, c. 423, s. 1; 1993, c. 539, s. 885; 1994, Ex. Sess., c. 24, s. 14(c).)

§ 115C-317.1. School social workers and transporting students.

A school social worker shall not be required to transport students without the existence of a written job description or local board policy that imposes this requirement. (2005-355, s. 1.)

§ 115C-318. Liability insurance for nonteaching public school personnel.

The State Board of Education shall provide funds for liability insurance for nonteaching public school personnel to the extent that such personnel's salaries are funded by the State. The insurance shall cover claims made for injury liability and property damage liability on account of an act done or an omission made in the course of the employee's duties. As provided by law or the rules and policies of the State Board of Education or the local school administrative unit, the State Board of Education shall comply with the State's laws in securing the insurance and shall provide it at the earliest possible date for the 1982-83 school year. Nothing in this section shall prevent the State Board from furnishing the same liability insurance protection for nonteaching public school personnel not supported by State funds, provided that the cost of the protection shall be funded from the same source that supports the salaries of these employees. (1981 (Reg. Sess., 1982), c. 1399, s. 3; 1993, c. 522, s. 4; 1995, c. 450, s. 22.)

Article 21A.

Privacy of Employee Personnel Records.

§ 115C-319. Personnel files not subject to inspection.

Personnel files of employees of local boards of education, former employees of local boards of education, or applicants for employment with local boards of education shall not be subject to inspection and examination as authorized by G.S. 132-6. For purposes of this Article, a personnel file consists of any information gathered by the local board of education which employs an individual, previously employed an individual, or considered an individual's application for employment, and which information relates to the individual's application, selection or nonselection, promotion, demotion, transfer, leave, salary, suspension, performance evaluation, disciplinary action, or termination of employment wherever located or in whatever form.

Nothing in this section shall be construed to prevent local boards of education from disclosing the certification status and other information about employees as required by Section 1111(h)(6) of P.L. 107-110. (1987, c. 571, s. 1; 2002-126, s. 7.36.)

§ 115C-320. Certain records open to inspection.

(a) Each local board of education shall maintain a record of each of its employees, showing the following information with respect to each employee:

(1) Name.

(2) Age.

(3) Date of original employment or appointment.

(4) The terms of any contract by which the employee is employed whether written or oral, past and current, to the extent that the board has the written contract or a record of the oral contract in its possession.

(5) Current position.

(6) Title.

(7) Current salary.

(8) Date and amount of each increase or decrease in salary with that local board of education.

(9) Date and type of each promotion, demotion, transfer, suspension, separation, or other change in position classification with that local board of education.

(10) Date and general description of the reasons for each promotion with that local board of education.

(11) Date and type of each dismissal, suspension, or demotion for disciplinary reasons taken by the local board of education. If the disciplinary action was a dismissal, a copy of the written notice of the final decision of the local board education setting forth the specific acts or omissions that are the basis of the dismissal.

(12) The office or station to which the employee is currently assigned.

(b) For the purposes of this section, the term "salary" includes pay, benefits, incentives, bonuses, and deferred and all other forms of compensation paid by the employing entity.

(c) Subject only to rules and regulations for the safekeeping of records adopted by the local board of education, every person having custody of the records shall permit them to be inspected and examined and copies made by any person during regular business hours. The name of a participant in the Address Confidentiality Program established pursuant to Chapter 15C of the

General Statutes shall not be open to inspection and shall be redacted from any record released pursuant to this section. Any person who is denied access to any record for the purpose of inspecting, examining or copying the record shall have a right to compel compliance with the provisions of this section by application to a court of competent jurisdiction for a writ of mandamus or other appropriate relief. (1987, c. 571, s. 1; 2002-171, s. 4; 2007-508, s. 1; 2010-169, s. 18(b).)

§ 115C-321. Confidential information in personnel files; access to information.

(a) All information contained in a personnel file, except as otherwise provided in this Chapter, is confidential and shall not be open for inspection and examination except to any of the following persons:

(1) The employee, applicant for employment, former employee, or his properly authorized agent, who may examine his own personnel file at all reasonable times in its entirety except for letters of reference solicited prior to employment.

(2) The superintendent and other supervisory personnel.

(3) Members of the local board of education and the board's attorney.

(4) A party by authority of a subpoena or proper court order may inspect and examine a particular confidential portion of an employee's personnel file.

(a1) Notwithstanding any other provision of this Chapter, information contained in a personnel file that is relevant to possible criminal misconduct may be made available to law enforcement and the district attorney to assist in the investigation of:

(1) A report made to law enforcement pursuant to G.S. 115C-288(g), or

(2) Any report to law enforcement regarding an arson, attempted arson, destruction of, theft from, theft of, embezzlement from, embezzlement of any personal or real property owned by the local board of education.

(a2) The employee shall be given five working days prior written notice of any disclosure under subsection (a1) of this section to permit the employee to apply to the district court for an in camera review prior to the date of disclosure to determine if the information is relevant to the possible criminal misconduct. Failure of the employee to apply for a review shall constitute a waiver by the employee of any relief under this subsection.

(a3) Statements or admissions made by the employee and produced under subsection (a1) of this section shall not be admissible in any subsequent criminal proceeding against the employee.

(b) Notwithstanding any other provision of this Chapter, any superintendent may, in his discretion, or shall at the direction of the Board of Education, inform any person or corporation of any promotion, demotion, suspension, reinstatement, transfer, separation, dismissal, employment or nonemployment of any applicant, employee or former employee employed by or assigned to the local board of education or whose personnel file is maintained by the board and the reasons therefor and may allow the personnel file of the person or any portion to be inspected and examined by any person or corporation provided that the board has determined that the release of the information or the inspection and examination of the file or any portion is essential to maintaining the integrity of the board or to maintaining the level or quality of services provided by the board; provided, that prior to releasing the information or making the file or any portion available as provided herein, the superintendent shall prepare a memorandum setting forth the circumstances which he and the board deem to require the disclosure and the information to be disclosed. The memorandum shall be retained in the files of the superintendent and shall be a public record.

(b1) Notwithstanding any provision of this section to the contrary, the Retirement Systems Division of the Department of State Treasurer may disclose the name and mailing address of former public school employees to domiciled, nonprofit organizations representing 10,000 or more retired State government, local government, or public school employees.

(c) A public official or employee who knowingly, willfully, and with malice permits any person to have access to information contained in a personnel file, except as permitted by this section, is guilty of a Class 3 misdemeanor and upon conviction shall only be fined an amount not in excess of five hundred dollars ($500.00).

(d) Any person, not specifically authorized by this section to have access to a personnel file, who shall knowingly and willfully examine in its official filing place, remove, or copy any portion of a personnel file shall be guilty of a Class 3 misdemeanor and upon conviction shall only be fined not in excess of five hundred dollars ($500.00). (1987, c. 571, s. 1; 2005-321, s. 1; 2007-192, s. 1; 2008-194, s. 11(b).)

§ 115C-322. Reserved for future codification purposes.

Article 22.

General Regulations.

Part 1. Health Certificate.

§ 115C-323. Employee health certificate.

(a) Any person initially employed in a public school or reemployed in a public school after an absence of more than one school year shall provide to the superintendent a certificate certifying that the person does not have any physical or mental disease, including tuberculosis in the communicable form or other communicable disease, that would impair the person's ability to perform his or her duties effectively. A local board or a superintendent may require any school employee to take a physical examination when considered necessary.

Any public school employee who has been absent for more than 40 successive school days because of a communicable disease shall, before returning to work, provide to the superintendent a certificate certifying that the individual is free from any communicable disease.

(b) One of the following individuals shall prepare any certificate required under this section:

(1) A physician licensed to practice in North Carolina.

(2) A nurse practitioner approved under G.S. 90-18(14).

(3) A physician's assistant licensed to practice in North Carolina.

(c) Notwithstanding subsection (b) of this section, in the case of a person initially employed in a public school, any of the following who holds a current unrestricted license or registration in another state may prepare the certificate so long as evidence of that license or registration is on the certificate:

(1) A physician.

(2) A nurse practitioner.

(3) A physician's assistant.

(d) The certificate shall be prepared on a form supplied by the Superintendent of Public Instruction. The certificate shall be issued only after a physical examination has been conducted, at the time of the certification, in accordance with rules adopted by the Superintendent of Public Instruction, with approval of the Secretary of Health and Human Services. These rules may require an X-ray chest examination for all new employees of the public school system.

(e) It shall be the duty of the superintendent of the school in which the person is employed to enforce the provisions of this section. Any person violating any of the provisions of this section shall be guilty of a Class 1 misdemeanor. (1955, c. 1372, art. 17, s. 1; 1957, c. 1357, ss. 2, 14; 1973, c. 476, s. 128; 1975, c. 72; 1981, c. 423, s. 1; 1985 (Reg. Sess., 1986), c. 975, s. 20; 1991, c. 342, s. 4; 1993, c. 539, s. 886; 1994, Ex. Sess., c. 24, s. 14(c); 1997-443, s. 11A.50; 2001-118, s. 1.)

Part 2. Payment of Wages After Death of Employee.

§ 115C-324. Disposition of payment due employees at time of death.

In the event of the death of any superintendent, teacher, principal, or other school employee to whom payment is due for or in connection with services rendered by such person or to whom has been issued any uncashed voucher for or in connection with services rendered, when there is no administration upon the estate of such person, such voucher may be cashed by the clerk of the superior court of the county in which such deceased person resided, or a voucher due for such services may be made payable to such clerk, who will treat such sums as a debt owed to the intestate under the provisions of G.S.

28A-25-6. (1955, c. 1372, art. 18, s. 8; 1965, c. 395; 1981, c. 423, s. 1; 2009-570, s. 38.)

Part 3. Principal and Teacher Employment Contracts.

§ 115C-325. (Repealed effective June 30, 2018 - see notes) System of employment for public school teachers.

(a) Definition of Terms. - As used in this section unless the context requires otherwise:

(1) Repealed by Session Laws 1997-221, s. 13(a).

(1a) "Career employee" as used in this section means:

a. An employee who has obtained career status with that local board as a teacher as provided in G.S. 115C-325(c);

b. An employee who has obtained career status with that local board in an administrative position as provided in G.S. 115C-325(d)(2);

c. A probationary teacher during the term of the contract as provided in G.S. 115C-325(m); and

d. A school administrator during the term of a school administrator contract as provided in G.S. 115C-287.1(c).

(1b) "Career school administrator" means a school administrator who has obtained career status in an administrative position as provided in G.S. 115C-325(d)(2).

(1c) "Career teacher" means a teacher who has obtained career status as provided in G.S. 115C-325(c).

(1d) Repealed by Session Laws 2011-348, s. 1, effective July 1, 2011, and applicable to persons recommended for dismissal or demotion on or after that date.

(2) Repealed by Session Laws 1997, c. 221, s. 13(a).

(3) "Day" means calendar day. In computing any period of time, Rule 6 of the North Carolina Rules of Civil Procedure shall apply.

(4) "Demote" means to reduce the salary of a person who is classified or paid by the State Board of Education as a classroom teacher or as a school administrator. The word "demote" does not include: (i) a suspension without pay pursuant to G.S. 115C-325(f)(1); (ii) the elimination or reduction of bonus payments, including merit-based supplements, or a systemwide modification in the amount of any applicable local supplement; or (iii) any reduction in salary that results from the elimination of a special duty, such as the duty of an athletic coach or a choral director.

(4a) "Disciplinary suspension" means a final decision to suspend a teacher or school administrator without pay for no more than 60 days under G.S. 115C-325(f)(2).

(4b) "Exchange teacher" means a nonimmigrant alien teacher participating in an exchange visitor program designated by the United States Department of State pursuant to 22 C.F.R. Part 62 or by the United States Department of Homeland Security pursuant to 8 C.F.R. Part 214.2(q).

(4c) "Hearing officer" means a person selected under G.S. 115C-325(h)(7).

(5) "Probationary teacher" means a licensed person, other than a superintendent, associate superintendent, or assistant superintendent, who has not obtained career-teacher status and whose major responsibility is to teach or to supervise teaching.

(5a) [Expired.]

(5b) "School administrator" means a principal, assistant principal, supervisor, or director whose major function includes the direct or indirect supervision of teaching or any other part of the instructional program as provided in G.S. 115C-287.1(a)(3).

(6) "Teacher" means a person who holds at least a current, not provisional or expired, Class A license or a regular, not provisional or expired, vocational license issued by the State Board of Education; whose major responsibility is to teach or directly supervises teaching or who is classified by the State Board of Education or is paid either as a classroom teacher or instructional support personnel; and who is employed to fill a full-time, permanent position.

(7) (See note) Redesignated.

(8) "Year" for purposes of computing time as a probationary teacher shall be not less than 120 workdays performed as a probationary teacher in a full-time permanent position in a school year. Workdays performed pending the outcome of a criminal history check as provided in G.S. 115C-332 are included in computing time as a probationary teacher.

(b) Personnel Files. - The superintendent shall maintain in his office a personnel file for each teacher that contains any complaint, commendation, or suggestion for correction or improvement about the teacher's professional conduct, except that the superintendent may elect not to place in a teacher's file (i) a letter of complaint that contains invalid, irrelevant, outdated, or false information or (ii) a letter of complaint when there is no documentation of an attempt to resolve the issue. The complaint, commendation, or suggestion shall be signed by the person who makes it and shall be placed in the teacher's file only after five days' notice to the teacher. Any denial or explanation relating to such complaint, commendation, or suggestion that the teacher desires to make shall be placed in the file. Any teacher may petition the local board of education to remove any information from his personnel file that he deems invalid, irrelevant, or outdated. The board may order the superintendent to remove said information if it finds the information is invalid, irrelevant, or outdated.

The personnel file shall be open for the teacher's inspection at all reasonable times but shall be open to other persons only in accordance with such rules and regulations as the board adopts. Any preemployment data or other information obtained about a teacher before his employment by the board may be kept in a file separate from his personnel file and need not be made available to him. No data placed in the preemployment file may be introduced as evidence at a hearing on the dismissal or demotion of a teacher, except the data may be used to substantiate G.S. 115C-325(e)(1)g. or G.S. 115C-325(e)(1)o. as grounds for dismissal or demotion.

(c) (1) (Repealed August 1, 2013, for teachers without career status on that date) Election of a Teacher to Career Status. - Except as otherwise provided in subdivision (3) of this subsection, when a teacher has been employed by a North Carolina public school system for four consecutive years, the board, near the end of the fourth year, shall vote upon whether to grant the teacher career status. The teacher has a right to notice and hearing prior to the board's vote as provided in G.S. 115C-325(m)(3) and G.S. 115C-325(m)(4). The board shall give the teacher written notice of that decision by June 15 or such later date as provided in G.S. 115C-325(m)(7). If a majority of the board votes to grant career status to the teacher, and if it has notified the teacher of the decision, it may not rescind that action but must proceed under the provisions of this section for the demotion or dismissal of a teacher if it decides to terminate the teacher's employment. If a majority of the board votes against granting career status, the teacher shall not teach beyond the current school term. If the board fails to vote on granting career status, the teacher shall be entitled to an additional month's pay for every 30 days or portion thereof after June 16 or such later date as provided in G.S. 115C-325(m)(7) if a majority of the board belatedly votes against granting career status.

(2) (Repealed August 1, 2013, for teachers without career status on that date) Employment of a Career Teacher. - A teacher who has obtained career status in any North Carolina public school system need not serve another probationary period of more than one year. The board may grant career status immediately upon employing the teacher, or after the first year of employment. The teacher has a right to notice and hearing prior to the board's vote as provided in G.S. 115C-325(m)(3) and G.S. 115C-325(m)(4). The board shall give the teacher written notice of that decision by June 15 or such later date as provided in G.S. 115C-325(m)(7). If a majority of the board votes against granting career status, the teacher shall not teach beyond the current term. If after one year of employment, the board fails to vote on the issue of granting career status, the teacher shall be entitled to one additional month's pay for every 30 days or portion thereof beyond June 16 or such later date as provided in G.S. 115C-325(m)(7) if a majority of the board belatedly voted against granting career status.

(2a) (Repealed August 1, 2013, for teachers without career status on that date) Notice of Teachers Eligible to Achieve Career Status. - At least 30 days prior to any board action granting career status, the superintendent shall submit to the board a list of the names of all teachers who are eligible to achieve career status. Notwithstanding any other provision of law, the list shall be a public record under Chapter 132 of the General Statutes.

(3) (Repealed August 1, 2013, for teachers without career status on that date) Ineligible for Career Status. - No employee of a local board of education except a teacher as defined by G.S. 115C-325(a)(6) is eligible to obtain career status or continue in a career status as a teacher if he no longer performs the responsibilities of a teacher as defined in G.S. 115C-325(a)(6). No person who is employed as a school administrator who did not acquire career status as a school administrator by June 30, 1997, shall have career status as an

administrator. Further, no director or assistant principal is eligible to obtain career status as a school administrator unless he or she has already been conferred that status by the local board of education.

(4) Leave of Absence. - A career teacher who has been granted a leave of absence by a board shall maintain his career status if he returns to his teaching position at the end of the authorized leave.

(5) (Repealed August 1, 2013, for teachers without career status on that date) Consecutive Years of Service. -

a. If a probationary teacher in a full-time permanent position does not work for at least 120 workdays in a school year because the teacher is on sick leave, disability leave, or both, that school year shall not be deemed to constitute (i) a consecutive year of service for the teacher or (ii) a break in the continuity in consecutive years of service for the teacher.

b. If a probationary teacher in a full-time permanent position is nonrenewed because of a decrease in the number of positions due to decreased funding, decreased enrollment, or a district reorganization, and is subsequently rehired by the same school system within three years, the intervening years when the teacher was not employed by the local school administrative unit shall not be deemed to constitute (i) a consecutive year of service for the teacher or (ii) a break in the continuity of years of service. However, if at the time of the teacher's nonrenewal for the reasons described in this subsection, the teacher was eligible for career status after being employed four consecutive years pursuant to G.S. 115C-325(c)(1), or one year pursuant to G.S. 115C-325(c)(2), and the board subsequently rehires the teacher within three years, the teacher will be eligible for a career status decision after one additional year of employment. Unless the superintendent unilaterally grants a teacher the benefit set forth in this subsection pursuant to a policy adopted by the board of education for this purpose, the teacher is entitled to such benefit only if the teacher notifies the head of human resources for the local school administrative unit in writing within 60 calendar days after the first day of employment upon being rehired that the teacher was nonrenewed because of a decrease in the number of positions triggered by decreased funding, decreased enrollment, or a district reorganization, and therefore the teacher's nonrenewal did not constitute a break in service for purposes of determining eligibility for career status. The local school administrative unit shall notify the teacher of the 60-day deadline as described herein in the employment application, contract, or in some other method reasonably calculated to provide the teacher actual notice within 30 calendar days after the first day of employment for the rehired teacher. The burden is on the teacher to submit information establishing that the teacher was nonrenewed because of a decrease in the number of positions triggered by decreased funding, decreased enrollment, or a district reorganization. If the local school administrative unit fails to provide notice to the teacher within this 30-day period, then the teacher's obligation to notify the local school administrative unit within 60 days does not commence until such time that the teacher is notified of the 60-day deadline.

The superintendent or designee will inform the teacher on whether the teacher qualifies for the benefit of this subsection within a reasonable period of time after receiving the information submitted by the teacher. This decision is final and the teacher has no right to a hearing or appeal except that the teacher may petition the board in writing within 10 calendar days after receiving the decision of the superintendent or designee, and the board or board panel shall review the matter on the record and provide the teacher a written decision. Notwithstanding any other provision of law, no appeal to court or otherwise is permitted in regard to the benefits provided under this subsection. This subsection creates no private right of action or basis for any liability on the part of the school system, nor does it create any reemployment rights for a nonrenewed probationary teacher.

The provisions of this subsection also shall apply to a probationary teacher in a full-time permanent position who resigns effective the end of the school year in good standing after receiving documentation that the teacher's position may be eliminated because of a decrease in the number of positions triggered by decreased funding, decreased enrollment, or a district reorganization, and is subsequently rehired by the same school system.

(6) (Repealed August 1, 2013, for teachers without career status on that date) Status of Exchange Teachers. - Exchange teachers shall not be eligible to obtain career status. However, for purposes of determining eligibility to receive employment benefits under this Chapter, including personal leave, annual vacation leave, and sick leave, an exchange teacher shall be considered a permanent teacher if employed with the expectation of at least six full consecutive monthly pay periods of employment and if employed at least 20 hours per week.

(d) Career Teachers and Career School Administrators.

(1) A career teacher or career school administrator shall not be subjected to the requirement of annual appointment nor shall he be dismissed, demoted, or employed on a part-time basis without his consent except as provided in subsection (e).

(2) a. The provisions of this subdivision do not apply to a person who is ineligible for career status as provided by G.S. 115C-325(c)(3).

b. Repealed by Session Laws 1997, c. 221, s. 13(a).

c. Subject to G.S. 115C-287.1, when a teacher has performed the duties of supervisor or principal for three consecutive years, the board, near the end of the third year, shall vote upon his employment for the next school year. The board shall give him written notice of that decision by June 1 of his third year of employment as a supervisor or principal. If a majority of the board votes to reemploy the teacher as a principal or supervisor, and it has notified him of that decision, it may not rescind that action but must proceed under the provisions of this section. If a majority of the board votes not to reemploy the teacher as a principal or supervisor, he shall retain career status as a teacher if that status was attained prior to assuming the duties of supervisor or principal. A supervisor or principal who has not held that position for three years and whose contract will not be renewed for the next school year shall be notified by June 1 and shall retain career status as a teacher if that status was attained prior to assuming the duties of supervisor or principal.

A year, for purposes of computing time as a probationary principal or supervisor, shall not be less than 145 workdays performed as a full-time, permanent principal or supervisor in a contract year.

A principal or supervisor who has obtained career status in that position in any North Carolina public school system may be required by the board of education in another school system to serve an additional three-year probationary period in that position before being eligible for career status. However, he may, at the option of the board of education, be granted career status immediately or after serving a probationary period of one or two additional years. A principal or supervisor with career status who resigns and within five years is reemployed by the same school system need not serve another probationary period in that position of more than two years and may, at the option of the board, be reemployed immediately as a career principal or supervisor or be given career status after only one year. In any event, if he is reemployed for a third consecutive year, he shall automatically become a career principal or supervisor.

(e) Grounds for Dismissal or Demotion of a Career Employee.

(1) Grounds. - No career employee shall be dismissed or demoted or employed on a part-time basis except for one or more of the following:

a. Inadequate performance.

b. Immorality.

c. Insubordination.

d. Neglect of duty.

e. Physical or mental incapacity.

f. Habitual or excessive use of alcohol or nonmedical use of a controlled substance as defined in Article 5 of Chapter 90 of the General Statutes.

g. Conviction of a felony or a crime involving moral turpitude.

h. Advocating the overthrow of the government of the United States or of the State of North Carolina by force, violence, or other unlawful means.

i. Failure to fulfill the duties and responsibilities imposed upon teachers or school administrators by the General Statutes of this State.

j. Failure to comply with such reasonable requirements as the board may prescribe.

k. Any cause which constitutes grounds for the revocation of the career teacher's teaching license or the career school administrator's administrator license.

l. A justifiable decrease in the number of positions due to district reorganization, decreased enrollment, or decreased funding, provided that there is compliance with subdivision (2).

m. Failure to maintain his or her license in a current status.

n. Failure to repay money owed to the State in accordance with the provisions of Article 60, Chapter 143 of the General Statutes.

o. Providing false information or knowingly omitting a material fact on an application for employment or in response to a preemployment inquiry.

(2) Reduction in Force. - Before recommending to a board the dismissal or demotion of the career employee pursuant to G.S. 115C-325(e)(1)l., the superintendent shall give written notice to the career employee by certified mail or personal delivery of his intention to make such recommendation and shall set forth as part of his or her recommendation the grounds upon which he or she believes such dismissal or demotion is justified. The notice shall include a statement to the effect that if the career employee within 15 days after receipt of the notice requests a review, he or she shall be entitled to have the proposed recommendations of the superintendent reviewed by the board. Within the 15-day period after receipt of the notice, the career employee may file with the superintendent a written request for a hearing before the board within 10 days. If the career employee requests a hearing before the board, the hearing procedures provided in G.S. 115C-325(j3) shall be followed. If no request is made within the 15-day period, the superintendent may file his or her recommendation with the board. If, after considering the recommendation of the superintendent and the evidence adduced at the hearing if there is one, the board concludes that the grounds for the recommendation are true and substantiated by a preponderance of the evidence, the board, if it sees fit, may by resolution order such dismissal. Provisions of this section which permit a hearing by a hearing officer shall not apply to a dismissal or demotion recommended pursuant to G.S. 115C-325(e)(1)l.

When a career employee is dismissed pursuant to G.S. 115C-325(e)(1)l., above, his or her name shall be placed on a list of available career employees to be maintained by the board.

(3) Inadequate Performance. - In determining whether the professional performance of a career employee is adequate, consideration shall be given to regular and special evaluation reports prepared in accordance with the published policy of the employing local school administrative unit and to any published standards of performance which shall have been adopted by the board. Failure to notify a career employee of an inadequacy or deficiency in performance shall be conclusive evidence of satisfactory performance. Inadequate performance for a teacher shall mean (i) the failure to perform at a proficient level on any standard of the evaluation instrument or (ii) otherwise

performing in a manner that is below standard. However, for a probationary teacher, a performance rating below proficient may or may not be deemed adequate at that stage of development by a superintendent or designee. For a career teacher, a performance rating below proficient shall constitute inadequate performance unless the principal noted on the instrument that the teacher is making adequate progress toward proficiency given the circumstances.

(4) Three-Year Limitation on Basis of Dismissal or Demotion. - Dismissal or demotion under subdivision (1) above, except paragraphs g. and o. thereof, shall not be based on conduct or actions which occurred more than three years before the written notice of the superintendent's intention to recommend dismissal or demotion is mailed to the career employee. The three-year limitation shall not apply to dismissals or demotions pursuant to subdivision (1)b. above when the charge of immorality is based upon a career employee's sexual misconduct toward or sexual harassment of students or staff.

(f) (1) Suspension without Pay. - If a superintendent believes that cause exists for dismissing a career employee for any reason specified in G.S. 115C-325(e)(1) and that immediate suspension of the career employee is necessary, the superintendent may suspend the career employee without pay. Before suspending a career employee without pay, the superintendent shall meet with the career employee and give him written notice of the charges against him, an explanation of the bases for the charges, and an opportunity to respond. Within five days after a suspension under this paragraph, the superintendent shall initiate a dismissal, demotion, or disciplinary suspension without pay as provided in this section. If it is finally determined that no grounds for dismissal, demotion, or disciplinary suspension without pay exist, the career employee shall be reinstated immediately, shall be paid for the period of suspension, and all records of the suspension shall be removed from the career employee's personnel file.

(2) Disciplinary Suspension Without Pay. - A career employee recommended for suspension without pay pursuant to G.S. 115C-325(a)(4a) may request a hearing before the board. If no request is made within 15 days, the superintendent may file his recommendation with the board. If, after considering the recommendation of the superintendent and the evidence adduced at the hearing if one is held, the board concludes that the grounds for the recommendation are true and substantiated by a preponderance of the evidence, the board, if it sees fit, may by resolution order such suspension.

a. Board hearing for disciplinary suspensions for more than 10 days or for certain types of intentional misconduct. - The procedures for a board hearing under G.S. 115C-325(j3) shall apply if any of the following circumstances exist:

1. The recommended disciplinary suspension without pay is for more than 10 days; or

2. The disciplinary suspension is for intentional misconduct, such as inappropriate sexual or physical conduct, immorality, insubordination, habitual or excessive alcohol or nonmedical use of a controlled substance as defined in Article 5 of Chapter 90 of the General Statutes, any cause that constitutes grounds for the revocation of the teacher's or school administrator's license, or providing false information.

b. Board hearing for disciplinary suspensions of no more that [than] 10 days. - The procedures for a board hearing under G.S. 115C-325(j2) shall apply to all disciplinary suspensions of no more than 10 days that are not for intentional misconduct as specified in G.S. 115C-325(f)(2)a.2.

(f1) Suspension with Pay. - If a superintendent believes that cause may exist for dismissing or demoting a career employee for any reasons specified in G.S. 115C-325(e)(1), but that additional investigation of the facts is necessary and circumstances are such that the career employee should be removed immediately from his duties, the superintendent may suspend the career employee with pay for a reasonable period of time, not to exceed 90 days. The superintendent shall notify the board of education within two days of his action and shall notify the career employee within two days of the action and the reasons for it. If the superintendent has not initiated dismissal or demotion proceedings against the career employee within the 90-day period, the career employee shall be reinstated to his duties immediately and all records of the suspension with pay shall be removed from the career employee's personnel file at his request. However, if the superintendent and the employee agree to extend the 90-day period, the superintendent may initiate dismissal or demotion proceedings against the career employee at any time during the period of the extension.

(f2) Procedure for Demotion of Career School Administrator. - If a superintendent intends to recommend the demotion of a career school administrator, the superintendent shall give written notice to the career school administrator by certified mail or personal delivery and shall include in the notice the grounds upon which the superintendent believes the demotion is justified.

The notice shall include a statement that if the career school administrator requests a hearing within 15 days after receipt of the notice, the administrator shall be entitled to have the grounds for the proposed demotion reviewed by the local board of education. If the career school administrator does not request a board hearing within 15 days, the superintendent may file the recommendation of demotion with the board. If, after considering the superintendent's recommendation and the evidence presented at the hearing if one is held, the board concludes that the grounds for the recommendation are true and substantiated by a preponderance of the evidence, the board may by resolution order the demotion. The procedures for a board hearing under G.S. 115C-325(j3) shall apply to all demotions of career school administrators.

(g)   Repealed by Session Laws 1997, c. 221, s. 13(a).

(h)   Procedure for Dismissal or Demotion of Career Employee.

(1)   a.   A career employee may not be dismissed, demoted, or reduced to part-time employment except upon the superintendent's recommendation.

b.   G.S. 115C-325(f2) shall apply to the demotion of a career school administrator.

(2)   Before recommending to a board the dismissal or demotion of the career employee, the superintendent shall give written notice to the career employee by certified mail or personal delivery of his or her intention to make such recommendation and shall set forth as part of his or her recommendation the grounds upon which he or she believes such dismissal or demotion is justified. The superintendent also shall meet with the career employee and provide written notice of the charges against the career employee, an explanation of the basis for the charges, and an opportunity to respond if the career employee has not done so under G.S. 115C-325(f)(1). The notice shall include a statement to the effect that if the career employee within 14 days after the date of receipt of the notice requests a review, he or she may request to have the grounds for the proposed recommendations of the superintendent reviewed by an impartial hearing officer appointed by the Superintendent of Public Instruction as provided for in G.S. 115C-325(h)(7). A copy of G.S. 115C-325 shall also be sent to the career employee. If the career employee does not request a hearing before a hearing officer within the 14 days provided, the superintendent may submit his or her recommendation to the board.

(3) Within the 14-day period after receipt of the notice, the career employee may file with the superintendent a written request for either (i) a hearing on the grounds for the superintendent's proposed recommendation by a hearing officer or (ii) a hearing within 10 days before the board on the superintendent's recommendation. If the career employee requests an immediate hearing before the board, he or she forfeits his or her right to a hearing by a hearing officer. If no request is made within that period, the superintendent may file his or her recommendation with the board. The board, if it sees fit, may by resolution (i) reject the superintendent's recommendation or (ii) accept or modify the superintendent's recommendation and dismiss, demote, reinstate, or suspend the employee without pay. If a request for review is made, the superintendent shall not file the recommendation for dismissal with the board until a report of the hearing officer is filed with the superintendent. Failure of the hearing officer to submit the report as required by G.S. 115C-325(i1)(1) shall entitle the career employee to a hearing before the board under the same procedures as provided in G.S.115C-325(j).

(4) Repealed by Session Laws 1997, c. 221, s. 13(a).

(5) Repealed by Session Laws 2011-348, s. 1, effective July 1, 2011, and applicable to persons recommended for dismissal or demotion on or after that date.

(6) If a career employee requests a review by a hearing officer, the superintendent shall notify the Superintendent of Public Instruction within five days of his or her receipt of the request.

(7) Within five days of being notified of the request for a hearing before a hearing officer, the Superintendent of Public Instruction shall submit to both parties a list of hearing officers trained and approved by the State Board of Education. Within five days of receiving the list, the parties may jointly select a hearing officer from that list, or, if the parties cannot agree to a hearing officer, each party may strike up to one-third of the names on the list and submit its strikeout list to the Superintendent of Public Instruction. The Superintendent of Public Instruction shall then appoint a hearing officer from those individuals remaining on the list. Further, the parties may jointly agree on another hearing officer not on the State Board of Eduation's [Education's] list, provided that individual is available to proceed in a timely manner and is willing to accept the terms of appointment required by the State Board of Education. No person eliminated by the career employee or superintendent shall be designated as the hearing officer for that case.

(8) The superintendent and career employee shall serve a copy to the other party of all documents submitted to the Superintendent of Public Instruction and to the designated hearing officer and include a signed certificate of service similar to that required in court pleadings.

(h1) Hearing Officers; Qualifications; Training; Compensation.

(1) The State Board of Education shall select and maintain a master list of no more than 15 qualified hearing officers. The State Board shall, except for good cause shown, remove a hearing officer from the list who has failed to conduct a hearing or prepare a report within the time specified in G.S. 115C-325(i1) or who has failed to submit a supplemental report in accordance with G.S. 115C-325(i1)(4) or (j1)(2). A hearing officer shall, except for good cause shown, also be removed from the list for failure to meet the terms and conditions of engagement established by the State Board. Additionally, if a hearing officer is not appointed to a case within a two-year period due to repeated strikes from the list by either party as provided in G.S. 115C-325(h)(7), the State Board may remove the hearing officer from the master list.

(2) Persons selected by the State Board as hearing officers shall be members in good standing of the North Carolina State Bar who have demonstrated experience and expertise in the areas of education law, due process, administrative law, or employment law within the last five years. The State Board shall give special consideration in its selection to persons jointly endorsed by the largest by membership of each statewide organization representing teachers, school administrators, and local boards of education. Following State Board selection, hearing officers must complete a special training course approved by the State Board of Education that includes training on the teacher evaluation instrument and performance standards before they are qualified to hear teacher dismissal or demotion cases.

(3) The State Board of Education shall determine the compensation for a hearing officer. The State Board shall pay the hearing officer's compensation and authorized expenses.

(i) Repealed by Session Laws 1997, c. 221, s. 13(a).

(i1) Report of Hearing Officer; Superintendent's Recommendation.

(1) The hearing officer shall complete the hearing held in accordance with G.S. 115C-325(j) and prepare the report within 90 days from the time of the designation. This time period may be extended only for extraordinary cause and upon written agreement by both parties. The State Board of Education shall determine an appropriate reduction in compensation to the hearing officer for failure to submit a timely report to the superintendent within the maximum 90-day period set forth in this subdivision, except upon a showing of good cause by the hearing officer.

(2) The hearing officer shall make all necessary findings of fact, based upon the preponderance of the evidence, on all issues related to each and every ground for dismissal and on all relevant matters related to the question of whether the superintendent's recommendation is justified. The hearing officer shall not make a recommendation as to conclusions of law or the disposition of the case. The hearing officer shall deliver copies of the report to the superintendent and the career employee.

(3) Within five days after receiving the hearing officer's report, the superintendent shall decide whether to submit a written recommendation to the local board for dismissal, demotion, or disciplinary suspension without pay to the board or to drop the charges against the career employee. The superintendent shall notify the career employee, in writing, of the decision.

(4) If the superintendent contends that the hearing officer's report fails to address a critical factual issue, the superintendent shall within five days' receipt of the hearing officer's report, request in writing with a copy to the career employee that the hearing officer prepare a supplement to the report. The superintendent shall specify what critical factual issue the superintendent contends the hearing officer failed to address. If the hearing officer determines that the report failed to address a critical factual issue, the hearing officer shall prepare a supplement to the report to address the issue and deliver the supplement to both parties before the board hearing. In no event shall the hearing officer take more than 30 days to provide a supplemental report. If the hearing officer fails to submit a timely supplemental report, the superintendent shall report the hearing officer to the State Board. The State Board shall determine an appropriate reduction in compensation to the hearing officer for failure to submit a timely supplemental report to both parties, except upon a showing of good cause by the hearing officer. The failure of the hearing officer to prepare a supplemental report or to address a critical factual issue shall not constitute a basis for appeal.

(j) Hearing by a Hearing Officer. - The following provisions shall apply to a hearing conducted by the hearing officer.

(1) The hearing shall be private.

(2) The hearing shall be conducted in accordance with reasonable rules and regulations adopted by the State Board of Education to govern such hearings.

(3) At the hearing the career employee and the superintendent or the superintendent's designee shall have the right to be present and to be heard, to be represented by counsel and to present through witnesses any competent testimony relevant to the issue of whether grounds for dismissal or demotion exist or whether the procedures set forth in G.S. 115C-325 have been followed.

(4) Rules of evidence shall not apply to a hearing conducted by a hearing officer. The hearing officer may give probative effect to evidence that is of a kind commonly relied on by reasonably prudent persons in the conduct of serious affairs.

(5) At least five days before the hearing, the superintendent shall provide to the career employee a list of witnesses the superintendent intends to present, a brief statement of the nature of the testimony of each witness and a copy of any documentary evidence the superintendent intends to present. At least three days before the hearing, the career employee shall provide to the superintendent a list of witnesses the career employee intends to present, a brief statement of the nature of the testimony of each witness and a copy of any documentary evidence the career employee intends to present. Additional witnesses or documentary evidence may not be presented except upon a finding by the hearing officer that the new evidence is critical to the matter at issue and the party making the request could not, with reasonable diligence, have discovered and produced the evidence according to the schedule provided in this subdivision.

(5a) The hearing shall be completed within three days after commencement, unless extended by the hearing officer on a showing of extraordinary cause. Neither party shall have more than eight hours to present its case in chief, which does not include cross-examination of witnesses, rebuttal evidence, or arguments of counsel.

(6) The hearing officer may issue subpoenas, at his or her discretion or upon written application by either party, and swear witnesses and may require them to give testimony and to produce records and documents relevant to the grounds for dismissal.

(7) The hearing officer shall decide all procedural issues, including limiting cumulative evidence, necessary for a fair and efficient hearing.

(8) The superintendent shall provide for making a transcript of the hearing. If the career employee contemplates a hearing before the board or to appeal the board's decision to a court of law, the career employee may request and shall receive at no charge a transcript of the proceedings before the hearing officer.

(j1) Board Determination. -

(1) Within five days after receiving the superintendent's notice of intent to recommend the career employee's dismissal to the board, the career employee shall decide whether to request a hearing before the board and shall notify the superintendent, in writing, of the decision. If the career employee can show that the request for a hearing was postmarked within the time provided, the career employee shall not forfeit the right to a board hearing. Within five days after receiving the career employee's request for a board hearing, the superintendent shall request that a transcript of the hearing be made. Within five days of receiving a copy of the transcript, the superintendent shall submit to the board the written recommendation and shall provide a copy of the recommendation to the career employee. The superintendent's recommendation shall state the grounds for the recommendation and shall be accompanied by a copy of the hearing officer's report and a copy of the transcript of the hearing.

(2) If the career employee contends that the hearing officer's report fails to address a critical factual issue the career employee shall, at the same time he or she notifies the superintendent of a request for a board hearing pursuant to G.S. 115C-325(j1)(1), request in writing with a copy to the superintendent that the hearing officer prepare a supplement to the hearing officer's report. The career employee shall specify the critical factual issue he or she contends the hearing officer failed to address. If the hearing officer determines that the report failed to address a critical factual issue, the hearing officer shall prepare a supplement to the report to address the issue and shall deliver the supplement to both parties before the board hearing. In no event shall the hearing officer take more than 30 days to provide a supplemental report. If the hearing officer fails to submit a timely supplemental report, the superintendent shall report the

hearing officer to the State Board. The State Board shall determine an appropriate reduction in compensation to the hearing officer for failure to submit a timely supplemental report to both parties, except upon a showing of good cause by the hearing officer. The failure of the hearing officer to prepare a supplemental report or to address a critical factual issue shall not constitute a basis for appeal.

(3) Within five days after receiving the superintendent's recommendation and before taking any formal action, the board shall set a time and place for the hearing and shall notify the career employee by certified mail or personal delivery of the date, time, and place of the hearing. The time specified shall not be less than 10 nor more than 30 days after the board has notified the career employee, unless both parties agree to an extension. If the career employee did not request a hearing, the board may, by resolution, reject the superintendent's decision, or accept or modify the decision and dismiss, demote, reinstate, or suspend the career employee without pay.

(4) If the career employee requests a board hearing, it shall be conducted in accordance with G.S. 115C-325(j2).

(5) The board shall make a determination and may (i) reject the superintendent's recommendation or (ii) accept or modify the recommendation and dismiss, demote, reinstate, or suspend the employee without pay.

(6) Within two days following the hearing, the board shall send a written copy of its findings and determination to the career employee and the superintendent.

(j2) Board Hearing. - The following procedures shall apply to a hearing conducted by the board:

(1) The hearing shall be private.

(2) If the career employee requested a hearing by a hearing officer, the board shall receive the following:

a. The whole record from the hearing held by the hearing officer, including a transcript of the hearing, as well as any other records, exhibits, and documentary evidence submitted to the case manager at the hearing.

b. The hearing officer's findings of fact, including any supplemental findings prepared by the hearing officer under G.S. 115C-325 (i1)(4) or G.S. 115C-325(j1)(2).

c. Repealed by Session Laws 2011-348, s. 1, effective July 1, 2011, and applicable to persons recommended for dismissal or demotion on or after that date.

d. The superintendent's recommendation and the grounds for the recommendation.

(3) If the career employee did not request a hearing by a hearing officer, the board shall receive the following:

a. Any documentary evidence the superintendent intends to use to support the recommendation. The superintendent shall provide the documentary evidence to the career employee seven days before the hearing.

b. Any documentary evidence the career employee intends to use to rebut the superintendent's recommendation. The career employee shall provide the superintendent with the documentary evidence three days before the hearing.

c. The superintendent's recommendation and the grounds for the recommendation.

(4) The superintendent and career employee may submit a written statement not less than three days before the hearing.

(5) The superintendent and career employee shall be permitted to make oral arguments to the board based on the record before the board.

(6) No new evidence may be presented at the hearing except upon a finding by the board that the new evidence is critical to the matter at issue and the party making the request could not, with reasonable diligence, have discovered and produced the evidence at the hearing before the hearing officer.

(7) The board shall accept the hearing officer's findings of fact unless a majority of the board determines that the findings of fact are not supported by substantial evidence when reviewing the record as a whole. In such an event, the board shall make alternative findings of fact. If a majority of the board determines that the hearing officer did not address a critical factual issue, the

board may remand the findings of fact to the hearing officer to complete the report to the board. If the hearing officer does not submit the report within seven days receipt of the board's request, the board may determine its own findings of fact regarding the critical factual issues not addressed by the hearing officer. The board's determination shall be based upon a preponderance of the evidence.

(8) The board is not required to provide a transcript of the hearing to the career employee. If the board elects to make a transcript and if the career employee contemplates an appeal to a court of law, the career employee may request and shall receive at no charge a transcript of the proceedings. A career employee may have the hearing transcribed by a court reporter at the career employee's expense.

(j3) Board Hearing for Certain Disciplinary Suspensions, Demotions of Career School Administrators, and for Reductions in Force. - The following procedures shall apply for a board hearing under G.S. 115C-325(e)(2), G.S. 115C-325(f2), and G.S. 115C-325(f)(2)a:

(1) The hearing shall be private.

(2) The hearing shall be conducted in accordance with reasonable rules adopted by the State Board of Education to govern such hearings.

(3) At the hearing, the career employee and the superintendent shall have the right to be present and to be heard, to be represented by counsel, and to present through witnesses any competent testimony relevant to the issue of whether grounds exist for a disciplinary suspension without pay under G.S. 115C-325(f)(2)a., a demotion of a career school administrator under G.S. 115C-325(f2), or whether the grounds for a dismissal or demotion due to a reduction in force is justified.

(4) Rules of evidence shall not apply to a hearing under this subsection and the board may give probative effect to evidence that is of a kind commonly relied on by reasonably prudent persons in the conduct of serious affairs.

(5) At least eight days before the hearing, the superintendent shall provide to the career employee a list of witnesses the superintendent intends to present, a brief statement of the nature of the testimony of each witness, and a copy of any documentary evidence the superintendent intends to present.

(6) At least six days before the hearing, the career employee shall provide the superintendent a list of witnesses the career employee intends to present, a brief statement of the nature of the testimony of each witness, and a copy of any documentary evidence the career employee intends to present.

(7) No new evidence may be presented at the hearing except upon a finding by the board that the new evidence is critical to the matter at issue and the party making the request could not, with reasonable diligence, have discovered and produced the evidence according to the schedule provided in this subsection.

(8) The board may subpoena and swear witnesses and may require them to give testimony and to produce records and documents relevant to the grounds for suspension without pay.

(9) The board shall decide all procedural issues, including limiting cumulative evidence, necessary for a fair and efficient hearing.

(10) The superintendent shall provide for making a transcript of the hearing. If the career employee contemplates an appeal of the board's decision to a court of law, the career employee may request and shall receive at no charge a transcript of the proceedings.

(k), (l) Repealed by Session Laws 1997, c. 221, s. 13(a).

(m) Probationary Teacher.

(1) The board of any local school administrative unit may not discharge a probationary teacher during the school year except for the reasons for and by the procedures by which a career employee may be dismissed as set forth in subsections (e), (f), (f1), and (h) to (j3) above.

(2) The board, upon recommendation of the superintendent, may refuse to renew the contract of any probationary teacher or to reemploy any teacher who is not under contract for any cause it deems sufficient: Provided, however, that the cause may not be arbitrary, capricious, discriminatory or for personal or political reasons.

(3) The superintendent shall provide written notice to a probationary teacher no later than May 15 of the superintendent's intent to recommend nonrenewal and the teacher's right, within 10 days of receipt of the superintendent's

recommendation, to (i) request and receive written notice of the reasons for the superintendent's recommendation for nonrenewal and the information that the superintendent may share with the board to support the recommendation for nonrenewal; and (ii) request a hearing for those teachers eligible for a hearing under G.S. 115C-325(m)(4). The failure to file a timely request within the 10 days shall result in a waiver of the right to this information and any right to a hearing. If a teacher files a timely request, the superintendent shall provide the requested information and arrange for a hearing, if allowed, and the teacher shall be permitted to submit supplemental information to the superintendent and board prior to the board making a decision or holding a hearing as provided in this section. The board shall adopt a policy to provide for the orderly exchange of information prior to the board's decision on the superintendent's recommendation for nonrenewal.

(4)   If the probationary teacher is eligible for career status pursuant to G.S. 115C-325(c)(1) and (c)(2) and the superintendent recommends not to give the probationary teacher career status, the probationary teacher has the right to a hearing before the board unless the reason is a justifiable board- or superintendent-approved decrease in the number of positions due to district reorganization, decreased enrollment, or decreased funding.

(5)   For probationary contracts that are not in the final year before the probationary teacher is eligible for career status, the probationary teacher shall have the right to petition the local board of education for a hearing, and the local board may grant a hearing regarding the superintendent's recommendation for nonrenewal. The local board of education shall notify the probationary teacher making the petition of its decision whether to grant a hearing.

(6)   Any hearing held according to this subsection shall be pursuant to the provisions of G.S. 115C-45(c).

(7)   The board shall notify a probationary teacher whose contract will not be renewed for the next school year of its decision by June 15; provided, however, if a teacher submits a request for information or a hearing, the board shall provide the nonrenewal notification by July 1 or such later date upon the written consent of the superintendent and teacher.

(n)   Appeal. - Any career employee who has been dismissed or demoted under G.S. 115C-325(e)(2), or under G.S. 115C-325(j2), or who has been suspended without pay under G.S. 115C-325(a)(4a), or any school administrator whose contract is not renewed in accordance with G.S. 115C-

287.1, or any probationary teacher whose contract is not renewed under G.S. 115C-325(m)(2) shall have the right to appeal from the decision of the board to the superior court for the superior court district or set of districts as defined in G.S. 7A-41.1 in which the career employee is employed. This appeal shall be filed within a period of 30 days after notification of the decision of the board. The cost of preparing the transcript shall be determined under G.S. 115C-325(j2)(8) or G.S. 115C-325(j3)(10). A career employee who has been demoted or dismissed, or a school administrator whose contract is not renewed, who has not requested a hearing before the board of education pursuant to this section shall not be entitled to judicial review of the board's action.

(o) Resignation. -

(1) If a career employee has been recommended for dismissal under G.S. 115C-325(e)(1) and the employee chooses to resign without the written agreement of the superintendent, then:

a. The superintendent shall report the matter to the State Board of Education.

b. The employee shall be deemed to have consented to (i) the placement in the employee's personnel file of the written notice of the superintendent's intention to recommend dismissal and (ii) the release of the fact that the superintendent has reported this employee to the State Board of Education to prospective employers, upon request. The provisions of G.S. 115C-321 shall not apply to the release of this particular information.

c. The employee shall be deemed to have voluntarily surrendered his or her license pending an investigation by the State Board of Education in a determination whether or not to seek action against the employee's license. This license surrender shall not exceed 45 days from the date of resignation. Provided further that the cessation of the license surrender shall not prevent the State Board of Education from taking any further action it deems appropriate. The State Board of Education shall initiate investigation within five working days of the written notice from the superintendent and shall make a final decision as to whether to revoke or suspend the employee's license within 45 days from the date of resignation.

(2) A teacher, career or probationary, who is not recommended for dismissal should not resign without the consent of the superintendent unless he or she has given at least 30 days' notice. If a teacher who is not recommended

for dismissal does resign without giving at least 30 days' notice, the board may request that the State Board of Education revoke the teacher's license for the remainder of that school year. A copy of the request shall be placed in the teacher's personnel file.

(p) Section Applicable to Certain Institutions. - Notwithstanding any law or regulation to the contrary, this section shall apply to all persons employed in teaching and related educational classes in the schools and institutions of the Departments of Health and Human Services and Public Instruction and the Divisions of Juvenile Justice and Adult Correction of the Department of Public Safety regardless of the age of the students.

(p1) Procedure for Dismissal of School Administrators and Teachers Employed in Low-Performing Residential Schools. -

(1) Notwithstanding any other provision of this section or any other law, this subdivision shall govern the dismissal by the Secretary of Health and Human Services of teachers, principals, assistant principals, directors, supervisors, and other licensed personnel assigned to a residential school that the State Board has identified as low-performing and to which the State Board has assigned an assistance team under Part 3A of Article 3 of Chapter 143B of the General Statutes. The Secretary shall dismiss a teacher, principal, assistant principal, director, supervisor, or other licensed personnel when the Secretary receives two consecutive evaluations that include written findings and recommendations regarding that person's inadequate performance from the assistance team. These findings and recommendations shall be substantial evidence of the inadequate performance of the teacher or school administrator.

The Secretary may dismiss a teacher, principal, assistant principal, director, supervisor, or other licensed personnel when:

a. The Secretary determines that the school has failed to make satisfactory improvement after the State Board assigned an assistance team to that school under Part 3A of Article 3 of Chapter 143B of the General Statutes; and

b. That assistance team makes the recommendation to dismiss the teacher, principal, assistant principal, director, supervisor, or other licensed personnel for one or more grounds established in G.S. 115C-325(e)(1) for dismissal or demotion of a career employee.

Within 30 days of any dismissal under this subdivision, a teacher, principal, assistant principal, director, supervisor, or other licensed personnel may request a hearing before a panel of three members designated by the Secretary. The Secretary shall adopt procedures to ensure that due process rights are afforded to persons recommended for dismissal under this subdivision. Decisions of the panel may be appealed on the record to the Secretary, with further right of judicial review under Chapter 150B of the General Statutes.

(2)   Notwithstanding any other provision of this section or any other law, this subdivision shall govern the dismissal by the Secretary of Health and Human Services of licensed staff members who have engaged in a remediation plan under G.S. 115C-105.38A(c) but who, after one retest, fail to meet the general knowledge standard set by the State Board. The failure to meet the general knowledge standard after one retest shall be substantial evidence of the inadequate performance of the licensed staff member.

Within 30 days of any dismissal under this subdivision, a licensed staff member may request a hearing before a panel of three members designated by the Secretary of Health and Human Services. The Secretary shall adopt procedures to ensure that due process rights are afforded to licensed staff members recommended for dismissal under this subdivision. Decisions of the panel may be appealed on the record to the Secretary, with further right of judicial review under Chapter 150B of the General Statutes.

(3)   The Secretary of Health and Human Services or the superintendent of a residential school may terminate the contract of a school administrator dismissed under this subsection. Nothing in this subsection shall prevent the Secretary from refusing to renew the contract of any person employed in a school identified as low-performing under Part 3A of Article 3 of Chapter 143B of the General Statutes.

(4)   Neither party to a school administrator contract is entitled to damages under this subsection.

(5)   The Secretary of Health and Human Services shall have the right to subpoena witnesses and documents on behalf of any party to the proceedings under this subsection.

(q)   Procedure for Dismissal of School Administrators and Teachers Employed in Low-Performing Schools. -

(1) Notwithstanding any other provision of this section or any other law, this subdivision governs the State Board's dismissal of principals assigned to low-performing schools to which the Board has assigned an assistance team:

a. The State Board through its designee may, at any time, recommend the dismissal of any principal who is assigned to a low-performing school to which an assistance team has been assigned. The State Board through its designee shall recommend the dismissal of any principal when the Board receives from the assistance team assigned to that principal's school two consecutive evaluations that include written findings and recommendations regarding the principal's inadequate performance.

b. If the State Board through its designee recommends the dismissal of a principal under this subdivision, the principal shall be suspended with pay pending a hearing before a panel of three members of the State Board. The purpose of this hearing, which shall be held within 60 days after the principal is suspended, is to determine whether the principal shall be dismissed.

c. The panel shall order the dismissal of the principal if it determines from available information, including the findings of the assistance team, that the low performance of the school is due to the principal's inadequate performance.

d. The panel may order the dismissal of the principal if (i) it determines that the school has not made satisfactory improvement after the State Board assigned an assistance team to that school; and (ii) the assistance team makes the recommendation to dismiss the principal for one or more grounds established in G.S. 115C-325(e)(1) for dismissal or demotion of a career employee.

e. If the State Board or its designee recommends the dismissal of a principal before the assistance team assigned to the principal's school has evaluated that principal, the panel may order the dismissal of the principal if the panel determines from other available information that the low performance of the school is due to the principal's inadequate performance.

f. In all hearings under this subdivision, the burden of proof is on the principal to establish that the factors leading to the school's low performance were not due to the principal's inadequate performance. In all hearings under sub-subdivision d. of this subdivision, the burden of proof is on the State Board to establish that the school failed to make satisfactory improvement after an assistance team was assigned to the school and to establish one or more of the grounds established for dismissal or demotion of a career employee under G.S. 115C-325(e)(1).

g. In all hearings under this subdivision, two consecutive evaluations that include written findings and recommendations regarding that person's inadequate performance from the assistance team are substantial evidence of the inadequate performance of the principal.

h. The State Board shall adopt procedures to ensure that due process rights are afforded to principals under this subdivision. Decisions of the panel may be appealed on the record to the State Board, with further right of judicial review under Chapter 150B of the General Statutes.

(2) Notwithstanding any other provision of this section or any other law, this subdivision shall govern the State Board's dismissal of teachers, assistant principals, directors, and supervisors assigned to schools that the State Board has identified as low-performing and to which the State Board has assigned an assistance team under Article 8B of this Chapter. The State Board shall dismiss a teacher, assistant principal, director, or supervisor when the State Board receives two consecutive evaluations that include written findings and recommendations regarding that person's inadequate performance from the assistance team. These findings and recommendations shall be substantial evidence of the inadequate performance of the teacher or school administrator.

The State Board may dismiss a teacher, assistant principal, director, or supervisor when:

a. The State Board determines that the school has failed to make satisfactory improvement after the State Board assigned an assistance team to that school under G.S. 115C-105.38; and

b. That assistance team makes the recommendation to dismiss the teacher, assistant principal, director, or supervisor for one or more grounds established in G.S. 115C-325(e)(1) for dismissal or demotion of a career teacher.

A teacher, assistant principal, director, or supervisor may request a hearing before a panel of three members of the State Board within 30 days of any dismissal under this subdivision. The State Board shall adopt procedures to ensure that due process rights are afforded to persons recommended for dismissal under this subdivision. Decisions of the panel may be appealed on the record to the State Board, with further right of judicial review under Chapter 150B of the General Statutes.

(2a) Notwithstanding any other provision of this section or any other law, this subdivision shall govern the State Board's dismissal of licensed staff members who have engaged in a remediation plan under G.S. 115C-105.38A(a) but who, after one retest, fail to meet the general knowledge standard set by the State Board. The failure to meet the general knowledge standard after one retest shall be substantial evidence of the inadequate performance of the licensed staff member.

A licensed staff member may request a hearing before a panel of three members of the State Board within 30 days of any dismissal under this subdivision. The State Board shall adopt procedures to ensure that due process rights are afforded to licensed staff members recommended for dismissal under this subdivision. Decisions of the panel may be appealed on the record to the State Board, with further right of judicial review under Chapter 150B of the General Statutes.

(3) The State Board of Education or a local board may terminate the contract of a school administrator dismissed under this subsection. Nothing in this subsection shall prevent a local board from refusing to renew the contract of any person employed in a school identified as low-performing under G.S. 115C-105.37.

(4) Neither party to a school administrator contract is entitled to damages under this subsection.

(5) The State Board shall have the right to subpoena witnesses and documents on behalf of any party to the proceedings under this subsection. (1955, c. 664; 1967, c. 223, s. 1; 1971, c. 883; c. 1188, s. 2; 1973, c. 315, s. 1; c. 782, ss. 1-30; 1979, c. 864, s. 2; 1981, c. 423, s. 1; c. 538, ss. 1-3; c. 731, s. 1; c. 1127, ss. 39, 40; 1981 (Reg. Sess., 1982), c. 1282, s. 30; 1983, c. 770, ss. 1-15; 1983 (Reg. Sess., 1984), c. 1034, s. 34; 1985, c. 791, s. 5(a), (b); 1985 (Reg. Sess., 1986), c. 1014, s. 60(a); 1987, c. 395, s. 2; c. 540, c. 571, s. 3; 1987 (Reg. Sess., 1988), c. 1037, s. 109; 1991 (Reg. Sess., 1992), c. 942, s. 1; c. 1038, s. 14; 1993, c. 169, s. 1; c. 210, ss. 1-3; 1993 (Reg. Sess., 1994), c. 677, ss. 10, 16(a); 1995, c. 369, s. 2; 1995 (Reg. Sess., 1996), c. 716, s. 8; 1997-221, ss. 11(a), 13(a); 1997-443, s. 11A.118(a); 1998-5, s. 2; 1998-59, s. 3; 1998-131, s. 6; 1998-202, s. 4(o); 1998-212, s. 28.24(c); 1998-217, s. 67.1(a); 1999-96, ss. 1-5; 1999-456, s. 34; 2000-67, s. 8.24(b); 2000-137, s. 4(r); 2000-

140, ss. 23, 24; 2001-376, s. 2; 2001-424, ss. 28.11(g), 32.25(b); 2001-487, s. 74(c); 2002-110, ss. 2, 3; 2002-126, ss. 7.38, 28.10(a), (c), (d); 2003-302, s. 1; 2004-81, s. 2; 2004-124, s. 31.18A(a), (c), (d); 2004-199, s. 57(b); 2005-144, ss. 7A.1, 7A.3, 7A.4; 2005-276, ss. 29.28(b), 29.28(d); 2007-145, s. 7(a), (c)-(e); 2007-326, ss. 2, 3(a), (c)-(e); 2007-484, s. 43.7E; 2009-326, s. 1; 2010-31, s. 7.14(a); 2010-163, s. 1; 2011-145, ss. 7.23(b), 7.25(e); 2011-348, ss. 1, 8.5(a), (b); 2012-83, s. 40; 2012-194, s. 21(a), (b); 2013-360, s. 9.6(f).)

§ 115C-325.1. (Effective July 1, 2014 - see Editor's note for applicability) Definitions.

As used in this Part, the following definitions apply:

(1) "Day" means calendar day. In computing any period of time, Rule 6 of the North Carolina Rules of Civil Procedure shall apply.

(2) "Demote" means to reduce the salary of a person who is classified or paid by the State Board of Education as a classroom teacher or as a school administrator during the time of the contract. The word "demote" does not include (i) a suspension without pay pursuant to G.S. 115C-325.5(a); (ii) the elimination or reduction of bonus payments, including merit-based supplements or a systemwide modification in the amount of any applicable local supplement; (iii) any reduction in salary that results from the elimination of a special duty, such as the duty of an athletic coach or a choral director; or (iv) any reduction of pay as compared to a prior term of contract.

(3) "Disciplinary suspension" means a final decision to suspend a teacher or school administrator without pay for no more than 60 days under G.S. 115C-325.5(b).

(4) "Residential school" means a school operated by the Department of Health and Human Services that provides residential services to students pursuant to Part 3A of Article 3 of Chapter 143B of the General Statutes or a school operated pursuant to Article 9C of Chapter 115C of the General Statutes.

(5) "School administrator" means a principal, assistant principal, supervisor, or director whose major function includes the direct or indirect supervision of teaching or any other part of the instructional program, as provided in G.S. 115C-287.1(a)(3).

(6) "Teacher" means a person meeting each of the following requirements:

a. Who holds at least one of the following licenses issued by the State Board of Education:

1. A current standard professional educator's license.

2. A current lateral entry teaching license.

3. A regular, not expired, vocational license.

b. Whose major responsibility is to teach or directly supervise teaching or who is classified by the State Board of Education or is paid either as a classroom teacher or instructional support personnel.

c. Who is employed to fill a full-time, permanent position.

(7) "Year" means a calendar year beginning July 1 and ending June 30. (2013-360, s. 9.6(b).)

§ 115C-325.2. (Effective July 1, 2014 - see Editor's note for applicability) Personnel files.

(a) Maintenance of Personnel File. - The superintendent shall maintain in his or her office a personnel file for each teacher that contains any complaint, commendation, or suggestion for correction or improvement about the teacher's professional conduct, except that the superintendent may elect not to place in a teacher's file (i) a letter of complaint that contains invalid, irrelevant, outdated, or false information or (ii) a letter of complaint when there is no documentation of an attempt to resolve the issue. The complaint, commendation, or suggestion shall be signed by the person who makes it and shall be placed in the teacher's file only after five days' notice to the teacher. Any denial or explanation relating to such complaint, commendation, or suggestion that the teacher desires to make shall be placed in the file. Any teacher may petition the local board of education to remove any information from the teacher's personnel file that the teacher deems invalid, irrelevant, or outdated. The board may order the superintendent to remove said information if it finds the information is invalid, irrelevant, or outdated.

(b) Inspection of Personnel Files. - The personnel file shall be open for the teacher's inspection at all reasonable times but shall be open to other persons only in accordance with such rules and regulations as the board adopts. Any preemployment data or other information obtained about a teacher before the teacher's employment by the board may be kept in a file separate from the teacher's personnel file and need not be made available to the teacher. No data placed in the preemployment file may be introduced as evidence at a hearing on the dismissal or demotion of a teacher, except the data may be used to substantiate G.S. 115C-325.4(a)(7) or G.S. 115C-325.4(a)(14) as grounds for dismissal or demotion. (2013-360, s. 9.6(b).)

§ 115C-325.3. (Effective July 1, 2014 - see Editor's note for applicability) Teacher contracts.

(a) Length of Contract. - A contract between the local board of education and a teacher who has been employed by the local board of education for less than three years shall be for a term of one school year. A contract or renewal of contract between the local board of education and a teacher who has been employed by the local board of education for three years or more shall be for a term of one, two, or four school years.

(b) Superintendent Recommendation to Local Board. - Local boards of education shall employ teachers upon the recommendation of the superintendent. If a superintendent intends to recommend to the local board of education that a teacher be offered a new or renewed contract, the superintendent shall submit the recommendation to the local board for action and shall include in the recommendation the length of the term of contract. A superintendent shall only recommend a teacher for a contract of a term longer than one school year if the teacher has shown effectiveness as demonstrated by proficiency on the evaluation instrument. The local board may approve the superintendent's recommendation, may decide not to offer the teacher a new or renewed contract, or may decide to offer the teacher a renewed contract for a different term than recommended by the superintendent.

(c) Dismissal During Term of Contract. - A teacher shall not be dismissed or demoted during the term of the contract except for the grounds and by the procedure set forth in G.S. 115C-325.4.

(d) Recommendation on Nonrenewal. - If a superintendent decides not to recommend that the local board of education offer a renewed contract to a teacher, the superintendent shall give the teacher written notice of the decision no later than June 1.

(e) Right to Petition for Hearing. - A teacher shall have the right to petition the local board of education for a hearing no later than 10 days after receiving written notice. The local board may, in its discretion, grant a hearing regarding the superintendent's recommendation for nonrenewal. The local board of education shall notify the teacher making the petition of its decision whether to grant a hearing. If the request for a hearing is granted, the local board shall conduct a hearing pursuant to the provisions of G.S. 115C-45(c) and make a final decision on whether to offer the teacher a renewed contract. The board shall notify a teacher whose contract will not be renewed for the next school year of its decision by June 15; provided, however, if a teacher submits a request for a hearing, the board shall provide the nonrenewal notification within 10 days of the hearing or such later date upon the written consent of the superintendent and teacher. A decision not to offer a teacher a renewed contract shall not be arbitrary, capricious, discriminatory, for personal or political reasons, or on any basis prohibited by State or federal law.

(f) Failure to Offer Contract or Notify on Nonrenewal of Contract. - If a teacher fails to receive a contract offer but does not receive written notification from the superintendent of a recommendation of nonrenewal, and the teacher continues to teach in the local school administrative unit without entering into a contract with the local board, upon discovery of the absence of contract, the board by majority vote shall do one of the following:

(1) Offer the teacher a one-year contract expiring no later than June 30 of the current school year.

(2) Dismiss the teacher and provide the teacher with the equivalent of one additional month's pay. A teacher dismissed as provided in this section shall be considered an at-will employee and shall not be entitled to a hearing or appeal of the dismissal.

(g) Local boards of education and teachers employed by the local board may mutually modify the terms of the contract to permit part-time employment. An individual that mutually modifies a full-time contract to permit part-time employment or enters into a part-time contract is not a teacher as defined in G.S. 115C-325.1(6). (2013-360, s. 9.6(b).)

§ 115C-325.4. (Effective July 1, 2014 - see Editor's note for applicability) Dismissal or demotion for cause.

(a) Grounds. - No teacher shall be dismissed, demoted, or reduced to employment on a part-time basis for disciplinary reasons during the term of the contract except for one or more of the following:

(1) Inadequate performance. In determining whether the professional performance of a teacher is adequate, consideration shall be given to regular and special evaluation reports prepared in accordance with the published policy of the employing local school administrative unit and to any published standards of performance which shall have been adopted by the board. Inadequate performance for a teacher shall mean (i) the failure to perform at a proficient level on any standard of the evaluation instrument or (ii) otherwise performing in a manner that is below standard.

(2) Immorality.

(3) Insubordination.

(4) Neglect of duty.

(5) Physical or mental incapacity.

(6) Habitual or excessive use of alcohol or nonmedical use of a controlled substance as defined in Article 5 of Chapter 90 of the General Statutes.

(7) Conviction of a felony or a crime involving moral turpitude.

(8) Advocating the overthrow of the government of the United States or of the State of North Carolina by force, violence, or other unlawful means.

(9) Failure to fulfill the duties and responsibilities imposed upon teachers or school administrators by the General Statutes of this State.

(10) Failure to comply with such reasonable requirements as the board may prescribe.

(11) Any cause which constitutes grounds for the revocation of the teacher's teaching license or the school administrator's administrator license.

(12) Failure to maintain his or her license in a current status.

(13) Failure to repay money owed to the State in accordance with the provisions of Article 60 of Chapter 143 of the General Statutes.

(14) Providing false information or knowingly omitting a material fact on an application for employment or in response to a preemployment inquiry.

(15) A justifiable decrease in the number of positions due to district reorganization, decreased enrollment, or decreased funding.

(b) Dismissal Procedure. - The procedures provided in G.S. 115C-325.6 shall be followed for dismissals, demotions, or reductions to part-time employment for disciplinary reasons for any reason specified in subsection (a) of this section. (2013-360, s. 9.6(b).)

§ 115C-325.5. (Effective July 1, 2014 - see Editor's note for applicability) Teacher suspension.

(a) Immediate Suspension Without Pay. - If a superintendent believes that cause exists for dismissing a teacher for any reason specified in G.S. 115C-325.4 and that immediate suspension of the teacher is necessary, the superintendent may suspend the teacher without pay. Before suspending a teacher without pay, the superintendent shall meet with the teacher and give him or her written notice of the charges against the teacher, an explanation of the basis for the charges, and an opportunity to respond. Within five days after a suspension under this subsection, the superintendent shall initiate a dismissal, demotion, or disciplinary suspension without pay as provided in this section. If it is finally determined that no grounds for dismissal, demotion, or disciplinary suspension without pay exist, the teacher shall be reinstated immediately, shall be paid for the period of suspension, and all records of the suspension shall be removed from the teacher's personnel file.

(b) Disciplinary Suspension Without Pay. - A teacher recommended for disciplinary suspension without pay may request a hearing before the board. The hearing shall be conducted as provided in G.S. 115C-325.7. If no request is made within 15 days, the superintendent may file his or her recommendation with the board. If, after considering the recommendation of the superintendent and the evidence adduced at the hearing if one is held, the board concludes that the grounds for the recommendation are true and substantiated by a preponderance of the evidence, the board, if it sees fit, may by resolution order such suspension.

(c) Suspension With Pay. - If a superintendent believes that cause may exist for dismissing or demoting a teacher for any reasons specified in G.S. 115C-325.4 but that additional investigation of the facts is necessary and circumstances are such that the teacher should be removed immediately from the teacher's duties, the superintendent may suspend the teacher with pay for a reasonable period of time, not to exceed 90 days. The superintendent shall notify the board of education within two days of the superintendent's action and shall notify the teacher within two days of the action and the reasons for it. If the superintendent has not initiated dismissal or demotion proceedings against the teacher within the 90-day period, the teacher shall be reinstated to the teacher's duties immediately, and all records of the suspension with pay shall be removed from the teacher's personnel file at the teacher's request. However, if the superintendent and the teacher agree to extend the 90-day period, the superintendent may initiate dismissal or demotion proceedings against the teacher at any time during the period of the extension. (2013-360, s. 9.6(b).)

§ 115C-325.6. (Effective July 1, 2014 - see Editor's note for applicability) Procedure for dismissal or demotion of a teacher for cause.

(a) Recommendation of Dismissal or Demotion. - A teacher may not be dismissed, demoted, or reduced to part-time employment for disciplinary reasons during the term of the contract except upon the superintendent's recommendation based on one or more of the grounds in G.S. 115C-325.4.

(b) Notice of Recommendation. - Before recommending to a board the dismissal or demotion of a teacher, the superintendent shall give written notice to the teacher by certified mail or personal delivery of the superintendent's intention to make such recommendation and shall set forth as part of the superintendent's recommendation the grounds upon which he or she believes such dismissal or demotion is justified. The superintendent also shall meet with the teacher and provide written notice of the charges against the teacher, an explanation of the basis for the charges, and an opportunity to respond if the teacher has not done so under G.S. 115C-325.5(a). The notice shall include a statement to the effect that the teacher, within 14 days after the date of receipt of the notice, may request a hearing before the board on the superintendent's recommendation. A copy of Part 3 of Article 22 of Chapter 115C of the General Statutes shall also be sent to the teacher.

(c) Request for Hearing. - Within 14 days after receipt of the notice of recommendation, the teacher may file with the superintendent a written request for a hearing before the board on the superintendent's recommendation. The superintendent shall submit his or her recommendation to the board. Within five days after receiving the superintendent's recommendation and before taking any formal action, the board shall set a time and place for the hearing and shall notify the teacher by certified mail or personal delivery of the date, time, and place of the hearing. The time specified shall not be less than 10 nor more than 30 days after the board has notified the teacher, unless both parties agree to an extension. The hearing shall be conducted as provided in G.S. 115C-325.7.

(d) No Request for Hearing. - If the teacher does not request a hearing before the board within the 14 days provided, the superintendent may submit his or her recommendation to the board. The board, if it sees fit, may by resolution (i) reject the superintendent's recommendation or (ii) accept or modify the superintendent's recommendation and dismiss, demote, reinstate, or suspend the teacher without pay. (2013-360, s. 9.6(b).)

§ 115C-325.7. (Effective July 1, 2014 - see Editor's note for applicability) Hearing before board.

The following procedures shall apply for a board hearing for dismissal, demotion, reduction to part-time employment for disciplinary reasons, or disciplinary suspension without pay:

(1) The hearing shall be private.

(2) The hearing shall be conducted in accordance with reasonable rules adopted by the State Board of Education to govern such hearings.

(3) At the hearing, the teacher and the superintendent shall have the right to be present and to be heard, to be represented by counsel, and to present through witnesses any competent testimony relevant to the issue of whether grounds exist for a dismissal, demotion, reduction to part-time employment for disciplinary reasons, or disciplinary suspension without pay.

(4) Rules of evidence shall not apply to a hearing under this subsection, and the board may give probative effect to evidence that is of a kind commonly relied on by reasonably prudent persons in the conduct of serious affairs.

(5) At least five days before the hearing, the superintendent shall provide to the teacher a list of witnesses the superintendent intends to present, a brief statement of the nature of the testimony of each witness, and a copy of any documentary evidence the superintendent intends to present.

(6) At least three days before the hearing, the teacher shall provide the superintendent a list of witnesses the teacher intends to present, a brief statement of the nature of the testimony of each witness, and a copy of any documentary evidence the teacher intends to present.

(7) No new evidence may be presented at the hearing except upon a finding by the board that the new evidence is critical to the matter at issue and the party making the request could not, with reasonable diligence, have discovered and produced the evidence according to the schedule provided in this section.

(8) The board may subpoena and swear witnesses and may require them to give testimony and to produce records and documents relevant to the grounds for dismissal, demotion, reduction to part-time employment for disciplinary reasons, or disciplinary suspension without pay.

(9) The board shall decide all procedural issues, including limiting cumulative evidence, necessary for a fair and efficient hearing.

(10) The superintendent shall provide for making a transcript of the hearing. The teacher may request and shall receive at no charge a transcript of the proceedings. (2013-360, s. 9.6(b).)

§ 115C-325.8. (Effective July 1, 2014 - see Editor's note for applicability) Right of appeal.

(a) A teacher who (i) has been dismissed, demoted, or reduced to employment on a part-time basis for disciplinary reasons during the term of the contract as provided in G.S. 115C-325.4, or has received a disciplinary suspension without pay as provided in G.S. 115C-325.5, and (ii) requested and participated in a hearing before the local board of education, shall have a further right of appeal from the final decision of the local board of education to the superior court of the State on one or more of the following grounds that the decision:

(1)   Is in violation of constitutional provisions.

(2)   Is in excess of the statutory authority or jurisdiction of the board.

(3)   Was made upon unlawful procedure.

(4)   Is affected by other error of law.

(5)   Is unsupported by substantial evidence in view of the entire record as submitted.

(6)   Is arbitrary or capricious.

(b)   An appeal pursuant to this section must be filed within 30 days of notification of the final decision of the local board of education and shall be decided on the administrative record. The superior court shall have authority to affirm or reverse the local board's decision or remand the matter to the local board of education. The superior court shall not have authority to award monetary damages or to direct the local board of education to enter into an employment contract of more than one year, ending June 30. (2013-360, s. 9.6(b).)

§ 115C-325.9. (Effective July 1, 2014 - see Editor's note for applicability) Teacher resignation.

(a)   Teacher Resignation Following Recommendation for Dismissal. - If a teacher has been recommended for dismissal under G.S. 115C-325.4 and the teacher chooses to resign without the written agreement of the superintendent, then:

(1)   The superintendent shall report the matter to the State Board of Education.

(2) The teacher shall be deemed to have consented to (i) the placement in the teacher's personnel file of the written notice of the superintendent's intention to recommend dismissal and (ii) the release of the fact that the superintendent has reported this teacher to the State Board of Education to prospective employers, upon request. The provisions of G.S. 115C-321 shall not apply to the release of this particular information.

(3) The teacher shall be deemed to have voluntarily surrendered his or her license pending an investigation by the State Board of Education in a determination whether or not to seek action against the teacher's license. This license surrender shall not exceed 45 days from the date of resignation. Provided further that the cessation of the license surrender shall not prevent the State Board of Education from taking any further action it deems appropriate. The State Board of Education shall initiate investigation within five working days of the written notice from the superintendent and shall make a final decision as to whether to revoke or suspend the teacher's license within 45 days from the date of resignation.

(b) Thirty Days' Notice Resignation Requirement. - A teacher who is not recommended for dismissal should not resign during the term of the contract without the consent of the superintendent unless he or she has given at least 30 days' notice. If a teacher who is not recommended for dismissal does resign during the term of the contract without giving at least 30 days' notice, the board may request that the State Board of Education revoke the teacher's license for the remainder of that school year. A copy of the request shall be placed in the teacher's personnel file. (2013-360, s. 9.6(b).)

§ 115C-325.10. (Effective July 1, 2014 - see Editor's note for applicability) Application to certain institutions.

Notwithstanding any law or regulation to the contrary, this Part shall apply to all persons employed in teaching and related educational classes in the schools and institutions of the Departments of Health and Human Services and Public Instruction and the Divisions of Juvenile Justice and Adult Correction of the Department of Public Safety, regardless of the age of the students. (2013-360, s. 9.6(b).)

§ 115C-325.11. (Effective July 1, 2014 - see Editor's note for applicability) Dismissal of school administrators and teachers employed in low-performing residential schools.

(a) Notwithstanding any other provision of this section or any other law, this section shall govern the dismissal by the State Board of Education of teachers, principals, assistant principals, directors, supervisors, and other licensed personnel assigned to a residential school that the State Board has identified as low-performing and to which the State Board has assigned an assistance team. The State Board shall dismiss a teacher, principal, assistant principal, director, supervisor, or other licensed personnel when the State Board receives two consecutive evaluations that include written findings and recommendations regarding that person's inadequate performance from the assistance team. These findings and recommendations shall be substantial evidence of the inadequate performance of the teacher or school administrator.

(b) The State Board may dismiss a teacher, principal, assistant principal, director, supervisor, or other licensed personnel when:

(1) The State Board determines that the school has failed to make satisfactory improvement after the State Board assigned an assistance team to that school.

(2) That assistance team makes the recommendation to dismiss the teacher, principal, assistant principal, director, supervisor, or other licensed personnel for one or more grounds established in G.S. 115C-325.4 for dismissal or demotion of a teacher.

Within 30 days of any dismissal under this subsection, a teacher, principal, assistant principal, director, supervisor, or other licensed personnel may request a hearing before a panel of three members designated by the State Board. The State Board shall adopt procedures to ensure that due process rights are afforded to persons recommended for dismissal under this subsection. Decisions of the panel may be appealed on the record to the State Board.

(c) Notwithstanding any other provision of this section or any other law, this subsection shall govern the dismissal by the State Board of licensed staff members who have engaged in a remediation plan under G.S. 115C-105.38A(c) but who, after one retest, fail to meet the general knowledge standard set by the State Board. The failure to meet the general knowledge standard after one retest shall be substantial evidence of the inadequate performance of the licensed staff member.

Within 30 days of any dismissal under this subsection, a licensed staff member may request a hearing before a panel of three members designated by the State Board. The State Board shall adopt procedures to ensure that due process rights are afforded to licensed staff members recommended for dismissal under this subsection. Decisions of the panel may be appealed on the record to the State Board.

(d) The State Board or the superintendent of a residential school may terminate the contract of a school administrator dismissed under this section. Nothing in this section shall prevent the State Board from refusing to renew the contract of any person employed in a school identified as low-performing.

(e) Neither party to a school administrator or teacher contract is entitled to damages under this section.

(f) The State Board shall have the right to subpoena witnesses and documents on behalf of any party to the proceedings under this section. (2013-360, s. 9.6(b).)

§ 115C-325.12. (Effective July 1, 2014 - see Editor's note for applicability) Procedure for dismissal of principals employed in low-performing schools.

(a) Dismissal of Principals Assigned to Low-Performing Schools With Assistance Teams. - Notwithstanding any other provision of this Part or any other law, this section governs the State Board's dismissal of principals assigned to low-performing schools to which the State Board has assigned an assistance team.

(b) Authority of State Board to Dismiss Principal. - The State Board through its designee may, at any time, recommend the dismissal of any principal who is assigned to a low-performing school to which an assistance team has been assigned. The State Board through its designee shall recommend the dismissal of any principal when the State Board receives from the assistance team assigned to that principal's school two consecutive evaluations that include written findings and recommendations regarding the principal's inadequate performance.

(c) Procedures for Dismissal of Principal. -

(1) If the State Board through its designee recommends the dismissal of a principal under this section, the principal shall be suspended with pay pending a hearing before a panel of three members of the State Board. The purpose of this hearing, which shall be held within 60 days after the principal is suspended, is to determine whether the principal shall be dismissed.

(2) The panel shall order the dismissal of the principal if it determines from available information, including the findings of the assistance team, that the low performance of the school is due to the principal's inadequate performance.

(3) The panel may order the dismissal of the principal if (i) it determines that the school has not made satisfactory improvement after the State Board assigned an assistance team to that school and (ii) the assistance team makes the recommendation to dismiss the principal for one or more grounds established in G.S. 115C-325.4 for dismissal or demotion of a teacher.

(4) If the State Board or its designee recommends the dismissal of a principal before the assistance team assigned to the principal's school has evaluated that principal, the panel may order the dismissal of the principal if the panel determines from other available information that the low performance of the school is due to the principal's inadequate performance.

(5) In all hearings under this section, the burden of proof is on the principal to establish that the factors leading to the school's low performance were not due to the principal's inadequate performance. In all hearings under this section, the burden of proof is on the State Board to establish that the school failed to make satisfactory improvement after an assistance team was assigned to the school and to establish one or more of the grounds established for dismissal or demotion of a teacher under G.S. 115C-325.4.

(6) In all hearings under this section, two consecutive evaluations that include written findings and recommendations regarding that principal's inadequate performance from the assistance team are substantial evidence of the inadequate performance of the principal.

(7) The State Board shall adopt procedures to ensure that due process rights are afforded to principals under this section. Decisions of the panel may be appealed on the record to the State Board.

(d) The State Board of Education or a local board may terminate the contract of a principal dismissed under this section.

(e) Neither party to a school administrator contract is entitled to damages under this section.

(f) The State Board shall have the right to subpoena witnesses and documents on behalf of any party to the proceedings under this section. (2013-360, s. 9.6(b).)

§ 115C-325.13. (Effective July 1, 2014 - see Editor's note for applicability) Procedure for dismissal of teachers employed in low-performing schools.

(a) Notwithstanding any other provision of this Part or any other law, this section shall govern the State Board's dismissal of teachers, assistant principals, directors, and supervisors assigned to schools that the State Board has identified as low-performing and to which the State Board has assigned an assistance team under Article 8B of this Chapter. The State Board shall dismiss a teacher, assistant principal, director, or supervisor when the State Board receives two consecutive evaluations that include written findings and recommendations regarding that person's inadequate performance from the assistance team. These findings and recommendations shall be substantial evidence of the inadequate performance of the teacher, assistant principal, director, or supervisor.

(b) The State Board may dismiss a teacher, assistant principal, director, or supervisor when:

(1) The State Board determines that the school has failed to make satisfactory improvement after the State Board assigned an assistance team to that school under G.S. 115C-105.38; and

(2) That assistance team makes the recommendation to dismiss the teacher, assistant principal, director, or supervisor for one or more grounds established in G.S. 115C-325.4 for dismissal or demotion for cause.

A teacher, assistant principal, director, or supervisor may request a hearing before a panel of three members of the State Board within 30 days of any dismissal under this section. The State Board shall adopt procedures to ensure that due process rights are afforded to persons recommended for dismissal under this section. Decisions of the panel may be appealed on the record to the State Board.

(c) Notwithstanding any other provision of this Part or any other law, this section shall govern the State Board's dismissal of licensed staff members who have engaged in a remediation plan under G.S. 115C-105.38A(c) but who, after one retest, fail to meet the general knowledge standard set by the State Board. The failure to meet the general knowledge standard after one retest shall be substantial evidence of the inadequate performance of the licensed staff member.

(d) A licensed staff member may request a hearing before a panel of three members of the State Board within 30 days of any dismissal under this section. The State Board shall adopt procedures to ensure that due process rights are afforded to licensed staff members recommended for dismissal under this section. Decisions of the panel may be appealed on the record to the State Board.

(e) The State Board of Education or a local board may terminate the contract of a teacher, assistant principal, director, or supervisor dismissed under this section.

(f) Neither party to a school administrator or teacher contract is entitled to damages under this section.

(g) The State Board shall have the right to subpoena witnesses and documents on behalf of any party to the proceedings under this section. (2013-360, s. 9.6(b).)

§ 115C-326: Repealed by Session Laws 1998-5, s. 3.

§ 115C-326.1: Repealed by Session Laws 1985, c. 479, s. 52.

Part 3A. Job Sharing by School Employees.

§ 115C-326.5. Job sharing by school employees.

(a) The General Assembly finds that there is a shortage of qualified public school employees available in certain geographical areas of the State. The elimination of administrative and fiscal limitations on job-sharing arrangements would make employment in a public school an attractive option for well-qualified persons who do not wish to work full time.

(b) A "school employee in a job-sharing position" is a person who is employed by a local board of education as a public school employee for at least fifty percent (50%) of the applicable workweek, as defined by that local board of education.

(c) The State Board of Education shall adopt rules to facilitate job sharing by public school employees. These rules shall provide that an employee in a job-sharing position shall receive paid legal holidays, annual vacation leave, sick leave, and personal leave on a pro rata basis. Such an employee shall also receive service credit under the Teachers' and State Employees' Retirement System as provided in G.S. 135-4(b) and insurance benefits as provided in Article 3 of Chapter 135 of the General Statutes. (2003-358, s. 2.)

Part 4. Personnel Administration Commission for Public School Employees.

§§ 115C-327 through 115C-329: Repealed by Session Laws 1997-18, s. 10.

Part 5. Employment of Handicapped.

§ 115C-330. Employment of handicapped.

The Board and each local educational agency shall make positive efforts to employ and advance in employment qualified handicapped individuals. (1977, c. 927, s. 1; 1981, c. 423, s. 1.)

§ 115C-331. Reserved for future codification purposes.

Part 6. Criminal History Checks.

§ 115C-332. School personnel criminal history checks.

(a) As used in this section:

(1) "Criminal history" means a county, state, or federal criminal history of conviction of a crime, whether a misdemeanor or a felony, that indicates the employee (i) poses a threat to the physical safety of students or personnel, or (ii) has demonstrated that he or she does not have the integrity or honesty to fulfill his or her duties as public school personnel. Such crimes include the following North Carolina crimes contained in any of the following Articles of Chapter 14 of the General Statutes: Article 5A, Endangering Executive and Legislative Officers; Article 6, Homicide; Article 7A, Rape and Kindred Offenses; Article 8, Assaults; Article 10, Kidnapping and Abduction; Article 13, Malicious Injury or Damage by Use of Explosive or Incendiary Device or Material; Article 14, Burglary and Other Housebreakings; Article 15, Arson and Other Burnings; Article 16, Larceny; Article 17, Robbery; Article 18, Embezzlement; Article 19, False Pretense and Cheats; Article 19A, Obtaining Property or Services by False or Fraudulent Use of Credit Device or Other Means; Article 20, Frauds; Article 21, Forgery; Article 26, Offenses Against Public Morality and Decency; Article 26A, Adult Establishments; Article 27, Prostitution; Article 28, Perjury; Article 29, Bribery; Article 31, Misconduct in Public Office; Article 35, Offenses Against the Public Peace; Article 36A, Riots, Civil Disorders, and Emergencies; Article 39, Protection of Minors; and Article 60, Computer-Related Crime. Such crimes also include possession or sale of drugs in violation of the North Carolina Controlled Substances Act, Article 5 of Chapter 90 of the General Statutes, and alcohol-related offenses such as sale to underage persons in violation of G.S. 18B-302 or driving while impaired in violation of G.S. 20-138.1 through G.S. 20-138.5. In addition to the North Carolina crimes listed in this subparagraph, such crimes also include similar crimes under federal law or under the laws of other states.

(2) "School personnel" means any:

a. Employee of a local board of education whether full-time or part-time, or

b. Independent contractor or employee of an independent contractor of a local board of education, if the independent contractor carries out duties customarily performed by school personnel, whether paid with federal, State, local, or other funds, who has significant access to students. School personnel includes substitute teachers, driver training teachers, bus drivers, clerical staff, and custodians.

(b)   Each local board of education shall adopt a policy on whether and under what circumstances an applicant for a school personnel position shall be required to be checked for a criminal history before the applicant is offered an unconditional job. Each local board of education shall apply its policy uniformly in requiring applicants for school personnel positions to be checked for a criminal history. A local board of education that requires a criminal history check for an applicant may employ an applicant conditionally while the board is checking the person's criminal history and making a decision based on the results of the check.

A local board of education shall not require an applicant to pay for the criminal history check authorized under this subsection.

(c)   The Department of Justice shall provide to the local board of education the criminal history from the State and National Repositories of Criminal Histories of any applicant for a school personnel position in the local school administrative unit for which a local board of education requires a criminal history check. The local board of education shall require the person to be checked by the Department of Justice to (i) be fingerprinted and to provide any additional information required by the Department of Justice to a person designated by the local board, or to the local sheriff or the municipal police, whichever is more convenient for the person, and (ii) sign a form consenting to the check of the criminal record and to the use of fingerprints and other identifying information required by the repositories The local board of education shall consider refusal to consent when making employment decisions and decisions with regard to independent contractors.

The local board of education shall not require an applicant to pay for being fingerprinted.

(d)   The local board of education shall review the criminal history it receives on a person. The local board shall determine whether the results of the review indicate that the applicant or employee (i) poses a threat to the physical safety of students or personnel, or (ii) has demonstrated that he or she does not have the integrity or honesty to fulfill his or her duties as public school personnel and shall use the information when making employment decisions and decisions with regard to independent contractors. The local board shall make written findings with regard to how it used the information when making employment decisions and decisions with regard to independent contractors. The local board may delegate any of the duties in this subsection to the superintendent.

(e) The local board of education, or the superintendent if designated by the local board of education, shall provide to the State Board of Education the criminal history it receives on a person who is certificated, certified, or licensed by the State Board of Education. The State Board of Education shall review the criminal history and determine whether the person's certificate or license should be revoked in accordance with State laws and rules regarding revocation.

(f) All the information received by the local board of education through the checking of the criminal history or by the State Board of Education in accordance with this section is privileged information and is not a public record but is for the exclusive use of the local board of education or the State Board of Education. The local board of education or the State Board of Education may destroy the information after it is used for the purposes authorized by this section after one calendar year.

(g) There shall be no liability for negligence on the part of a local board of education, or its employees, or the State Board of Education, or its employees, arising from any act taken or omission by any of them in carrying out the provisions of this section. The immunity established by this subsection shall not extend to gross negligence, wanton conduct, or intentional wrongdoing that would otherwise be actionable. The immunity established by this subsection shall be deemed to have been waived to the extent of indemnification by insurance, indemnification under Articles 31A and 31B of Chapter 143 of the General Statutes, and to the extent sovereign immunity is waived under the Tort Claims Act, as set forth in Chapter 31 of Chapter 143 of the General Statutes.

(h) Any applicant for employment who willfully furnishes, supplies, or otherwise gives false information on an employment application that is the basis for a criminal history record check under this section shall be guilty of a Class A1 misdemeanor. (1995, c. 373, s. 1; 2001-376, s. 1; 2012-12, s. 2(rr).)

§ 115C-332.1. Sex offender registries checks for certain contractual personnel.

(a) For purposes of this section, the term "contractual personnel" includes any individual or entity under contract with the local board of education whose contractual job involves direct interaction with students as part of the job. For purposes of this section, the term "contractual personnel" does not include any person covered under G.S. 115C-332.

(b) Each local board of education shall require, as a term of any contract the local board of education enters, that employers of a person who is contractual personnel conduct an annual check of that person on the State Sex Offender and Public Protection Registration Program, the State Sexually Violent Predator Registration Program, and the National Sex Offender Registry. As a term of any contract, a local board of education shall prohibit any contractual personnel listed on the State Sex Offender and Public Protection Registration Program, the State Sexually Violent Predator Registration Program, and the National Sex Offender Registry from having direct interaction with students. (2008-117, s. 21.)

Part 7. Personnel Evaluations.

§ 115C-333. Evaluation of licensed employees including certain superintendents; mandatory improvement plans; State board notification upon dismissal of employees.

(a) (Effective until July 1, 2014) Annual Evaluations; Low-Performing Schools. - Local school administrative units shall evaluate at least once each year all licensed employees assigned to a school that has been identified as low-performing. The evaluation shall occur early enough during the school year to provide adequate time for the development and implementation of a mandatory improvement plan if one is recommended under subsection (b) of this section. If the employee is a teacher as defined under G.S. 115C-325(a)(6), either the principal, the assistant principal who supervises the teacher, or an assistance team assigned under G.S. 115C-105.38 shall conduct the evaluation. If the employee is a school administrator as defined under G.S. 115C-287.1(a)(3), either the superintendent or the superintendent's designee shall conduct the evaluation.

All teachers in low-performing schools who have not attained career status shall be observed at least three times annually by the principal or the principal's designee and at least once annually by a teacher and shall be evaluated at least once annually by a principal. This section shall not be construed to limit the duties and authority of an assistance team assigned to a low-performing school under G.S. 115C-105.38.

A local board shall use the performance standards and criteria adopted by the State Board and may adopt additional evaluation criteria and standards. All other provisions of this section shall apply if a local board uses an evaluation other than one adopted by the State Board.

(a) (Effective July 1, 2014, until June 30, 2018) Annual Evaluations; Low-Performing Schools. - Local school administrative units shall evaluate at least once each year all licensed employees assigned to a school that has been identified as low-performing. The evaluation shall occur early enough during the school year to provide adequate time for the development and implementation of a mandatory improvement plan if one is recommended under subsection (b) of this section. If the employee is a teacher with career status as defined under G.S. 115C-325(a)(6), or a teacher as defined under G.S. 115C-325.1(6), either the principal, the assistant principal who supervises the teacher, or an assistance team assigned under G.S. 115C-105.38 shall conduct the evaluation. If the employee is a school administrator as defined under G.S. 115C-287.1(a)(3), either the superintendent or the superintendent's designee shall conduct the evaluation.

All teachers in low-performing schools who have been employed for less than three consecutive years shall be observed at least three times annually by the principal or the principal's designee and at least once annually by a teacher and shall be evaluated at least once annually by a principal. This section shall not be construed to limit the duties and authority of an assistance team assigned to a low-performing school under G.S. 115C-105.38.

A local board shall use the performance standards and criteria adopted by the State Board and may adopt additional evaluation criteria and standards. All other provisions of this section shall apply if a local board uses an evaluation other than one adopted by the State Board.

(a) (Effective June 30, 2018) Annual Evaluations; Low-Performing Schools. - Local school administrative units shall evaluate at least once each year all licensed employees assigned to a school that has been identified as low-performing. The evaluation shall occur early enough during the school year to provide adequate time for the development and implementation of a mandatory improvement plan if one is recommended under subsection (b) of this section. If the employee is a teacher as defined under G.S. 115C-325.1(6) either the principal, the assistant principal who supervises the teacher, or an assistance team assigned under G.S. 115C-105.38 shall conduct the evaluation. If the employee is a school administrator as defined under G.S. 115C-287.1(a)(3), either the superintendent or the superintendent's designee shall conduct the evaluation.

All teachers in low-performing schools who have been employed for less than three consecutive years shall be observed at least three times annually by the principal or the principal's designee and at least once annually by a teacher and shall be evaluated at least once annually by a principal. This section shall not be construed to limit the duties and authority of an assistance team assigned to a low-performing school under G.S. 115C-105.38.

A local board shall use the performance standards and criteria adopted by the State Board and may adopt additional evaluation criteria and standards. All other provisions of this section shall apply if a local board uses an evaluation other than one adopted by the State Board.

(b) Mandatory Improvement Plans. -

(1) Repealed by Session Laws 2011-348, s. 2, effective July 1, 2011, and applicable to persons recommended for dismissal or demotion on or after that date.

(1a) A mandatory improvement plan is an instrument designed to improve a teacher's performance or the performance of any licensed employee in a low-performing school by providing the individual with notice of specific performance areas that have substantial deficiencies and a set of strategies, including the specific support to be provided to the individual, so that the individual, within a reasonable period of time, should satisfactorily resolve such deficiencies.

(2) Repealed by Session Laws 2011-348, s. 2, effective July 1, 2011, and applicable to persons recommended for dismissal or demotion on or after that date.

(2a) (Effective until July 1, 2014) If a licensed employee in a low-performing school receives a rating on any standard on an evaluation that is below proficient or otherwise represents unsatisfactory or below standard performance in an area that the licensed employee was expected to demonstrate, the individual or team that conducted the evaluation shall recommend to the superintendent that (i) the employee receive a mandatory improvement plan designed to improve the employee's performance or (ii) the superintendent recommend to the local board that the employee be dismissed or demoted. If the individual or team that conducted the evaluation elects not to make either of the above recommendations, the said individual or team shall notify the superintendent of this decision. The superintendent shall determine whether to develop a mandatory improvement plan or to recommend a dismissal proceeding.

(2a)   (Effective July 1, 2014, until June 30, 2018) If a licensed employee in a low-performing school receives a rating on any standard on an evaluation that is below proficient or otherwise represents unsatisfactory or below standard performance in an area that the licensed employee was expected to demonstrate, the individual or team that conducted the evaluation shall recommend to the superintendent that (i) the employee receive a mandatory improvement plan designed to improve the employee's performance, (ii) the superintendent recommend to the local board that if the employee is a career status teacher the employee be dismissed or demoted and if the employee is a teacher on contract the teacher's contract not be recommended for renewal, or (iii) if the employee engaged in inappropriate conduct or performed inadequately to such a degree that such conduct or performance causes substantial harm to the educational environment that a proceeding for immediate dismissal or demotion be instituted. If the individual or team that conducted the evaluation elects not to make any of the above recommendations, the said individual or team shall notify the superintendent of this decision. The superintendent shall determine whether to develop a mandatory improvement plan, to not recommend renewal of the employee's contract, or to recommend a dismissal proceeding.

(2a)   (Effective June 30, 2018) If a licensed employee in a low-performing school receives a rating on any standard on an evaluation that is below proficient or otherwise represents unsatisfactory or below standard performance in an area that the licensed employee was expected to demonstrate, the individual or team that conducted the evaluation shall recommend to the superintendent that (i) the employee receive a mandatory improvement plan designed to improve the employee's performance, (ii) the superintendent recommend to the local board that employee's contract not be recommended for renewal, or (iii) if the employee engaged in inappropriate conduct or performed inadequately to such a degree that such conduct or performance causes substantial harm to the educational environment that a proceeding for immediate dismissal or demotion be instituted. If the individual or team that conducted the evaluation elects not to make any of the above recommendations, the said individual or team shall notify the superintendent of this decision. The superintendent shall determine whether to develop a mandatory improvement plan, to not recommend renewal of the employee's contract, or to recommend a dismissal proceeding.

(3) If at any time a licensed employee engages in inappropriate conduct or performs inadequately to such a degree that such conduct or performance causes substantial harm to the educational environment, and immediate dismissal or demotion is not appropriate, then the principal may immediately institute a mandatory improvement plan regardless of any ratings on previous evaluations. The principal shall document the exigent reason for immediately instituting such a plan.

(4) Mandatory improvement plans shall be developed by the person who evaluated the licensed employee or the employee's supervisor unless the evaluation was conducted by an assistance team. If the evaluation was conducted by an assistance team, that team shall develop the mandatory improvement plan in collaboration with the employee's supervisor. Mandatory improvement plans shall be designed to be completed within 90 instructional days or before the beginning of the next school year. The State Board shall develop guidelines that include strategies to assist local boards in evaluating licensed employees and developing effective mandatory improvement plans within the time allotted under this section. Local boards may adopt policies for the development and implementation of mandatory improvement plans and policies for the implementation of monitored and directed growth plans.

(c) (Effective until July 1, 2014) Reassessment of Employee in a Low-Performing School. - After the expiration of the time period for the mandatory improvement plan under subdivision (2a) of subsection (b) of this section, the superintendent, the superintendent's designee, or the assistance team shall assess the performance of the employee of the low-performing school a second time. If the superintendent, superintendent's designee, or assistance team determines that the employee has failed to become proficient in any of the performance standards articulated in the mandatory improvement plan or demonstrate sufficient improvement toward such standards, the superintendent shall recommend that the employee be dismissed or demoted under G.S. 115C-325. The results of the second assessment shall constitute substantial evidence of the employee's inadequate performance.

(c) (Effective July 1, 2014, until June 30, 2018) Reassessment of Employee in a Low-Performing School. - After the expiration of the time period for the mandatory improvement plan under subdivision (2a) of subsection (b) of this section, the superintendent, the superintendent's designee, or the assistance team shall assess the performance of the employee of the low-performing school a second time. If the superintendent, superintendent's designee, or assistance team determines that the employee has failed to become proficient in any of the performance standards articulated in the mandatory improvement plan or demonstrate sufficient improvement toward such standards, the superintendent shall recommend that if the employee is a teacher with career status the teacher be dismissed or demoted under G.S. 115C-325, or if the employee is a teacher on contract the employee's contract not be renewed or if the employee has engaged in inappropriate conduct or performed inadequately to such a degree that such conduct or performance causes substantial harm to the educational environment, that the employee be immediately dismissed or demoted under G.S. 115C-325.4. The results of the second assessment shall constitute substantial evidence of the employee's inadequate performance.

(c) (Effective June 30, 2018) Reassessment of Employee in a Low-Performing School. - After the expiration of the time period for the mandatory improvement plan under subdivision (2a) of subsection (b) of this section, the superintendent, the superintendent's designee, or the assistance team shall assess the performance of the employee of the low-performing school a second time. If the superintendent, superintendent's designee, or assistance team determines that the employee has failed to become proficient in any of the performance standards articulated in the mandatory improvement plan or demonstrate sufficient improvement toward such standards, the superintendent shall recommend that the employee's contract not be renewed or if the employee has engaged in inappropriate conduct or performed inadequately to such a degree that such conduct or performance causes substantial harm to the educational environment, that the employee be immediately dismissed or demoted under G.S. 115C-325.4. The results of the second assessment shall constitute substantial evidence of the employee's inadequate performance.

(d) (Effective until July 1, 2014) State Board Notification. - If a local board dismisses an employee of a low-performing school for any reason except a reduction in force under G.S. 115C-325(e)(1)l., it shall notify the State Board of the action, and the State Board annually shall provide to all local boards the names of those individuals. If a local board hires one of these individuals, within 60 days the superintendent or the superintendent's designee shall observe the employee, develop a mandatory improvement plan to assist the employee, and submit the plan to the State Board. The State Board shall review the mandatory improvement plan and may provide comments and suggestions to the superintendent. If on the next evaluation the employee receives a rating on any standard that was identified as an area of concern on the mandatory improvement plan that is again below proficient or otherwise represents unsatisfactory or below standard performance, the local board shall notify the State Board and the State Board shall initiate a proceeding to revoke the employee's license under G.S. 115C-296(d). If on this next evaluation the employee receives at least a proficient rating on all of the performance standards that were identified as areas of concern on the mandatory improvement plan, the local board shall notify the State Board that the employee is in good standing and the State Board shall not continue to provide the individual's name to local boards under this subsection unless the employee is subsequently dismissed under G.S. 115C-325 except for a reduction in force.

(d) (Effective July 1, 2014, until June 30, 2018) State Board Notification. - If a local board dismisses an employee of a low-performing school who is a teacher with career status for any reason except a reduction in force under G.S. 115C-325(e)(1)l., or dismisses an employee who is a teacher on contract for cause or elects to not renew an employee's contract as a result of a superintendent's recommendation under subsection (b) or (c) of this section, it shall notify the State Board of the action, and the State Board annually shall provide to all local boards the names of those individuals. If a local board hires one of these individuals, within 60 days the superintendent or the superintendent's designee shall observe the employee, develop a mandatory improvement plan to assist the employee, and submit the plan to the State Board. The State Board shall review the mandatory improvement plan and may provide comments and suggestions to the superintendent. If on the next evaluation the employee receives a rating on any standard that was identified as an area of concern on the mandatory improvement plan that is again below proficient or otherwise represents unsatisfactory or below standard performance, the local board shall notify the State Board and the State Board shall initiate a proceeding to revoke the employee's license under G.S. 115C-296(d). If on this next evaluation the employee receives at least a proficient rating on all of the performance standards that were identified as areas of concern on the mandatory improvement plan, the local board shall notify the State Board that the employee is in good standing and the State Board shall not continue to provide the individual's name to local boards under this subsection unless the employee is a teacher with career status and is subsequently dismissed under G.S. 115C-325 except for a reduction in force, or the employee is a teacher on contract subsequently dismissed under G.S. 115C-325.4.

(d) (Effective June 30, 2018) State Board Notification. - If a local board dismisses an employee of a low-performing school for cause or elects to not renew an employee's contract as a result of a superintendent's recommendation under subsection (b) or (c) of this section, it shall notify the State Board of the action, and the State Board annually shall provide to all local boards the names of those individuals. If a local board hires one of these individuals, within 60 days the superintendent or the superintendent's designee shall observe the employee, develop a mandatory improvement plan to assist the employee, and submit the plan to the State Board. The State Board shall review the mandatory improvement plan and may provide comments and suggestions to the superintendent. If on the next evaluation the employee receives a rating on any standard that was identified as an area of concern on the mandatory improvement plan that is again below proficient or otherwise represents unsatisfactory or below standard performance, the local board shall notify the State Board and the State Board shall initiate a proceeding to revoke the employee's license under G.S. 115C-296(d). If on this next evaluation the employee receives at least a proficient rating on all of the performance standards that were identified as areas of concern on the mandatory improvement plan, the local board shall notify the State Board that the employee is in good standing and the State Board shall not continue to provide the individual's name to local boards under this subsection unless the employee is subsequently dismissed under G.S. 115C-325.4.

(e) Civil Immunity. - There shall be no liability for negligence on the part of the State Board of Education or a local board of education, or their employees, arising from any action taken or omission by any of them in carrying out the provisions of this section. The immunity established by this subsection shall not extend to gross negligence, wanton conduct, or intentional wrongdoing that would otherwise be actionable. The immunity established by this subsection shall be deemed to have been waived to the extent of indemnification by insurance, indemnification under Articles 31A and 31B of Chapter 143 of the General Statutes, and to the extent sovereign immunity is waived under the Tort Claims Act, as set forth in Article 31 of Chapter 143 of the General Statutes.

(f) Local Board Evaluation of Certain Superintendents. - Each year the local board of education shall evaluate the superintendent employed by the local school administrative unit and report to the State Board the results of that evaluation if during that year the State Board designated as low-performing:

(1) One or more schools in a local school administrative unit that has no more than 10 schools.

(2) Two or more schools in a local school administrative unit that has no more than 20 schools.

(3) Three or more schools in a local school administrative unit that has more than 20 schools. (1998-5, s. 4; 1998-220, ss. 14, 15; 2011-348, s. 2; 2013-360, s. 9.7(i), (s).)

§ 115C-333.1. Evaluation of teachers in schools not identified as low-performing; mandatory improvement plans; State Board notification upon dismissal of teachers.

(a) (Effective until July 1, 2014) Annual Evaluations. - All teachers who are assigned to schools that are not designated as low-performing and who have not attained career status shall be observed at least three times annually by the principal or the principal's designee and at least once annually by a teacher and shall be evaluated at least once annually by a principal. All teachers with career status who are assigned to schools that are not designated as low-performing shall be evaluated annually unless a local board adopts rules that allow teachers with career status to be evaluated more or less frequently, provided that such rules are not inconsistent with State or federal requirements. Local boards also may adopt rules requiring the annual evaluation of nonlicensed employees. A local board shall use the performance standards and criteria adopted by the State Board and may adopt additional evaluation criteria and standards. All other provisions of this section shall apply if a local board uses an evaluation other than one adopted by the State Board.

(a) (Effective July 1, 2014, until June 30, 2018) Annual Evaluations. - All teachers who are assigned to schools that are not designated as low-performing and who have not been employed for at least three consecutive years shall be observed at least three times annually by the principal or the principal's designee and at least once annually by a teacher and shall be evaluated at least once annually by a principal. All teachers with career status or on a four-year contract who are assigned to schools that are not designated as low-performing shall be evaluated annually unless a local board adopts rules that allow teachers with career status or on a four-year contract to be evaluated more or less frequently, provided that such rules are not inconsistent with State or federal requirements. Local boards also may adopt rules requiring the annual evaluation of nonlicensed employees. A local board shall use the performance standards and criteria adopted by the State Board and may adopt additional evaluation criteria and standards. All other provisions of this section shall apply if a local board uses an evaluation other than one adopted by the State Board.

(a) (Effective June 30, 2018) Annual Evaluations. - All teachers who are assigned to schools that are not designated as low-performing and who have not been employed for at least three consecutive years shall be observed at least three times annually by the principal or the principal's designee and at least once annually by a teacher and shall be evaluated at least once annually by a principal. All teachers who have been employed for three or more years who are assigned to schools that are not designated as low-performing shall be evaluated annually unless a local board adopts rules that allow teachers employed for three or more years to be evaluated more or less frequently, provided that such rules are not inconsistent with State or federal requirements. Local boards also may adopt rules requiring the annual evaluation of nonlicensed employees. A local board shall use the performance standards and criteria adopted by the State Board and may adopt additional evaluation criteria and standards. All other provisions of this section shall apply if a local board uses an evaluation other than one adopted by the State Board.

(b) Mandatory Improvement Plans for Teachers. - If, in an observation report or year-end evaluation, a teacher receives a rating that is below proficient or otherwise represents unsatisfactory or below standard performance on any standard that the teacher was expected to demonstrate, the principal may place the teacher on a mandatory improvement plan as defined in G.S. 115C-333(b)(1a). The mandatory improvement plan shall be utilized only if the superintendent or superintendent's designee determines that an individual, monitored, or directed growth plan will not satisfactorily address the deficiencies.

If at any time a teacher engages in inappropriate conduct or performs inadequately to such a degree that such conduct or performance causes substantial harm to the educational environment, and immediate dismissal or demotion is not appropriate, then the principal may immediately institute a mandatory improvement plan regardless of any ratings on previous evaluations. The principal shall document the exigent reason for immediately instituting such a plan. The mandatory improvement plan shall be developed by the principal in consultation with the teacher. The teacher shall have five instructional days from receipt of the proposed mandatory improvement plan to request a modification of such plan before it is implemented, and the principal shall consider such suggested modifications before finalizing the plan. The teacher shall have at least 60 instructional days to complete the mandatory improvement plan. The

State Board shall develop guidelines that include strategies to assist local boards in evaluating teachers and developing effective mandatory improvement plans. Local boards may adopt policies for the implementation of mandatory improvement plans under this section.

(c) Observation by a Qualified Observer. -

(1) The term "qualified observer" as used in this section is any administrator or teacher who is licensed by the State Board of Education and working in North Carolina; any employee of the North Carolina Department of Public Instruction who is trained in evaluating licensed employees; or any instructor or professor who teaches in an accredited North Carolina school of education and holds an educator's license.

(2) The local board of education shall create a list of qualified observers who are employed by that board and available to do observations of employees on mandatory improvement plans. This list shall be limited to names of administrators and teachers selected by the local board of education. The local board of education shall strive to select administrators and teachers with excellent reputations for competence and fairness.

(3) Any teacher, other than a teacher assigned to a school designated as low-performing, who has been placed on a mandatory improvement plan shall have a right to be observed by a qualified observer in the area or areas of concern identified in the mandatory improvement plan. The affected teacher and the principal shall jointly choose the qualified observer within 20 instructional days after the commencement of the mandatory improvement plan. If the teacher and the principal cannot agree on a qualified observer within this time period, they each shall designate a person from the list of qualified observers created pursuant to subdivision (2) of this subsection, and these two designated persons shall choose a qualified observer within five instructional days of their designation. The qualified observer shall draft a written report assessing the teacher in the areas of concern identified in the mandatory improvement plan. The report shall be submitted to the principal before the end of the mandatory improvement plan period. If a teacher or administrator from the same local school administrative unit is selected to serve as the qualified observer, the administration of the local school administrative unit shall provide such qualified observer with the time necessary to conduct the observation and prepare a report. If someone who is not employed by the same local school administrative unit is selected to serve as the qualified observer, the teacher who is the subject of the mandatory improvement plan will be responsible for any expenses related

to the observations and reports prepared by the qualified observer. The qualified observer shall not unduly disrupt the classroom when conducting an observation.

(4) No local board of education or employee of a local board of education shall discharge, threaten, or otherwise retaliate against another employee of the board regarding that employee's compensation, terms, conditions, location, or privileges of employment because of the employee's service or completion of a report as an objective observer pursuant to this subsection, unless the employee's report contained material information that the employee knew was false.

(d) (Effective until July 1, 2014) Reassessment of the Teacher. - Upon completion of a mandatory improvement plan under subsection (b) of this section, the principal shall assess the performance of the teacher a second time. The principal shall also review and consider any report provided by the qualified observer under subsection (c) of this section if one has been submitted before the end of the mandatory improvement plan period. If, after the second assessment of the teacher and consideration of any report from the qualified observer, the superintendent or superintendent's designee determines that the teacher has failed to become proficient in any of the performance standards identified as deficient in the mandatory improvement plan or demonstrate sufficient improvement toward such standards, the superintendent may recommend that the teacher be dismissed or demoted under G.S. 115C-325. The results of the second assessment produced pursuant to the terms of this subsection shall constitute substantial evidence of the teacher's inadequate performance.

(d) (Effective July 1, 2014, until June 30, 2018) Reassessment of the Teacher. - Upon completion of a mandatory improvement plan under subsection (b) of this section, the principal shall assess the performance of the teacher a second time. The principal shall also review and consider any report provided by the qualified observer under subsection (c) of this section if one has been submitted before the end of the mandatory improvement plan period. If, after the second assessment of the teacher and consideration of any report from the qualified observer, the superintendent or superintendent's designee determines that the teacher has failed to become proficient in any of the performance standards identified as deficient in the mandatory improvement plan or demonstrate sufficient improvement toward such standards, the superintendent may recommend that a teacher with career status be dismissed or demoted under G.S. 115C-325, or if the teacher is on contract that the teacher's contract not be renewed or if the teacher has engaged in inappropriate conduct or performed inadequately to such a degree that such conduct or performance causes substantial harm to the educational environment, that the teacher be immediately dismissed or demoted under G.S. 115C-325.4. The results of the second assessment produced pursuant to the terms of this subsection shall constitute substantial evidence of the teacher's inadequate performance.

(d) (Effective June 30, 2018) Reassessment of the Teacher. - Upon completion of a mandatory improvement plan under subsection (b) of this section, the principal shall assess the performance of the teacher a second time. The principal shall also review and consider any report provided by the qualified observer under subsection (c) of this section if one has been submitted before the end of the mandatory improvement plan period. If, after the second assessment of the teacher and consideration of any report from the qualified observer, the superintendent or superintendent's designee determines that the teacher has failed to become proficient in any of the performance standards identified as deficient in the mandatory improvement plan or demonstrate sufficient improvement toward such standards, the superintendent may recommend that the teacher's contract not be renewed, or if the teacher has engaged in inappropriate conduct or performed inadequately to such a degree that such conduct or performance causes substantial harm to the educational environment, that the teacher be immediately dismissed or demoted under G.S. 115C-325.4. The results of the second assessment produced pursuant to the terms of this subsection shall constitute substantial evidence of the teacher's inadequate performance.

(e) (Effective until July 1, 2014) Dismissal Proceedings Without a Mandatory Improvement Plan. - The absence of a mandatory improvement plan as described in this section shall not prohibit a superintendent from initiating a dismissal proceeding against a teacher under the provisions of G.S. 115C-325. However, the superintendent shall not be entitled to the substantial evidence provision in subsection (d) of this section if such mandatory improvement plan is not utilized.

(e) (Effective July 1, 2014, until June 30, 2018) Dismissal Proceedings Without a Mandatory Improvement Plan. - The absence of a mandatory improvement plan as described in this section shall not prohibit a superintendent from initiating a dismissal proceeding against a teacher under the provisions of G.S. 115C-325 or G.S. 115C-325.4. However, the superintendent shall not be entitled to the substantial evidence provision in subsection (d) of this section if such mandatory improvement plan is not utilized.

(e) (Effective June 30, 2018) Dismissal Proceedings Without a Mandatory Improvement Plan. - The absence of a mandatory improvement plan as described in this section shall not prohibit a superintendent from initiating a dismissal proceeding against a teacher under the provisions of G.S. 115C-325.4. However, the superintendent shall not be entitled to the substantial evidence provision in subsection (d) of this section if such mandatory improvement plan is not utilized.

(f) (Effective until July 1, 2014) State Board Notification. - If a local board dismisses a teacher for any reason except a reduction in force under G.S. 115C-325(e)(1)l., it shall notify the State Board of the action, and the State Board annually shall provide to all local boards the names of those teachers. If a local board hires one of these teachers, within 60 days the superintendent or the superintendent's designee shall observe the teacher, develop a mandatory improvement plan to assist the teacher, and submit the plan to the State Board. The State Board shall review the mandatory improvement plan and may provide comments and suggestions to the superintendent. If on the next evaluation the teacher receives a rating on any standard that was an area of concern on the mandatory improvement plan that is again below proficient or a rating that otherwise represents unsatisfactory or below standard performance, the local board shall notify the State Board, and the State Board shall initiate a proceeding to revoke the teacher's license under G.S. 115C-296(d). If on the next evaluation the teacher receives at least a proficient rating on all of the overall performance standards that were areas of concern on the mandatory improvement plan, the local board shall notify the State Board that the teacher is in good standing, and the State Board shall not continue to provide the teacher's name to local boards under this subsection unless the teacher is subsequently dismissed under G.S. 115C-325 except for a reduction in force. If, however, on this next evaluation the teacher receives a developing rating on any standards that were areas of concern on the mandatory improvement plan, the teacher shall have one more year to bring the rating to proficient. If, by the end of this second year, the teacher is not proficient in all standards that were areas of concern on the mandatory improvement plan, the local board shall notify the State Board, and the State Board shall initiate a proceeding to revoke the teacher's license under G.S. 115C-296(d).

(f) (Effective July 1, 2014, until June 30, 2018) State Board Notification. - If a local board dismisses a teacher with career status for any reason except a reduction in force under G.S. 115C-325(e)(1)l., or dismisses a teacher on contract for cause or elects to not renew a teacher's contract as a result of a superintendent's recommendation under subsection (d) of this section, it shall notify the State Board of the action, and the State Board annually shall provide to all local boards the names of those teachers. If a local board hires one of these teachers, within 60 days the superintendent or the superintendent's designee shall observe the teacher, develop a mandatory improvement plan to assist the teacher, and submit the plan to the State Board. The State Board shall review the mandatory improvement plan and may provide comments and suggestions to the superintendent. If on the next evaluation the teacher receives a rating on any standard that was an area of concern on the mandatory improvement plan that is again below proficient or a rating that otherwise represents unsatisfactory or below standard performance, the local board shall notify the State Board, and the State Board shall initiate a proceeding to revoke the teacher's license under G.S. 115C-296(d). If on the next evaluation the teacher receives at least a proficient rating on all of the overall performance standards that were areas of concern on the mandatory improvement plan, the local board shall notify the State Board that the teacher is in good standing, and the State Board shall not continue to provide the teacher's name to local boards under this subsection unless the teacher has career status and is subsequently dismissed under G.S. 115C-325 except for a reduction in force or is a teacher on contract who is subsequently dismissed under G.S. 115C-325.4. If, however, on this next evaluation the teacher receives a developing rating on any standards that were areas of concern on the mandatory improvement plan, the teacher shall have one more year to bring the rating to proficient if the local board elects to renew the teacher's contract. If by the end of this second year the teacher is not proficient in all standards that were areas of concern on the mandatory improvement plan, the local board shall notify the State Board, and the State Board shall initiate a proceeding to revoke the teacher's license under G.S. 115C-296(d).

(f) (Effective June 30, 2018) State Board Notification. - If a local board dismisses a teacher for cause or elects to not renew a teacher's contract as a result of a superintendent's recommendation under subsection (d) of this section, it shall notify the State Board of the action, and the State Board annually shall provide to all local boards the names of those teachers. If a local board hires one of these teachers, within 60 days the superintendent or the superintendent's designee shall observe the teacher, develop a mandatory improvement plan to assist the teacher, and submit the plan to the State Board. The State Board shall review the mandatory improvement plan and may provide comments and suggestions to the superintendent. If on the next evaluation the teacher receives a rating on any standard that was an area of concern on the mandatory improvement plan that is again below proficient or a rating that otherwise represents unsatisfactory or below standard performance, the local board shall notify the State Board, and the State Board shall initiate a proceeding to revoke the teacher's license under G.S. 115C-296(d). If on the next evaluation the teacher receives at least a proficient rating on all of the overall performance standards that were areas of concern on the mandatory improvement plan, the local board shall notify the State Board that the teacher is in good standing, and the State Board shall not continue to provide the teacher's name to local boards under this subsection unless the teacher has career status and is subsequently dismissed under G.S. 115C-325.4. If, however, on this next evaluation the teacher receives a developing rating on any standards that were areas of concern on the mandatory improvement plan, if the local board elects to renew the teacher's contract. If by the end of this second year the teacher is not proficient in all standards that were areas of concern on the mandatory improvement plan, the local board shall notify the State Board, and the State Board shall initiate a proceeding to revoke the teacher's license under G.S. 115C-296(d).

(g) Civil Immunity. - There shall be no liability for negligence on the part of the State Board of Education or a local board of education, or their employees, arising from any action taken or omission by any of them in carrying out the provisions of this section. The immunity established by this subsection shall not extend to gross negligence, wanton conduct, or intentional wrongdoing that would otherwise be actionable. The immunity established by this subsection shall be deemed to have been waived to the extent of indemnification by insurance, indemnification under Articles 31A and 31B of Chapter 143 of the General Statutes, and to the extent sovereign immunity is waived under the Tort Claims Act, as set forth in Article 31 of Chapter 143 of the General Statutes. (2011-348, ss. 3, 8.6; 2013-360, s. 9.7(j), (t).)

§ 115C-334. Assessment teams.

The State Board shall develop guidelines for local boards to use to create assessment teams. A local board shall assign an assessment team to every low-performing school in the local school administrative unit that has not received an assistance team. Local boards shall ensure that assessment team members are trained in the proper administration of the employee evaluation used by the local school administrative unit. If service on an assessment team is an additional duty for an employee of a local board, the board may pay the employee for that additional work.

Assessment teams shall have the following duties:

(1)   Conduct evaluations of licensed employees in low-performing schools;

(2)   Provide technical assistance and training to principals, assistant principals, superintendents, and superintendents' designees who conduct evaluations of licensed employees;

(3)   Develop mandatory improvement plans for licensed employees; and

(4)   Assist principals, assistant principals, superintendents, and superintendents' designees in the development and implementation of mandatory improvement plans. (1998-5, s. 4; 2011-348, s. 7.)

§ 115C-335. Development of performance standards and criteria for licensed employees; training and remediation programs.

(a)   Development of Performance Standards. - The State Board, in consultation with local boards of education, shall revise and develop uniform performance standards and criteria to be used in evaluating certified public school employees, including school administrators. These standards and criteria shall include improving student achievement, employee skills, and employee knowledge. The standards and criteria for school administrators also shall include building-level gains in student learning and effectiveness in providing for school safety and enforcing student discipline. The State Board shall develop rules regarding the use of these standards and criteria. The State Board also shall develop guidelines for evaluating superintendents. The guidelines shall include criteria for evaluating a superintendent's effectiveness in providing safe schools and enforcing student discipline.

(b)   (Effective until July 1, 2014) Training. - The State Board, in collaboration with the Board of Governors of The University of North Carolina, shall develop programs designed to train principals and superintendents in the proper administration of the employee evaluations developed by the State Board. The Board of Governors shall use the professional development programs for public school employees that are under its authority to make this training available to all principals and superintendents at locations that are geographically convenient to local school administrative units. The programs shall include methods to determine whether an employee's performance has improved student learning, the development and implementation of appropriate professional growth and mandatory improvement plans, the process for contract nonrenewal, and the dismissal process under G.S. 115C-325. The Board of Governors shall ensure that the subject matter of the training programs is incorporated into the masters in school administration programs offered by the constituent institutions. The State Board, in collaboration with the Board of Governors, also shall develop in-service programs for licensed public school employees that may be included in a mandatory improvement plan created under G.S. 115C-333(b) or G.S. 115C-333.1(b). The Board of Governors shall use the professional development programs for public school employees that are under its authority to make this training available at locations that are geographically convenient to local school administrative units.

(b) (Effective July 1, 2014) Training. - The State Board, in collaboration with the Board of Governors of The University of North Carolina, shall develop programs designed to train principals and superintendents in the proper administration of the employee evaluations developed by the State Board. The Board of Governors shall use the professional development programs for public school employees that are under its authority to make this training available to all principals and superintendents at locations that are geographically convenient to local school administrative units. The programs shall include methods to determine whether an employee's performance has improved student learning, the development and implementation of appropriate professional growth and mandatory improvement plans, the process for contract nonrenewal, and the dismissal process under Part 3 of Article 22 of this Chapter. The Board of Governors shall ensure that the subject matter of the training programs is incorporated into the masters in school administration programs offered by the constituent institutions. The State Board, in collaboration with the Board of Governors, also shall develop in-service programs for licensed public school employees that may be included in a mandatory improvement plan created under G.S. 115C-333(b) or G.S. 115C-333.1(b). The Board of Governors shall use the professional development programs for public school employees that are under its authority to make this training available at locations that are geographically convenient to local school administrative units. (1998-5, s. 4; 2011-348, s. 8; 2013-360, s. 9.7(k).)

§§ 115C-335.1 through 115C-335.4. Reserved for future codification purposes.

Part 8. Sexual Harassment Policies.

§ 115C-335.5. Policies addressing harassment of school employees; protection against retaliation for reporting harassment.

(a) Each local board of education may adopt a policy addressing the sexual harassment of local board employees by students, other local board employees, or school board members. The policy may, at a minimum, set out (i) the consequences of sexually harassing school employees and (ii) a procedure for reporting incidents of sexual harassment.

(b) No local board of education or employee of a local board shall discharge, threaten, or otherwise retaliate against another employee of the board regarding that employee's compensation, terms, conditions, location, or privileges of employment because the employee files a written complaint alleging sexual harassment by students, other local board employees, or school board members, unless the employee reporting the harassment knew or should have known the report was false. (1999-352, s. 1; 2001-173, s. 1.)

Part 9. Equal Access Act.

§ 115C-335.9. Equal access for all education employee associations.

(a) As used in this section, the following definitions apply:

(1) "Education employee association" includes teacher associations, teacher organizations, and classified education employees' associations.

(2) "School" means a charter school or a school operated by a local school administrative unit, the State Board of Education or a State agency.

(b) It is the intent of the General Assembly that all education employee associations have equal access to employees at schools and that schools not favor nor endorse an education employee association; therefore, neither a local school administrative unit nor a school shall do any of the following:

(1) Grant access to employees' physical or electronic mailboxes to an education employee association unless it gives such access to all education employee associations operating in the local school administrative unit.

(2) Permit an education employee association to attend new teacher or employee orientations to recruit members unless it permits all education employee associations operating in the local school administrative unit to attend.

(3) Give an education employee association preferential treatment through procedures, policies, or any other means. This subdivision does not authorize any payroll deduction for any association unless authorized by law for that association.

(4) Endorse one education employee association over another.

(5) Refer to days or breaks in a school calendar by the name of an employee education association.

(c) A school shall not discourage or prohibit an employee from joining an organization or showing preferences toward any educational association. (2012-179, s. 1(b).)

Article 23.

Employment Benefits.

§ 115C-336. Sick leave.

(a) All public school employees shall be permitted a minimum of five days per school term of sick leave, pursuant to rules and regulations promulgated by the State Board of Education as provided in G.S. 115C-12(8).

(b) The State Board of Education shall adopt rules and regulations for the establishment of voluntary sick leave banks by local boards of education, from which an employee, upon exhaustion of accumulated sick leave and annual leave, when allowable, may withdraw sick leave days in the event of emergency or catastrophic illness. These rules may include, but not be limited to, (i) requirements of minimum service and minimum balance of sick leave before an employee may join the sick leave bank, (ii) enrollment periods for present employees and new hires, (iii) time limits for rejoining the sick leave bank, (iv) limitation on number of days which can be withdrawn by any employee, (v) waiting period before being eligible to withdraw sick leave, (vi) exclusion of illness or injury covered by Workers' Compensation Benefits, (vii) certification by physician attesting to member's illness or accident, (viii) administration of each sick leave bank by a Sick Leave Bank Committee to be made up of representatives of different classifications of employees, and (ix) other requirements to prevent any adverse selection by employees. The rules concerning the establishment of sick leave banks shall include provisions for notifying employees who donate sick leave to and employees who withdraw sick leave from the sick leave bank, of the State retirement credit consequences as to the donated sick leave.

(c) The State Board of Education shall also adopt rules and regulations to authorize an employee who requires a substitute to use annual leave on days that students are in attendance if the employee has exhausted all of the employee's sick leave and if the employee's absence is due to the catastrophic illness of the employee. The employee shall not be required to pay the substitute.

(d) The State Board of Education shall adopt rules relating to the reinstatement of unused sick leave when an employee who was employed on a 10-month contract at the time of separation returns to employment on a 10-month contract. Under these rules, the maximum period of separation after which unused sick leave is reinstated shall be three calendar months longer for school personnel employed on a 10-month contract than for school personnel employed on a 12-month contract. (1981, c. 423, s. 1; 1993, c. 321, s. 72(a); 1995, c. 324, s. 17.4; 2009-144, s. 1.)

§ 115C-336.1. Parental leave.

A school employee may use annual leave or leave without pay to care for a newborn child or for a child placed with the employee for adoption or foster care. A school employee may also use up to 30 days of sick leave to care for a child placed with the employee for adoption. The leave may be for consecutive workdays during the first 12 months after the date of birth or placement of the child, unless the school employee and the local board of education agree otherwise. (2002-159, s. 37.5(b).)

§ 115C-337. Workers' compensation for school employees.

(a) Workers' Compensation Act Applicable to School Employees. - The provisions of the Workers' Compensation Act shall be applicable to all school employees, and the State Board of Education shall make arrangements necessary to carry out the provisions of the Workers' Compensation Act applicable to these employees paid from State school funds. Liability of the State for compensation shall be confined to school employees paid by the State from State school funds for injuries or death caused by accident arising out of and in the course of their employment in connection with the state-operated school term. The State shall be liable for this compensation on the basis of the average weekly wage of the employees as defined in the Workers' Compensation Act, to the extent of the proportionate part of each employee's salary that is paid from State funds. The State shall also be liable for workers' compensation for all school employees employed in connection with the teaching of vocational agriculture, home economics, trades and industries, and other vocational subjects, supported in part by State and federal funds, which liability shall cover the entire period of service of these employees, to the extent of the proportionate part of each employee's salary that is paid from State funds. The local school administrative units shall be liable for workers' compensation for school employees, including lunchroom employees, whose salaries or wages are paid by the local units from local or special funds. The local units may provide insurance to cover this compensation liability and to include the cost of this insurance in their annual budgets.

The provisions of this subsection shall not apply to any person, firm, or corporation making voluntary contributions to schools for any purpose, and the person, firm, or corporation shall not be liable for the payment of any sum of money under this Chapter.

(b) Payment of Awards to School Bus Drivers Pursuant to the Workers' Compensation Act. - In the event that the Industrial Commission shall make an award pursuant to the Workers' Compensation Act against any local board of education on account of injuries to or the death of a school bus driver arising out of and in the course of his employment as such driver, the local board of education shall draw a requisition upon the State Board of Education for the amount required to pay such award. The State Board of Education shall honor such requisition to the extent that it shall have in its hands, or subject to its control, available funds which have been or shall thereafter be appropriated by the General Assembly for the support of the school term. It shall be the duty of the local board of education to apply all funds received by it from the State

Board of Education pursuant to such requisition to the payment of such award. Neither the State nor the State Board of Education shall be deemed the employer of such school bus driver, nor shall the State or the State Board of Education be liable to any school bus driver or any other person for the payment of any claim, award, or judgment under the provisions of the Workers' Compensation Act or of any other law of this State for any injury or death arising out of or in the course of the operation by such driver of a public school bus. Neither the local board of education, the local school administrative unit, nor the tax levying authorities for the local school administrative unit shall be liable for the payment of any award made pursuant to the provisions of this subsection in excess of the amount paid upon such requisition by the State Board of Education, nor shall the local school board of education, the local school administrative unit, nor the said tax levying authorities be required to provide or carry workers' compensation insurance for such purpose. (1955, c. 1292; c. 1372, art. 18, s. 9; 1979, c. 714, s. 2; 1981, c. 423, s. 1; 1995, c. 324, s. 17(b).)

§ 115C-338. Salaries for employees injured during an episode of violence.

(a) For the purpose of this section, "employee" shall mean any teacher, helping teacher, librarian, principal, supervisor, superintendent of public schools or any full-time employee, city or county, superintendent of public instruction, or any full-time employee of Department of Public Instruction, president, dean or teacher, or any full-time employee in any educational institution supported by and under the control of the State: Provided, that the term "teacher" shall not include any part-time, temporary, or substitute teacher or employee, and shall not include those participating in an optional retirement program provided for in G.S. 135-5.1. In all cases of doubt, the Board of Trustees, as defined in G.S. 135-1(7), shall determine whether any person is a teacher as herein defined.

(b) Any employee who while engaged in the course of his employment or in any activities incidental thereto, suffers any injury or disability resulting from or arising out of any episode of violence by one or more persons shall be entitled to receive his full salary during the shortest of these periods: one year, the continuation of his disability, or the time during which he is unable to engage in his employment because of injury. An episode of violence shall be defined to mean but shall not be limited to any acts of violence directed toward any school building or facility, or to any employee or any student by any person including but not limited to another student. These benefits shall be in lieu of all other income or disability benefits payable under workers' compensation to such employee only during the period prescribed herein. Thereafter, such teacher shall be paid such income or disability payments to which he might be entitled under workers' compensation. If the employment of a substitute is necessitated by the disability of the injured employee the salary of such substitute shall be paid from the same source of funds from which the employee is paid. This section shall in no way limit the right of the injured employee to receive the benefits of medical, hospital, drug and related expense payments from any source, including workers' compensation: Provided, further, that this section shall not apply to any employee who is injured while he participates in or provokes such episode of violence except as is incident to the maintenance or restoration of order or classroom discipline or to defend himself: Provided, further, that this section shall be given liberal construction and interpretation as to any and all definitions, conditions, and factual circumstances set forth herein.

(c) Any employee claiming the benefits of this section shall file claim with the board of education employing such employee within one year after the occurrence giving rise to his alleged injury. That board of education shall, within 30 days after receipt of such claim, decide whether and to what extent that employee is entitled to the benefits of this section and shall forthwith transmit its decision in writing to such employee. That employee shall, however, have the right to appeal the decision of that board of education to the North Carolina Industrial Commission by serving that board of education and the North Carolina Industrial Commission with written notice thereof within 30 days after receipt of the board's written decision. In determining all appeals under this section the North Carolina Industrial Commission shall constitute a court for the purpose of hearing de novo and passing upon all claims thereby presented in accordance with procedures utilized by the Commission in determining claims under the Workers' Compensation Act. The decision of the Industrial Commission in each instance shall be subject to appeal to the North Carolina Court of Appeals as provided in G.S. 143-293 and 143-294. (1971, c. 640, ss. 1, 2; 1973, c. 753; 1979, c. 714, s. 2; 1981, c. 423, s. 1.)

§ 115C-339. Retirement plan.

Provisions for retirement plans for public school employees may be found in Chapter 135 of the General Statutes. (1981, c. 423, s. 1.)

§ 115C-340. Health insurance.

(a) The State Board of Education may authorize and empower any local board of education, the board of trustees of any community college, or other governing authority, within the State, to establish a voluntary payroll deduction plan for premiums for any type of group insurance, including health insurance, established and authorized by the laws of this State.

(b) Any employee of any local board of education, any community college, or of any educational association, may enter into a written agreement with his employer for the purpose of carrying out the provisions of this section. The State Board of Education is authorized and empowered to make and promulgate rules and regulations to carry out the purposes of this section. (1969, c. 591; 1981, c. 423, s. 1; 1987, c. 564, ss. 12, 16.)

§ 115C-341. Annuity contracts from local boards of education.

Notwithstanding the provisions of this Chapter for the adoption of State and local salary schedules for the pay of teachers, principals, superintendents, and other school employees, local boards of education may enter into annual contracts with any employee of such board which provide for a reduction in salary below the total established compensation or salary schedule for a term of one year. The local board of education shall use the funds derived from the reduction in the salary of the employee to purchase a nonforfeitable annuity contract for the benefit of said employee. An employee who has agreed to a salary reduction for this purpose shall not have the right to receive the amount of the salary reduction in cash or in any other way except the annuity contract. Funds used by the local boards of education for the purchase of an annuity contract shall not be in lieu of any amount earned by the employee before his election for a salary reduction has become effective.

The agreement for salary reductions referred to herein shall be effected under any necessary regulations and procedures adopted by the State Board of Education and on forms prepared by the State Board of Education.

Notwithstanding any other provisions of this section, the amount by which the salary of any employee is reduced pursuant to this section shall be included in computing and making payroll deductions for social security and retirement system purposes, and in computing and providing matching funds for retirement system purposes.

In lieu of the annuity contracts provided for under this section, interests in custodial accounts pursuant to Section 401(f), Section 403(b)(7), and related sections of the Internal Revenue Code of 1986 as amended may be purchased by local boards of education for the benefit of qualified employees under this section with the funds derived from the reduction in the salaries of such employees. (1963, c. 582; 1981, c. 423, s. 1; 1989, c. 526, s. 1; 2011-310, s. 1.)

§ 115C-341.1. Flexible Compensation Plan.

Notwithstanding any other provisions of law relating to the salaries of employees of local boards of education, the State Board of Education is authorized to provide a plan of flexible compensation to eligible employees of local school administrative units for benefits available under Section 125 and related sections of the Internal Revenue Code of 1986 as amended. This plan shall not include those benefits provided to employees under Articles 1, 3B, and 6 of Chapter 135 of the General Statutes nor any vacation leave, sick leave, or any other leave that may be carried forward from year to year by employees as a form of deferred compensation. If a plan of flexible compensation is offered, then a TRICARE supplement shall be offered. In providing a plan of flexible compensation, the State Board may authorize local school administrative units to enter into agreements with their employees for reductions in the salaries of employees electing to participate in the plan of flexible compensation provided by this section. With the approval of the Director of the Budget, savings in the employer's share of contributions under the Federal Insurance Contributions Act on account of the reduction in salary may be used to pay some or all of the administrative expenses of the program. Should the State Board decide to contract with a third party to administer the terms and conditions of a plan of flexible compensation as provided by this section, it may select such a contractor only upon a thorough and completely advertised competitive procurement process. (1989 (Reg. Sess., 1990), c. 1059, s. 1; 1991 (Reg. Sess., 1992), c. 1044, s. 14(f); 1993, c. 561, s. 42; 1993 (Reg. Sess., 1994), c. 769, s. 7.28A; 1997-443, s. 33.20(a); 1999-237, s. 28.27(a); 2013-292, s. 1.)

§ 115C-341.2. Department of State Treasurer sponsored 403(b) option.

(a) In addition to the opportunities for local boards of education to offer section 403(b) of the Internal Revenue Code of 1986 retirement annuities and/or mutual funds to their employees under G.S. 115C-341, the Department of State Treasurer may establish an approved third-party vendor of retirement offerings as described in section 403(b) of the Internal Revenue Code of 1986, as now and hereafter amended, pursuant to which employees of local school boards may enter into nonforfeitable 403(b) plan options by way of salary reduction through the auspices of the Department of State Treasurer. This statewide plan shall be known as the "North Carolina Public School Teachers' and Professional Educators' Investment Plan." The vendor authorized under this section shall be selected by use of State procurement procedures, with the goal of attaining lower administrative fees and enhanced services for participants and employer compliance with applicable law and regulations. Eligible employees of local school boards shall all be allowed to use this vendor for the tax-deferred 403(b) option of their choice.

(b) The criteria in this subsection apply to the Department of State Treasurer's 403(b) offerings to employees of local school boards under this section.

(1) Annuity contracts, trust accounts, and/or custodial accounts shall be administered by a qualified third-party administrator that shall, under written agreement with the Department of State Treasurer, provide custodial, record-keeping, and administrative services. The third-party administrator may also be the selected vendor for the North Carolina Public School Teachers' and Professional Educators' Investment Plan.

For employers choosing to participate in the North Carolina Public School Teachers' and Professional Educators' Investment Plan, the third-party administrator shall, at a minimum, provide the following:

a. Maintain a written plan document.

b. Review hardship withdrawal requests, loan requests, and other disbursements permitted under section 403(b) of the Internal Revenue Code of 1986.

c. Maintain specimen salary reduction agreements for the employer and employees of that employer to initiate payroll deferrals.

d. Monitor maximum contributions.

e. Coordinate responses to the Internal Revenue Service in any case of an IRS audit.

f. Generate educational communication materials to employees concerning the enrollment process, program eligibility, and investment options.

g. Maintain internal reports to ensure compliance with Section 403(b) of the Internal Revenue Code and Title 26 of the Code of Federal Regulations.

h. Provide compliance monitoring/oversight for all 403(b) plans established under G.S. 115C-341 within each participating local board of education plan by creating and establishing the necessary connections and processes with existing and future vendors.

i. Keep an updated schedule of vendor fees and commissions as to the Department's statewide plan.

(2) Governance and oversight of the North Carolina Public School Teachers' and Professional Educators' Investment Plan will be performed by the Department of State Treasurer and the Board of Trustees for the North Carolina Supplemental Retirement Plans established pursuant to G.S. 135-96. Because of the administrative and record-keeping duties enumerated in subdivision (1) of this subsection, any existing vendor of a 403(b) with a participating employer must either agree to share data with the State's 403(b) vendor under this provision (so as to permit oversight over contribution limits, loans, and hardship withdrawals) or be directed by the participating employer to cease accepting new contributions, loans, and hardship withdrawals.

(3) Investment options shall be solely determined by the Department of State Treasurer and Board of Trustees for the North Carolina Supplemental Retirement Plans consistent with section 403(b) of the Internal Revenue Code of 1986, as amended.

(4) Investment staff of the Department of State Treasurer may make recommendations to the State Treasurer and Board of Trustees for the North Carolina Supplemental Retirement Plans as to appropriate investment options. The State Treasurer and Board of Trustees shall have sole responsibility for the selection of the service provider for the North Carolina Public School Teachers' and Professional Educators' Investment Plan.

(5) All contributions made in accordance with the provisions of section 403(b) of the Internal Revenue Code of 1986, as amended, and this section shall be remitted directly to the administrator and held by the administrator in a custodial account on behalf of each participating employee. Any investment gains or losses shall be credited to those accounts. The forms of payment and disbursement procedures shall be consistent with those generally offered by similar annuity contracts, trust accounts, and custodial accounts and applicable federal and State statutes governing those contracts and accounts.

(6) Any local board of education may elect to make contributions to the employee's account on behalf of the employee. The employer shall take whatever action is necessary to implement this section.

(7) The design and administration of annuity contracts, trust accounts, and custodial accounts under this provision shall comply with all applicable provisions of the Internal Revenue Code of 1986, as amended. (2011-310, s. 2.)

§ 115C-342. Group insurance and credit unions.

(a) The State Board of Education may authorize and empower any local board of education, the board of trustees of any community college, or other governing authority, within the State, to establish a voluntary payroll deduction plan for:

(1) Premiums for any type of group insurance established and authorized by the laws of this State.

(2) Amounts authorized by members of the State Employees' Credit Union or any local teachers' credit unions to be deposited with such organizations.

(3) Loans made to teachers by credit unions.

(b) Any employee of any local board of education, any community college, or of any educational association, may enter into a written agreement with his employer for the purpose of carrying out the provisions of this section. The State Board of Education is authorized and empowered to make and promulgate rules and regulations to carry out the purposes of this section.

(c) Any public school teacher who is a member of a credit union organized and established under Chapter 54 of the General Statutes may, by executing a written consent to the local school administrative unit by whom employed, authorize periodical payment or obligation to such credit union to be deducted from their salaries or wages, and such deductions shall be made and paid to said credit union as and when said salaries and wages are payable. (1969, c. 591; 1981, c. 423, s. 1; 1987, c. 564, ss 12, 16.)

§ 115C-343: Repealed by Session Laws 2011-210, s. 2, effective June 23, 2011.

§ 115C-344. Employment benefits for exchange teachers.

An exchange teacher is a nonimmigrant alien teacher participating in an exchange visitor program designated by the United States Department of State pursuant to 22 C.F.R. Part 62 or by the United States Department of Homeland Security pursuant to 8 C.F.R. Part 214.2(q). For purposes of determining eligibility to receive employment benefits under this Chapter, including personal leave, annual vacation leave, and sick leave, an exchange teacher shall be considered a permanent teacher if employed with the expectation of at least six full consecutive monthly pay periods of employment and if employed at least 20 hours per week. An exchange teacher is not a teacher for purposes of the Teachers' and State Employees' Retirement System of North Carolina as provided in G.S. 135-1(25). (2013-360, s. 9.7(u).)

§ 115C-345. Reserved for future codification purposes.

§ 115C-346. Reserved for future codification purposes.

§ 115C-347. Reserved for future codification purposes.

§ 115C-348. Reserved for future codification purposes.

Article 24.

Interstate Agreement on Qualifications of Educational Personnel.

§ 115C-349. Purpose, findings, and policy.

(a) The states party to this agreement, desiring by common action to improve their respective school systems by utilizing the teacher or other professional educational person wherever educated, declare that it is the policy of each of them, on the basis of cooperation with one another, to take advantage of the preparation and experience of such persons wherever gained, thereby serving the best interests of society, of education, and of the teaching profession. It is the purpose of this agreement to provide for the development and execution of such programs of cooperation as will facilitate the movement of teachers and other professional educational personnel among the states party to it, and to authorize specific interstate educational personnel contracts to achieve that end.

(b) The party states find that included in the large movement of population among all sections of the nation are many qualified educational personnel who move for family and other personal reasons but who are hindered in using their professional skill and experience in their new locations. Variations from state to state in requirements for qualifying educational personnel discourage such personnel from taking the steps necessary to qualify in other states. As a consequence, a significant number of professionally prepared and experienced educators is lost to our school systems. Facilitating the employment of qualified educational personnel, without reference to their states of origin, can increase the available educational resources. Participation in this Compact can increase the availability of educational manpower. (1969, c. 631, s. 1; 1981, c. 423, s. 1.)

§ 115C-350. Definitions.

As used in this agreement and contracts made pursuant to it, unless the context clearly requires otherwise:

(1) "Accept" or any variant thereof, means to recognize and give effect to one or more determinations of another state relating to the qualifications of educational personnel in lieu of making or requiring a like determination that would otherwise be required by or pursuant to the laws of a receiving state.

(2) "Designated state official" means the educational official of a state selected by that state to negotiate and enter into, on behalf of his state, contracts pursuant to this agreement.

(3) "Educational personnel" means persons who must meet requirements pursuant to state law as a condition of employment in educational programs.

(4) "Originating state" means a state (and the subdivision thereof, if any) whose determination that certain educational personnel are qualified to be employed for specific duties in schools, is acceptable in accordance with the terms of a contract made pursuant to G.S. 115C-351.

(5) "Receiving state" means a state (and the subdivisions thereof) which accepts educational personnel in accordance with the terms of a contract made pursuant to G.S. 115C-351.

(6) "State" means a state, territory, or possession of the United States; the District of Columbia; or the Commonwealth of Puerto Rico. (1969, c. 631, s. 1; 1981, c. 423, s. 1.)

§ 115C-351. Interstate educational personnel contracts.

(a) The designated state official of a party state may make one or more contracts on behalf of his state with one or more other party states providing for the acceptance of educational personnel. Any such contract for the period of its duration shall be applicable to and binding on the states whose designated state officials enter into it, and the subdivisions of those states, with the same force and effect as if incorporated in this agreement. A designated state official may enter into a contract pursuant to this section only with states in which he finds that there are programs of education, certification standards or other acceptable qualifications that assure preparation or qualification of educational personnel on a basis sufficiently comparable, even though not identical to that prevailing in his own state.

(b) Any such contract shall provide for:

(1) Its duration.

(2) The criteria to be applied by an originating state in qualifying educational personnel for acceptance by a receiving state.

(3) Such waivers, substitutions, and conditional acceptances as shall aid the practical effectuation of the contract without sacrifice of basic educational standards.

(4) Any other necessary matters.

(c) No contract made pursuant to this agreement shall be for a term longer than five years but any such contract may be renewed for like or lesser periods.

(d) Any contract dealing with acceptance of educational personnel on the basis of their having completed an educational program shall specify the earliest date or dates on which originating state approval of the program or programs involved can have occurred. No contract made pursuant to this agreement shall require acceptance by a receiving state of any persons qualified because of successful completion of a program prior to January 1, 1954.

(e) The certification or other acceptance of a person who has been accepted pursuant to the terms of a contract shall not be revoked or otherwise impaired because the contract has expired or been terminated. However, any certificate or other qualifying document may be revoked or suspended on any ground which would be sufficient for revocation or suspension of a certificate or other qualifying document initially granted or approved in the receiving state.

(f) A contract committee composed of the designated state officials of the contracting states or their representatives shall keep the contract under continuous review, study means of improving its administration, and report no less frequently than once a year to the heads of the appropriate education agencies of the contracting states. (1969, c. 631, s. 1; 1981, c. 423, s. 1.)

§ 115C-352. Approved and accepted programs.

(a) Nothing in this agreement shall be construed to repeal or otherwise modify any law or regulation of a party state relating to the approval of programs of educational preparation having effect solely on the qualification of educational personnel within that state.

(b) To the extent that contracts made pursuant to this agreement deal with the educational requirements for the proper qualification of educational personnel, acceptance of a program of educational preparation shall be in accordance with such procedures and requirements as may be provided in the applicable contract. (1969, c. 631, s. 1; 1981, c. 423, s. 1.)

§ 115C-353. Interstate cooperation.

The party states agree that:

(1) They will, so far as practicable, prefer the making of multilateral contracts pursuant to G.S. 115C-351 of this agreement.

(2) They will facilitate and strengthen cooperation in interstate certification and other elements of educational personnel qualification and for this purpose shall cooperate with agencies, organizations, and associations interested in certification and other elements of educational personnel qualification. (1969, c. 631, s. 1; 1981, c. 423, s. 1.)

§ 115C-354. Agreement evaluation.

The designated state officials of any party state(s) may meet from time to time as a group to evaluate progress under the agreement, and to formulate recommendations for changes. (1969, c. 631, s. 1; 1981, c. 423, s. 1.)

§ 115C-355. Other arrangements.

Nothing in this agreement shall be construed to prevent or inhibit other arrangements or practices of any party state or states to facilitate the interchange of educational personnel. (1969, c. 631, s. 1; 1981, c. 423, s. 1.)

§ 115C-356. Effect and withdrawal.

(a) This agreement shall become effective when enacted into law by two states. Thereafter it shall become effective as to any state upon its enactment of this agreement.

(b) Any party state may withdraw from this agreement by enacting a statute repealing the same, but no such withdrawal shall take effect until one year after the governor of the withdrawing state has given notice in writing of the withdrawal to the governors of all other party states.

(c) No withdrawal shall relieve the withdrawing state of any obligation imposed upon it by a contract to which it is a party. The duration of contracts and the methods and conditions of withdrawal therefrom shall be those specified in their terms. (1969, c. 631, s. 1; 1981, c. 423, s. 1.)

§ 115C-357. Construction and severability.

This agreement shall be liberally construed so as to effectuate the purposes thereof. The provisions of this agreement shall be severable and if any phrase, clause, sentence, or provision of this agreement is declared to be contrary to the constitution of any state or of the United States, or the application thereof to any government, agency, person, or circumstance is held invalid, the validity of the remainder of this agreement and the applicability thereof to any government, agency, person, or circumstance shall not be affected thereby. If this agreement shall be held contrary to the constitution of any state participating therein, the agreement shall remain in full force and effect as to the state affected as to all severable matters. (1969, c. 631, s. 1; 1981, c. 423, s. 1.)

§ 115C-358. Designated state official.

For the purposes of the agreement set forth in this Article the "designated state official" for this State shall be the Superintendent of Public Instruction. He shall enter into contracts pursuant to G.S. 115C-351 only with the approval of the specific text thereof by the State Board of Education. (1969, c. 631, s. 2; 1981, c. 423, s. 1.)

§§ 115C-359 through 115C-361. Reserved for future codification purposes.

Article 24A.

Certified Personnel Evaluation Pilot Program.

§ 115C-362: Repealed by Session Laws 1989, c. 500, s. 12.

Article 24B.

Career Development Pilot Program.

§§ 115C-363 through 115C-363.14: Repealed by Session Laws 1991 (Regular Session, 1992), c. 900, s. 75.1(j).

Article 24C.

Teacher Enhancement Program

Part 1. Office of Teacher Recruitment

§§ 115C-363.15 through 115C-363.21: Repealed by Session Laws 1993, c. 321, s. 128.

Part 2. North Carolina Teaching Fellows Commission.

§ 115C-363.22. (Repealed effective July 1, 2015) North Carolina Teaching Fellows Commission established.

There is established the North Carolina Teaching Fellows Commission. This Commission shall exercise its powers and functions independently of the State Board of Education and the Department of Public Instruction. The Public School Forum of North Carolina, Inc., shall provide staff and office space to the

Commission. Staff to the Commission are not State employees. (1985 (Reg. Sess., 1986), c. 1014, s. 63(a); 2011-266, s. 1.38(a).)

§ 115C-363.23. (Repealed effective July 1, 2015) Membership.

(a) The Commission shall consist of 11 nonlegislative members as follows:

(1) The Chairman of the State Board of Education, or his designee;

(2) The Lieutenant Governor, or his designee;

(3) Three persons appointed by the Governor;

(4) Three persons appointed by the General Assembly on the recommendation of the President Pro Tempore of the Senate, as provided in G.S. 120-121; and

(5) Three persons appointed by the General Assembly on the recommendation of the Speaker of the House of Representatives, as provided in G.S. 120-121.

Terms of commission members appointed under this section expire on June 30 of the year of expiration. In 1990, three members shall be appointed by the General Assembly upon the recommendation of the Speaker of the House of Representatives, one for a term to expire June 30, 1992, one for a term to expire June 30, 1993, and one for a term to expire June 30, 1994. In 1990, three members shall be appointed by the General Assembly upon the recommendation of the President of the Senate, one for a term to expire June 30, 1991, one for a term to expire June 30, 1992, and one for a term to expire June 30, 1993. In 1990, three members shall be appointed by the Governor, one for a term to expire June 30, 1992, one for a term to expire June 30, 1993, and one for a term to expire June 30, 1994. Subsequent appointments are for a term of four years.

(b) Each of the appointing entities shall seek to achieve a balanced membership representing, to the maximum extent possible, the State as a whole. The Commission members shall be chosen from among individuals who have demonstrated a commitment to education.

(c) Commission members shall be appointed for four-year terms, with the first appointments to expire July 1, 1990.

(d) In the event a vacancy occurs for any reason, the vacancy shall be filled by appointment by the entity that made the appointment, except that vacancies in appointments by the General Assembly shall be filled under G.S. 120-122. The new appointee shall serve for the remainder of the unexpired term.

(e) The Lieutenant Governor or his designee shall serve as chairman.

(f) Members of the Commission shall receive per diem and necessary travel and subsistence expenses in accordance with Chapter 138 of the General Statutes.

(g) The Commission shall meet regularly at times and places the chairman deems necessary. (1985 (Reg. Sess., 1986), c. 1014, s. 63(a); 1989 (Reg. Sess., 1990), c. 1038, s. 19; 1995, c. 490, s. 58; 2011-266, s. 1.38(a).)

§ 115C-363.23A. (Repealed effective July 1, 2015) Teaching Fellows Program established; administration.

(a) A Teaching Fellows Program shall be administered by the North Carolina Teaching Fellows Commission. The Teaching Fellows Program shall be used to provide a four-year scholarship loan of six thousand five hundred dollars ($6,500) per year to North Carolina high school seniors interested in preparing to teach in the public schools of the State. The Commission shall adopt very stringent standards, including minimum grade point average and scholastic aptitude test scores, for awarding these scholarship loans to ensure that only the best high school seniors receive them.

(b) The Commission shall administer the program in cooperation with teacher training institutions selected by the Commission. Teaching Fellows should be exposed to a range of extra-curricular activities while in college. These activities should be geared to instilling a strong motivation not only to remain in teaching but to provide leadership for tomorrow's schools.

(c) The Commission shall form regional review committees to assist it in identifying the best high school seniors for the program. The Commission and the review committees shall make an effort to identify and encourage minority students and students who may not otherwise consider a career in teaching to enter the program.

(d) All scholarship loans shall be evidenced by notes made payable to the Commission that shall bear interest at the rate of ten percent (10%) per year beginning September 1 after completion of the program, or immediately after termination of the scholarship loan, whichever is earlier. The scholarship loan may be terminated by the recipient withdrawing from school or by the recipient not meeting the standards set by the Commission.

(e) The Commission shall forgive the loan if, within seven years after graduation, the recipient teaches for four years at a North Carolina public school or at a school operated by the United States government in North Carolina. The Commission shall also forgive the loan if, within seven years after graduation, the recipient teaches for three consecutive years, unless the recipient takes an approved leave of absence, at a North Carolina public school in a local school administrative unit that, at the time the recipient accepts employment with the unit, is a low-performing school system identified in accordance with Article 6A of this Chapter or is on warning status as defined by the State Board of Education. The Commission shall also forgive the loan if it finds that it is impossible for the recipient to teach for four years, within seven years after graduation, at a North Carolina public school or at a school operated by the United States government in North Carolina, because of the death or permanent disability of the recipient.

(f) All funds appropriated to or otherwise received by the Teaching Fellows Program for scholarships, all funds received as repayment of scholarship loans, and all interest earned on these funds, shall be placed in a revolving fund. This revolving fund shall be used for scholarship loans granted under the Teaching Fellows Program. With the prior approval of the General Assembly in the Current Operations Appropriations Act, the revolving fund may also be used for campus and summer program support, and costs related to disbursement of awards and collection of loan repayments.

The Public School Forum, as administrator for the Teaching Fellows Program, may use up to six hundred thousand dollars ($600,000) annually from the fund balance for costs associated with administration of the Teaching Fellows Program.

(g) The State Education Assistance Authority is responsible for the collection of a loan awarded under this section if the loan repayment is outstanding for more than 30 days. (1985 (Reg. Sess., 1986), c. 1014, s. 63(a); 1989 (Reg. Sess., 1990), c. 1066, s. 101(a), (b); 1991 (Reg. Sess., 1992), c. 1030, s. 29; 1993, c. 330, s. 1; 1998-212, s. 9.19(a); 1999-237, s. 8.12; 2002-126, ss. 9.2(c), (d); 2006-66, s. 7.19(a); 2007-323, s. 7.25(a); 2011-145, s. 7.24; 2011-266, s. 1.38(a).)

§ 115C-363.24. Repealed by Session Laws 1989, c. 500, s. 15.

§§ 115C-363.25 through 115C-363.27. Reserved for future codification purposes.

Article 24D.

Lead Teacher Pilot Program.

§ 115C-363.28: Repealed by Session Laws 1991 (Regular Session, 1992), c. 900, s. 75.1(k).

SUBCHAPTER VI. STUDENTS.

Article 25.

Admission and Assignment of Students.

§ 115C-364. Admission requirements.

(a) A child who is presented for enrollment at any time during the first 120 days of a school year is entitled to initial entry into the public schools if:

(1) The child reaches or reached the age of 5 on or before August 31 of that school year; or

(2) The child did not reach the age of 5 on or before August 31 of that school year, but has been attending school during that school year in another state in accordance with the laws or rules of that state before the child moved to and became a resident of North Carolina.

(3) The child did not reach the age of five on or before August 31 of that school year, but would be eligible to attend school during that school year in another state in accordance with the laws or rules of that state, if all of the following apply:

a. The child's parent is a legal resident of North Carolina who is an active member of the uniformed services assigned to a permanent duty station in another state.

b. The child's parent is the sole legal custodian of the child.

c. The child's parent is deployed for duty away from the permanent duty station.

d. The child resides with an adult who is a domiciliary of a local school administrative unit in North Carolina as a result of the parent's deployment away from the permanent duty station.

(b) A local board may allow a child who is presented for enrollment at any time after the first 120 days of a school year to be eligible for initial entry into the public schools if:

(1) The child reached the age of 5 on or before August 31 of that school year; or

(2) The child did not reach the age of 5 on or before August 31 of that school year, but has been attending school during that school year in another state in accordance with the laws or rules of that state before the child moved to and became a resident of North Carolina.

(c) The initial point of entry into the public school system shall be at the kindergarten level. If the principal of a school finds as fact subsequent to initial entry that a child, by reason of maturity can be more appropriately served in the first grade rather than in kindergarten, the principal may act under G.S. 115C-288 to implement this educational decision without regard to chronological age. The principal of any public school shall require the parent or guardian of any child presented for admission for the first time to that school to furnish (i) a certified copy of the child's birth certificate, which shall be furnished by the register of deeds of the county having on file the record of the birth of the child, or other satisfactory evidence of date of birth, as provided in Article 4 of Chapter 130A of the General Statutes and (ii) a certificate of immunization as required by G.S. 130A-155.

(d)   A child who has passed the fourth anniversary of the child's birth on or before April 16 may enter kindergarten if the child is presented for enrollment no later than the end of the first month of the school year and if the principal of the school finds, based on information submitted by the child's parent or guardian, that the child is gifted and that the child has the maturity to justify admission to the school. The State Board of Education shall establish guidelines for the principal to use in making this finding. (1955, c. 1372, art. 19, s. 2; 1969, c. 1213, s. 4; 1973, c. 603, s. 3; 1981, c. 423, s. 1; 1983, c. 656, s. 1; 1997-204, s. 1; 1997-269, s. 1; 2007-173, s. 1; 2010-111, s. 2; 2011-388, s. 2.)

§ 115C-365: Repealed by Session Laws 1991, c. 719, s. 1.

§ 115C-366. Assignment of student to a particular school.

(a)   All students under the age of 21 years who are domiciled in a school administrative unit who have not been removed from school for cause, or who have not obtained a high school diploma, are entitled to all the privileges and advantages of the public schools to which they are assigned by the local boards of education. The assignment of students living in one local school administrative unit or district to a school located in another local school administrative unit or district, shall have no effect upon the right of the local school administrative unit or district to which the students are assigned to levy and collect any supplemental tax heretofore or hereafter voted in that local school administrative unit or district.

(a1)   Children living in and cared for and supported by an institution established, operated, or incorporated for the purpose of rearing and caring for children who do not live with their parents are considered legal residents of the local school administrative unit in which the institution is located. These children are eligible for admission to the public schools of the local school administrative unit as provided in this section.

(a2) It is the policy of the State that every child of a homeless individual and every homeless child and youth has access to a free, appropriate public education. The State Board of Education and every local board of education shall ensure compliance with the federal McKinney-Vento Homeless Education Assistance Improvements Act of 2001. A local board of education shall not charge a homeless child or youth tuition for enrollment. An unaccompanied youth or a homeless child's or youth's parent, guardian, or legal custodian may apply to the State Board of Education for a determination of whether a particular local board of education shall enroll the homeless child or youth, and this determination shall be binding on the local board of education, subject to judicial review.

(a3) A student who is not a domiciliary of a local school administrative unit may attend, without the payment of tuition, the public schools of that unit if all of the following apply:

(1) The student resides with an adult, who is a domiciliary of that unit, as a result of any one of the following:

a. The death, serious illness, or incarceration of a parent or legal guardian.

b. The abandonment by a parent or legal guardian of the complete control of the student as evidenced by the failure to provide substantial financial support and parental guidance.

c. Abuse or neglect by the parent or legal guardian.

d. The physical or mental condition of the parent or legal guardian is such that he or she cannot provide adequate care and supervision of the student.

e. The relinquishment of physical custody and control of the student by the student's parent or legal guardian upon the recommendation of the department of social services or the Division of Mental Health.

f. The loss or uninhabitability of the student's home as the result of a natural disaster.

g. The parent or legal guardian is one of the following:

1. On active military duty and is deployed out of the local school administrative unit in which the student resides. For purposes of this sub-sub-subdivision, the term "active duty" does not include periods of active duty for training for less than 30 days.

2. A member or veteran of the uniformed services who is severely injured and medically discharged or retired, but only for a period of one year after the medical discharge or retirement of the parent or guardian.

3. A member of the uniformed services who dies on active duty or as a result of injuries sustained on active duty, but only for a period of one year after death. For purposes of this sub-sub-subdivision, the term "active duty" is as defined in G.S. 115C-407.5

Assignment under this sub-subdivision is only available if some evidence of the deployment, medical discharge, retirement, or death is tendered with the affidavits required under subdivision (3) of this subsection.

(2) The student is:

a. Not currently under a term of suspension or expulsion from a school for conduct that could have led to a suspension or an expulsion from the local school administrative unit, or

b. Currently under a term of suspension or expulsion from a school for conduct that could have led to a suspension or an expulsion from the local school administrative unit and is identified as eligible for special education and related services under the Individuals with Disabilities Education Improvement Act, 20 U.S.C. § 1400, et seq., (2004). Assignment under this sub-subdivision is available only if evidence of current eligibility is tendered with the affidavit required under subdivision (3) of this subsection.

(3) The caregiver adult and the student's parent, guardian, or legal custodian have each completed and signed separate affidavits that do all of the following:

a. Confirm the qualifications set out in this subsection establishing the student's residency.

b. Attest that the student's claim of residency in the unit is not primarily related to attendance at a particular school within the unit.

c. Attest that the caregiver adult has been given and accepts responsibility for educational decisions for the student.

If the student's parent, guardian, or legal custodian is unable, refuses, or is otherwise unavailable to sign the affidavit, then the caregiver adult shall attest to that fact in the affidavit. If the student is a minor, the caregiver adult must make educational decisions concerning the student and has the same legal authority and responsibility regarding the student as a parent or legal custodian would have even if the parent, guardian, or legal custodian does not sign the affidavit. The minor student's parent, legal guardian, or legal custodian retains liability for the student's acts.

Upon receipt of both affidavits or an affidavit from the caregiver adult that includes an attestation that the student's parent, guardian, or legal custodian is unable, refuses, or is otherwise unavailable to sign an affidavit, the local board shall admit and assign as soon as practicable the student to an appropriate school, as determined under the local board's school assignment policy, pending the results of any further procedures for verifying eligibility for attendance and assignment within the local school administrative unit.

If it is found that the information contained in either or both affidavits is false, then the local board may, unless the student is otherwise eligible for school attendance under other laws or local board policy, remove the student from school. If a student is removed from school, the board shall provide an opportunity to appeal the removal under the appropriate policy of the local board and shall notify any person who signed the affidavit of this opportunity. If it is found that a person willfully and knowingly provided false information in the affidavit, the maker of the affidavit shall be guilty of a Class 1 misdemeanor and shall pay to the local board an amount equal to the cost of educating the student during the period of enrollment. Repayment shall not include State funds.

Affidavits shall include, in large print, the penalty, including repayment of the cost of educating the student, for providing false information in an affidavit.

(a4) When a student transfers into the public schools of a local school administrative unit, that local board shall require the student's parent, guardian, or legal custodian to provide a statement made under oath or affirmation before a qualified official indicating whether the student is, at the time, under suspension or expulsion from attendance at a private or public school in this or any other state or has been convicted of a felony in this or any other state. This subsection does not apply to the enrollment of a student who has never been enrolled in or attended a private or public school in this or any other state.

(a5) Notwithstanding any other law, a local board may deny admission to or place reasonable conditions on the admission of a student who has been suspended from a school under G.S. 115C-390.5 through G.S. 115C-390.10 or who has been suspended from a school for conduct that could have led to a suspension from a school within the local school administrative unit where the student is seeking admission until the period of suspension has expired. Also, a local board may deny admission to or place reasonable conditions on the admission of a student who has been expelled from a school under G.S. 115C-390.11 or who has been expelled from a school for behavior that indicated the student's continued presence in school constituted a clear threat to the safety of other students or staff as found by clear and convincing evidence, or who has been convicted of a felony in this or any other state. If the local board denies admission to a student who has been expelled or convicted of a felony, the student may request the local board to reconsider that decision in accordance with G.S. 115C-390.12. When a student who has been identified as eligible to receive special education and related services under the Individuals with Disabilities Education Act, 20 U.S.C. § 1400, et seq., is denied admission under this subsection, the local board shall provide educational services to the student to the same extent it would if the student were enrolled in the local school administrative unit at the time of the suspension or expulsion, as required by G.S. 115C-107.1(a)(3).

(a6) A child who is placed in or assigned to a licensed facility is eligible for admission, without the payment of tuition, to the public schools of the local school administrative unit in which the licensed facility is located. If an agency or person, other than the student's parent or guardian, is the student's legal custodian and if that person or agency placed or assigned the student to a licensed facility under this subsection, then that agency or person must provide in writing to the school the name, address, and phone number of the individual who has authority and the responsibility to make educational decisions for the student. This individual shall reside or be employed within the local school administrative unit and shall provide in writing to the school a signed statement that the individual understands and accepts this authority and responsibility to make educational decisions for the student. If the student's parent or legal guardian retains legal custody of a child who is placed in or assigned to a licensed facility under this subsection, then the requirements of subsection (a3) of this section must be met.

(a7) A student who is a resident of a local school administrative unit because the student resides with a parent, guardian, or legal custodian who is a (i) student, employee, or faculty member of a college or university or (ii) visiting scholar at the National Humanities Center is considered domiciled in that unit for purposes of this section.

(a8) A student is considered domiciled in a local school administrative unit for purposes of this section if the student resides (i) with a legal custodian who is not the student's parent or guardian and the legal custodian is domiciled in the local school administrative unit, or (ii) in a preadoptive home following placement by a county department of social services or a licensed child-placing agency.

(b) Each local board of education shall assign to a public school each student qualified for assignment under this section. Except as otherwise provided by law, the authority of each board of education in the matter of assignment of children to the public schools shall be full and complete, and its decision as to the assignment of any child to any school shall be final.

(c) Any child who is qualified under the laws of this State for admission to a public school and who has a place of residence in a local school administrative unit incident to the child's parent's or guardian's service in the General Assembly, other than the local school administrative unit in which the child is domiciled, is entitled to attend school in the local school administrative unit of that residence as if the child were domiciled there, subject to the payment of applicable out-of-county fees in effect at the time.

(d) A student domiciled in one local school administrative unit may be assigned either with or without the payment of tuition to a public school in another local school administrative unit upon the terms and conditions agreed to in writing between the local boards of education involved and entered in the official records of the boards. The assignment shall be effective only for the current school year, but may be renewed annually in the discretion of the boards involved.

(e) The boards of education of adjacent local school administrative units may operate schools in adjacent units upon written agreements between the respective boards of education and approval by the county commissioners and the State Board of Education.

(f) This section shall not be construed to allow students to transfer from one local school administrative unit to another for athletic participation purposes in violation of eligibility requirements established by the State Board of Education and the North Carolina High School Athletic Association.

(g) Any local school administrative unit may use the actual address of a program participant for any purpose related to admission or assignment under this Article as long as the address is kept confidential from the public under Chapter 15C of the General Statutes. The substitute address designated by the Attorney General under the Address Confidentiality Program shall not be used as an address for admission or assignment purposes.

(h) The following definitions apply in this section:

(1) Abused or neglected. - A student is considered abused or neglected if there has been an adjudication of that issue. The State Board may adopt an additional definition of abuse and neglect, and that definition also shall apply to this section.

(2) Caregiver adult. - The adult with whom the child resides. For children placed or assigned in a licensed facility, a caregiver adult also may be the child's caretaker, foster parent, or other clearly identifiable adult who resides in the county where the licensed facility is located.

(3) Educational decisions. - Decisions or actions recommended or required by the school concerning the student's academic course of study, extracurricular activities, and conduct. These decisions or actions include enrolling the student, receiving and responding to notices of discipline under G.S. 115C-390.5 through G.S. 115C-390.12, attending conferences with school personnel, granting permission for school-related activities, granting permission for emergency medical care, receiving and taking appropriate action in connection with student records, and any other decisions or actions recommended or required by the school in connection to that student.

(4) Facility. - A group home, a family foster home as defined in G.S. 131D-10.2(8), or a therapeutic foster home as defined in G.S. 131D-10.2(14).

(5) Homeless. - Individuals who lack a fixed, regular, and adequate nighttime residence or are included in the definition of homeless children and youths in the McKinney-Vento Homeless Education Assistance Improvements

Act of 2001. The term does not include persons who are imprisoned or otherwise detained pursuant to federal or State law.

(6) Legal custodian. - The person or agency that has been awarded legal custody of the student by a court.

(7) Licensed facility. - A facility licensed under Article 2 of Chapter 122C of the General Statutes or under Article 1A of Chapter 131D of the General Statutes.

(8) McKinney-Vento Homeless Education Assistance Improvements Act of 2001. - 20 U.S.C. § 11431, et seq., as amended, and federal regulations adopted under this act.

(9) Program participant. - An individual accepted into the Address Confidentiality Program under Chapter 15C of the General Statutes.

(10) Unaccompanied youth. - Youths who are not in the physical custody of a parent or guardian as defined in the McKinney-Vento Homeless Education Assistance Improvements Act of 2001. (1955, c. 366, s. 1; c. 1372, art. 19, s. 3; 1956, Ex. Sess., c. 7, s. 1; 1971, c. 153; 1981, c. 423, s. 1; c. 567, s. 1; 1991, c. 407, s. 1; c. 719, s. 2; 1997-271, s. 1; 1997-443, s. 8.29(d); 2002-171, s. 5; 2006-65, s. 1; 2007-283, s. 1; 2008-185, s. 2; 2008-187, s. 19; 2009-331, ss. 1, 2; 2011-282, s. 12; 2013-410, s. 21.)

§ 115C-366.1. Local boards of education; tuition charges.

(a) Local boards of education may charge tuition to the following persons:

(1) Persons of school age who are not domiciliaries of the State.

(2) Persons of school age who are domiciliaries of the State but who do not reside within the school administrative unit or district.

(3) Persons of school age who reside on a military or naval reservation located within the State and who are not domiciliaries of the State. Provided, however, that no person of school age residing on a military or naval reservation located within the State and who attends the public schools within the State may be charged tuition if federal funds designed to compensate for the impact on

public schools of military dependent persons of school age are funded by the federal government at not less than fifty percent (50%) of the total per capita cost of education in the State, exclusive of capital outlay and debt service, for elementary or secondary pupils, as the case may be, of such school administrative unit.

(4)   Persons who are 21 years of age or older before the beginning of the school year in which they wish to enroll.

(b)   The tuition charge for a student shall not exceed the amount of per pupil local funding.

(c)   The tuition required in this section shall be determined by local boards of education each August 1 prior to the beginning of a new school year. (1981, c. 567, ss. 2-4; 1982, Ex. Sess., c. 2, ss. 1, 2; 1983 (Reg. Sess., 1984), c. 1034, s. 22; 1985, c. 780, s. 2.)

§ 115C-366.2: Repealed by Session Laws 2006-65, s. 2, effective July 1, 2006.

§ 115C-366.3. Classroom placement of multiple birth siblings.

(a)   As used in this section, the term "multiple birth siblings" means twins, triplets, quadruplets, or other siblings resulting from a multiple birth.

(b)   The parent of multiple birth siblings who are assigned to the same grade level and school may request a consultative meeting with the school principal to consider that the initial school placement of the siblings be in the same classroom or in separate classrooms. The request must be made no later than five days before the first day of each school year or five days after the first day of attendance of students during the school year if the students are enrolled in the school after the school year commences. The school may recommend to the parent the appropriate classroom placement for multiple birth siblings and may provide professional educational advice to assist the parent with the decision regarding appropriate classroom placement.

(c) Except as provided in subsection (d), (e), or (f) of this section, a school shall provide the multiple birth siblings with the classroom placement requested by the parent.

(d) A school is not required to place multiple birth siblings in separate classrooms if the request would require the school district to add an additional class to the grade level of the multiple birth siblings.

(e) At the end of the first grading period following the multiple birth siblings' enrollment in the school, if the principal of the school, in consultation with the teacher of each classroom in which the multiple birth siblings are placed, determines that the requested classroom placement is disruptive to the school, the principal may determine the appropriate classroom placement for the siblings.

(f) This section does not affect the right of a school administrative unit, principal, or teacher to remove a student from a classroom pursuant to the student discipline policies of that school administrative unit. (2011-354, s. 1.)

§ 115C-366.4. Assignment of students convicted of cyber-bullying.

A student who is convicted under G.S. 14-458.2 of cyber-bullying a school employee shall be transferred to another school within the local school administrative unit. If there is no other appropriate school within the local school administrative unit, the student shall be transferred to a different class or assigned to a teacher who was not involved as a victim of the cyber-bullying. Notwithstanding the provisions in this section, the superintendent may modify, in writing, the required transfer of an individual student on a case-by-case basis. (2012-149, s. 9.)

§ 115C-367. Assignment on certain bases prohibited.

No person shall be refused admission to or be excluded from any public school in this State on account of race, creed, color or national origin. No school attendance district or zone shall be drawn for the purpose of segregating persons of various races, creeds, colors or national origins from the community.

Where local school administrative units have divided the geographic area into attendance districts or zones, pupils shall be assigned to schools within such attendance districts: Provided, however, that the board of education of a local school administrative unit may assign any pupil to a school outside of such attendance district or zone in order that such pupil may attend a school of a specialized kind including but not limited to a vocational school or school operated for, or operating programs for, pupils mentally or physically handicapped, or for any other reason which the board of education in its sole discretion deems sufficient.

The provisions of Part 1D of Article 9 of this Chapter, G.S. 115C-366(b), and G.S. 115C-367 to G.S. 115C-370 shall not apply to a temporary assignment due to the unsuitability of a school for its intended purpose nor to any assignment or transfer necessitated by overcrowded conditions or other circumstances which, in the sole discretion of the school board, require assignment or reassignment.

The provisions of Part 1D of Article 9 of this Chapter, G.S. 115C-366(b), and G.S. 115C-367 to G.S. 115C-370 shall not apply to an application for the assignment or reassignment by the parent, guardian or person standing in loco parentis of any pupil or to any assignment made pursuant to a choice made by any pupil who is eligible to make such choice pursuant to the provisions of a freedom of choice plan voluntarily adopted by the board of education of a local school administrative unit. (1969, c. 1274; 1981, c. 423, s. 1; 2006-69, s. 3(j).)

§ 115C-368. Notice of assignment.

In exercising the authority conferred by G.S. 115C-366(b), each local board of education may, in making assignments of pupils, give individual written notice of assignment, on each pupil's report card or by written notice by any other feasible means, to the parent or guardian of each child or the person standing in loco parentis to the child, or may give notice of assignment of groups or categories of pupils by publication at least two times in some newspaper having general circulation in the local administrative unit. (1955, c. 366, s. 2; 1956, Ex. Sess., c. 7, s. 2; 1981, c. 423, s. 1.)

§ 115C-369. Application for reassignment; notice of disapproval; hearing before board.

(a) The parent or guardian of any child, or the person standing in loco parentis to any child, who is dissatisfied with the assignment made by a local board of education may, within 10 days after notification of the assignment, or the last publication thereof, apply in writing to the local board of education for the reassignment of the child to a different public school. Application for reassignment shall be made on forms prescribed by the local board of education pursuant to rules and regulations adopted by the board of education. If the application for reassignment is disapproved, the local board of education shall give notice to the applicant by registered or certified mail, and the applicant may within five days after receipt of such notice apply to the local board for a hearing. The applicant shall be entitled to a prompt and fair hearing on the question of reassignment of such child to a different school.

(b) The local board of education shall make a final determination on the question of reassignment. The board of education may establish initial hearings prior to the final determination. If the board of education establishes initial hearings, the board of education shall designate hearing panels composed of not less than two members of the board to hear such appeals in the name of the board of education, and may designate a hearing officer to hear such appeals for fact-finding and a recommended decision, or may designate both. If both are designated, an applicant must select the entity to hold the hearing. The hearing panel's recommendations or the hearing officer's recommended findings of fact and recommended decision shall be submitted to the board of education for final determination.

(c) At the hearing the local board of education shall consider the best interest of the child, the orderly and efficient administration of the public schools, the proper administration of the school to which reassignment is requested and the instruction, health, and safety of the pupils there enrolled, and shall assign said child in accordance with such factors. The local board shall render prompt decision upon the hearing, and notice of the decision shall be given to the applicant by mail, telephone, telefax, e-mail, or any other method reasonably designed to achieve notice. (1955, c. 366, s. 3; 1956, Ex. Sess., c. 7, s. 3; 1981, c. 423, s. 1; 1987, cc. 406, 791; 2007-501, s. 1.)

§ 115C-370. Judicial review of board's decision.

A decision of a local board under G.S. 115C-369 is final and, except as provided in this section, is subject to judicial review in accordance with Article 4 of

Chapter 150B of the General Statutes. A person seeking judicial review shall file a petition in the superior court of the county where the local board made its decision. (1955, c. 366, s. 4; 1969, c. 44, s. 73; 1981, c. 423, s. 1; 1987, c. 827, s. 51.)

§ 115C-371. Assignment to special education programs.

Assignment of students to special education programs is subject to Article 9 of this Chapter. (1981, c. 423, s. 1; 2006-69, s. 3(k).)

§ 115C-372. Assignment to school bus.

Assignment of students to school buses is subject to the provisions of G.S. 115C-244. (1981, c. 423, s. 1.)

§ 115C-373: Reserved for future codification purposes.

§ 115C-374: Reserved for future codification purposes.

§ 115C-375: Reserved for future codification purposes.

Article 25A.

Special Medical Needs of Students.

§ 115C-375.1. To provide some medical care to students.

It is within the scope of duty of teachers, including substitute teachers, teacher assistants, student teachers, or any other public school employee when authorized by the board of education or its designee, (i) to administer any drugs or medication prescribed by a doctor upon written request of the parents, (ii) to give emergency health care when reasonably apparent circumstances indicate that any delay would seriously worsen the physical condition or endanger the life of the pupil, and (iii) to perform any other first aid or lifesaving techniques in which the employee has been trained in a program approved by the State Board of Education. No employee, however, shall be required to administer drugs or medication or attend lifesaving techniques programs.

Any public school employee, authorized by the board of education or its designee to act under (i), (ii), or (iii) above, shall not be liable in civil damages for any authorized act or for any omission relating to that act unless the act or omission amounts to gross negligence, wanton conduct, or intentional wrongdoing. Any person, serving in a voluntary position at the request of or with the permission or consent of the board of education or its designee, who has been given the authority by the board of education or its designee to act under (ii) above shall not be liable in civil damages for any authorized act or for any omission relating to the act unless the act amounts to gross negligence, wanton conduct, or intentional wrongdoing.

At the commencement of each school year, but before the beginning of classes, and thereafter as circumstances require, the principal of each school shall determine which persons will participate in the medical care program. (2005-22, s. 2(b); 2006-264, ss. 57(a), (c).)

§ 115C-375.2. Possession and self-administration of asthma medication by students with asthma or students subject to anaphylactic reactions, or both.

(a) Local boards of education shall adopt a policy authorizing a student with asthma or a student subject to anaphylactic reactions, or both, to possess and self-administer asthma medication on school property during the school day, at school-sponsored activities, or while in transit to or from school or school-sponsored events. As used in this section, "asthma medication" means a medicine prescribed for the treatment of asthma or anaphylactic reactions and includes a prescribed asthma inhaler or epinephrine auto-injector. The policy shall include a requirement that the student's parent or guardian provide to the school:

(1) Written authorization from the student's parent or guardian for the student to possess and self-administer asthma medication.

(2) A written statement from the student's health care practitioner verifying that the student has asthma or an allergy that could result in an anaphylactic reaction, or both, and that the health care practitioner prescribed medication for

use on school property during the school day, at school-sponsored activities, or while in transit to or from school or school-sponsored events.

(3) A written statement from the student's health care practitioner who prescribed the asthma medication that the student understands, has been instructed in self-administration of the asthma medication, and has demonstrated the skill level necessary to use the asthma medication and any device that is necessary to administer the asthma medication.

(4) A written treatment plan and written emergency protocol formulated by the health care practitioner who prescribed the medicine for managing the student's asthma or anaphylaxis episodes and for medication use by the student.

(5) A statement provided by the school and signed by the student's parent or guardian acknowledging that the local school administrative unit and its employees and agents are not liable for an injury arising from a student's possession and self-administration of asthma medication.

(6) Other requirements necessary to comply with State and federal laws.

(b) The student must demonstrate to the school nurse, or the nurse's designee, the skill level necessary to use the asthma medication and any device that is necessary to administer the medication.

(c) The student's parent or guardian shall provide to the school backup asthma medication that shall be kept at the student's school in a location to which the student has immediate access in the event of an asthma or anaphylaxis emergency.

(d) Information provided to the school by the student's parent or guardian shall be kept on file at the student's school in a location easily accessible in the event of an asthma or anaphylaxis emergency.

(e) If a student uses asthma medication prescribed for the student in a manner other than as prescribed, a school may impose on the student disciplinary action according to the school's disciplinary policy. A school may not impose disciplinary action that limits or restricts the student's immediate access to the asthma medication.

(f) The requirement that permission granted for a student to possess and self-administer asthma medication shall be effective only for the same school and for 365 calendar days and must be renewed annually.

(g) No local board of education, nor its members, employees, designees, agents, or volunteers, shall be liable in civil damages to any party for any act authorized by this section, or for any omission relating to that act, unless that act or omission amounts to gross negligence, wanton conduct, or intentional wrongdoing. (2005-22, s. 1; 2006-264, s. 57(b).)

§ 115C-375.3. Guidelines to support and assist students with diabetes.

Local boards of education and boards of directors of charter schools shall ensure that the guidelines adopted by the State Board of Education under G.S. 115C-12(31) are implemented in schools in which students with diabetes are enrolled. In particular, the boards shall require the implementation of the procedures set forth in those guidelines for the development and implementation of individual diabetes care plans. The boards also shall make available necessary information and staff development to teachers and school personnel in order to appropriately support and assist students with diabetes in accordance with their individual diabetes care plans. Local boards of education and boards of directors of charter schools shall report to the State Board of Education annually, on or before August 15, whether they have students with diabetes enrolled and provide information showing compliance with the guidelines adopted by the State Board of Education under G.S. 115C-12(31). These reports shall be in compliance with the federal Family Educational Rights and Privacy Act, 20 U.S.C. § 1232g. (2005-22, s 3(a), (b); 2009-563, s. 1.)

§ 115C-375.4. Meningococcal Meningitis and Influenza and Their Vaccines.

Local boards of education shall ensure that schools provide parents and guardians with information about meningococcal meningitis and influenza and their vaccines at the beginning of every school year. This information shall include the causes, symptoms, and how meningococcal meningitis and influenza are spread and the places where parents and guardians may obtain additional information and vaccinations for their children. (2005-22, s. 4(a), (b).)

§ 115C-375.5. Education for pregnant and parenting students.

(a) Pregnant and parenting students shall receive the same educational instruction or its equivalent as other students. A local school administrative unit may provide programs to meet the special scheduling and curriculum needs of pregnant and parenting students. However, student participation in these programs shall be voluntary, and the instruction and curriculum must be comparable to that provided other students.

(b) Local boards of education shall adopt a policy to ensure that pregnant and parenting students are not discriminated against or excluded from school or any program, class, or extracurricular activity because they are pregnant or parenting students and to provide assistance and support to encourage pregnant and parenting students to remain enrolled in school and graduate. The policy shall include, at a minimum, all of the following:

(1) Local school administrative units shall use, as needed, supplemental funds from the At-Risk Student Services allotment to support programs for pregnant and parenting students.

(2) Notwithstanding Part 1 of Article 26 of this Chapter, pregnant and parenting students shall be given excused absences from school for pregnancy and related conditions for the length of time the student's physician finds medically necessary. This includes absences due to the illness or medical appointment during school hours of a child of whom the student is the custodial parent.

(3) Homework and make-up work shall be made available to pregnant and parenting students to ensure that they have the opportunity to keep current with assignments and avoid losing course credit because of their absence from school and, to the extent necessary, a homebound teacher shall be assigned. (2006-69, s. 4(a); 2009-330, s. 3.)

§ 115C-376: Reserved for future codification purposes.

§ 115C-377: Reserved for future codification purposes.

Article 26.

Attendance.

Part 1. Compulsory Attendance.

§ 115C-378. Children required to attend.

(a) Every parent, guardian or custodian in this State having charge or control of a child between the ages of seven and 16 years shall cause the child to attend school continuously for a period equal to the time which the public school to which the child is assigned shall be in session. Every parent, guardian, or custodian in this State having charge or control of a child under age seven who is enrolled in a public school in grades kindergarten through two shall also cause the child to attend school continuously for a period equal to the time which the public school to which the child is assigned shall be in session unless the child has withdrawn from school.

(b) No person shall encourage, entice or counsel any child of compulsory school age to be unlawfully absent from school. The parent, guardian, or custodian of a child shall notify the school of the reason for each known absence of the child, in accordance with local school board policy.

(c) The principal, superintendent, or a designee of the principal or superintendent shall have the right to excuse a child temporarily from attendance on account of sickness or other unavoidable cause that does not constitute unlawful absence as defined by the State Board of Education. The term "school" as used in this section includes all public schools and any nonpublic schools which have teachers and curricula that are approved by the State Board of Education.

(d) All nonpublic schools receiving and instructing children of compulsory school age shall be required to make, maintain, and render attendance records of those children and maintain the minimum curriculum standards required of public schools. If a nonpublic school refuses or neglects to make, maintain, and render required attendance records, attendance at that school shall not be accepted in lieu of attendance at the public school of the district to which the child shall be assigned. Instruction in a nonpublic school shall not be regarded as meeting the requirements of the law unless the courses of instruction run concurrently with the term of the public school in the district and extend for at least as long a term.

(e) The principal or the principal's designee shall notify the parent, guardian, or custodian of his or her child's excessive absences after the child has accumulated three unexcused absences in a school year. After not more than six unexcused absences, the principal or the principal's designee shall notify the parent, guardian, or custodian by mail that he or she may be in violation of the Compulsory Attendance Law and may be prosecuted if the absences cannot be justified under the established attendance policies of the State and local boards of education. Once the parents are notified, the school attendance counselor shall work with the child and the child's family to analyze the causes of the absences and determine steps, including adjustment of the school program or obtaining supplemental services, to eliminate the problem. The attendance counselor may request that a law enforcement officer accompany him or her if the attendance counselor believes that a home visit is necessary.

(f) After 10 accumulated unexcused absences in a school year, the principal or the principal's designee shall review any report or investigation prepared under G.S. 115C-381 and shall confer with the student and the student's parent, guardian, or custodian, if possible, to determine whether the parent, guardian, or custodian has received notification pursuant to this section and made a good faith effort to comply with the law. If the principal or the principal's designee determines that the parent, guardian, or custodian has not made a good faith effort to comply with the law, the principal shall notify the district attorney and the director of social services of the county where the child resides. If the principal or the principal's designee determines that the parent, guardian, or custodian has made a good faith effort to comply with the law, the principal may file a complaint with the juvenile court counselor pursuant to Chapter 7B of the General Statutes that the child is habitually absent from school without a valid excuse. Upon receiving notification by the principal or the principal's designee, the director of social services shall determine whether to undertake an investigation under G.S. 7B-302.

(g) Documentation that demonstrates that the parents, guardian, or custodian were notified and that the child has accumulated 10 absences which cannot be justified under the established attendance policies of the local board shall constitute prima facie evidence that the child's parent, guardian, or custodian is responsible for the absences. (1955, c. 1372, art. 20, s. 1; 1956, Ex. Sess., c. 5; 1963, c. 1223, s. 6; 1969, c. 339; c. 799, s. 1; 1971, c. 846; 1975, c. 678, s. 2; c. 731, s. 3; 1979, c. 847; 1981, c. 423, s. 1; 1985, c. 297; 1991 (Reg. Sess., 1992), c. 769, s. 2; 1998-202, s. 13(aa); 2001-490, s. 2.38; 2003-304, s. 3; 2009-404, s. 1.)

§ 115C-379. Method of enforcement.

It shall be the duty of the State Board of Education to formulate the rules that may be necessary for the proper enforcement of the provisions of this Part. The Board shall prescribe (i) what shall constitute unlawful absence, (ii) what causes may constitute legitimate excuses for temporary nonattendance due to a student's physical or mental inability to attend or a student's participation in a valid educational opportunity such as service as a legislative page or a Governor's page, and (iii) under what circumstances teachers, principals, or superintendents may excuse pupils for nonattendance due to immediate demands of the farm or the home in certain seasons of the year in the several sections of the State.

The rules shall require school principals to authorize a minimum of two excused absences each academic year for religious observances required by the faith of a student or the student's parents. The rules may require that the student's parents give the principal written notice of the request for an excused absence a reasonable time prior to the religious observance. The student shall be given the opportunity to make up any tests or other work missed due to an excused absence for a religious observance.

It shall be the duty of all school officials to carry out such instructions from the State Board of Education, and any school official failing to carry out such instructions shall be guilty of a Class 3 misdemeanor: Provided, that the compulsory attendance law herein prescribed shall not be in force in any local school administrative unit that has a higher compulsory attendance feature than that provided herein. (1955, c. 1372, art. 20, s. 2; 1963, c. 1223, s. 7; 1981, c. 423, s. 1; 1993, c. 539, s. 887; 1994, Ex. Sess., c. 24, s. 14(c); 2007-186, s. 1; 2010-112, s. 1.)

§ 115C-380. Penalty for violation.

Except as otherwise provided in G.S. 115C-379, any parent, guardian or other person violating the provisions of this Part shall be guilty of a Class 1 misdemeanor. (1955, c. 1372, art. 20, s. 4; 1969, c. 799, s. 2; 1981, c. 423, s. 1; 1993, c. 539, s. 888; 1994, Ex. Sess., c. 24, s. 14(c); 2005-318, s. 1.)

§ 115C-381. School social workers; reports; prosecutions.

The Superintendent of Public Instruction shall prepare such rules and procedures and furnish such blanks for teachers and other school officials as may be necessary for reporting such case of unlawful absence or lack of attendance to the school social worker of the respective local school administrative units. Such rules shall provide, among other things, for a notification in writing, to the person responsible for the nonattendance of any child, that the case is to be reported to the school social worker of the local school administrative unit unless the law is complied with immediately. Upon recommendation of the superintendent, local boards of education may employ school social workers and such school social workers shall have authority to report and verify on oath the necessary criminal warrants or other documents for the prosecutions of violations of this Part: Provided, that local school administrative units shall provide in their local operating budgets for travel and necessary office expense for such school social workers as may be employed through State or local funds, or both. The State Board of Education shall determine the process for allocating school social workers to the various local school administrative units, establish their qualifications, and develop a salary schedule which shall be applicable to such personnel: Provided, that persons now employed by local boards of education as attendance counselors shall be deemed qualified as school social workers under the terms of this Part subject to the approval of said local boards of education.

The school social worker shall investigate all violators of the provisions of this Part. The reports of unlawful absence required to be made by teachers and principals to the school social worker shall, in his hands, in case of any prosecution, constitute prima facie evidence of the violation of this Part and the burden of proof shall be upon the defendant to show the lawful attendance of the child or children upon an authorized school. (1955, c. 1372, art. 20, ss. 3, 5; 1957, c. 600; 1961, c. 186; 1963, c. 1223, ss. 8, 9; 1981, c. 423, s. 1; 1985, c. 686, s. 3.)

§ 115C-382. Investigation of indigency.

If affidavit shall be made by the parent of a child or by any other person that any child who is required to attend school under G.S. 115C-378 is not able to attend school by reason of necessity to work or labor for the support of himself or the support of the family, then the school social worker shall diligently inquire into the matter and bring it to the attention of some court allowed by law to act as a juvenile court, and said court shall proceed to find whether as a matter of fact such parents, or persons standing in loco parentis, are unable to send said child to school for the term of compulsory attendance for the reasons given. If the court shall find, after careful investigation, that the parents have made or are making bona fide effort to comply with the compulsory attendance law, and by reason of illness, lack of earning capacity, or any other cause which the court may deem valid and sufficient, are unable to send said child to school, then the court shall find and state what help is needed for the family to enable compliance with the attendance law. The court shall transmit its findings to the director of social services of the county or city in which the case may arise for such social services officer's consideration and action. (1955, c. 1372, art. 20, s. 6; 1961, c. 186; 1963, c. 1223, s. 10; 1969, c. 982; 1981, c. 423, s. 1; 1985, c. 686, s. 4; 1991 (Reg. Sess., 1992), c. 769, s. 3.)

§ 115C-383: Repealed by Session Laws 2013-247, s. 1(a), effective July 3, 2013.

Part 2. Student Records and Fees.

§ 115C-384. Student records and fees.

(a) In General. - The local board of education has the power to regulate fees, charges and solicitations subject to the provisions of G.S. 115C-47(6).

(b) Refund of Fees upon Transfer of Pupils.

(1) As used in this subsection:

a. "Month" shall mean 20 school days.

b. "First semester" shall mean the first 90 teaching days of the 180 days of the school year.

c. "Second semester" shall mean the last 90 teaching days of the 180 days of the school year.

d. "Term" shall have the same meaning as that of first semester or second semester.

(2) In all cases where pupils of a local school administrative unit of the public school system transfer to some other public school in another local school administrative unit or such pupils are compelled to leave the school in which they are enrolled because of some serious or permanent illness, or for any other good and valid reason, then such pupils or their parents shall be entitled to a refund of the fees and charges paid by them as follows:

a. If the transfer or departure of the pupils from the school in which they are enrolled takes place within one month after enrollment, then all such fees and charges shall be refunded in full.

b. If the transfer or leaving the school on the part of said pupils takes place after the first month and before the middle of the first semester, then one half of the fees for the first semester shall be refunded, and all fees and charges for the second semester shall be refunded.

c. If the pupils transfer or leave the school after the middle of the first semester, then no first semester fees or charges shall be refunded.

d. If the fees and charges on the part of such pupils have been paid for a year and such pupils transfer or leave the school at the end of the first semester or within the first month of the second semester, then all second semester fees and charges shall be refunded in full.

e. If the fees and charges herein described and set forth have been paid for one year, and the pupils transfer or leave the school before the middle of the second semester, then one half of the second semester fees shall be refunded.

f. The words "fees" and "charges" as used in this subsection shall not include any fees or charges paid for insurance or fees charged for expendable materials.

g. If the pupils transfer or leave the school after the middle of the second semester, then no fees shall be refunded.

h. If the amount of total refund as determined by this subsection shall be less than one dollar ($1.00), no refund shall be paid.

(3) The principal shall be responsible for refunding fees and charges at the place of the collection of the fees and charges by check made payable to the

parent or guardian of pupils leaving the school as noted in subdivision (2) above.

(c)   Rental Fees for Textbooks Prohibited; Damage Fees Authorized. - No rental fees are permitted for the use of textbooks, but damage fees may be collected pursuant to the provisions of G.S. 115C-100. (1969, c. 756; 1981, c. 423, s. 1.)

§§ 115C-385 through 115C-389. Reserved for future codification purposes.

Article 27.

Discipline.

§ 115C-390: Repealed by Session Laws 2011-282, s. 1, effective June 23, 2011, and applicable beginning with the 2011-2012 school year.

§ 115C-390.1. State policy and definitions.

(a)   In order to create and maintain a safe and orderly school environment conducive to learning, school officials and teachers need adequate tools to maintain good discipline in schools. However, the General Assembly also recognizes that removal of students from school, while sometimes necessary, can exacerbate behavioral problems, diminish academic achievement, and hasten school dropout. School discipline must balance these interests to provide a safe and productive learning environment, to continually teach students to respect themselves, others, and property, and to conduct themselves in a manner that fosters their own learning and the learning of those around them.

(b)   The following definitions apply in this Article:

(1)   Alternative education services. - Part or full-time programs, wherever situated, providing direct or computer-based instruction that allow a student to

progress in one or more core academic courses. Alternative education services include programs established by the local board of education in conformity with G.S. 115C-105.47A and local board of education policies.

(2) Corporal punishment. - The intentional infliction of physical pain upon the body of a student as a disciplinary measure.

(3) Destructive device. - An explosive, incendiary, or poison gas:

a. Bomb.

b. Grenade.

c. Rocket having a propellant charge of more than four ounces.

d. Missile having an explosive or incendiary charge of more than one-quarter ounce.

e. Mine.

f. Device similar to any of the devices listed in this subdivision.

(4) Educational property. - Any school building or bus, school campus, grounds, recreational area, athletic field, or other property under the control of any local board of education or charter school.

(5) Expulsion. - The indefinite exclusion of a student from school enrollment for disciplinary purposes.

(6) Firearm. - Any of the following:

a. A weapon, including a starter gun, which will or is designed to or may readily be converted to expel a projectile by the action of an explosive.

b. The frame or receiver of any such weapon.

c. Any firearm muffler or firearm silencer.

The term shall not include an inoperable antique firearm, a BB gun, stun gun, air rifle, or air pistol.

(7) Long-term suspension. - The exclusion for more than 10 school days of a student from school attendance for disciplinary purposes from the school to which the student was assigned at the time of the disciplinary action. If the offense leading to the long-term suspension occurs before the final quarter of the school year, the exclusion shall be no longer than the remainder of the school year in which the offense was committed. If the offense leading to the long-term suspension occurs during the final quarter of the school year, the exclusion may include a period up to the remainder of the school year in which the offense was committed and the first semester of the following school year.

(8) Parent. - Includes a parent, legal guardian, legal custodian, or other caregiver adult who is acting in the place of a parent and is entitled to enroll the student in school under Article 25 of this Chapter.

(9) Principal. - Includes the principal and the principal's designee.

(10) School official. - A superintendent or any other central office administrator to whom the superintendent has delegated duties under this Article and any principal or assistant principal.

(11) School personnel. - Any of the following:

a. An employee of a local board of education.

b. Any person working on school grounds or at a school function under a contract or written agreement with the public school system to provide educational or related services to students.

c. Any person working on school grounds or at a school function for another agency providing educational or related services to students.

(12) Short-term suspension. - The exclusion of a student from school attendance for disciplinary purposes for up to 10 school days from the school to which the student was assigned at the time of the disciplinary action.

(13) Substantial evidence. - Such relevant evidence as a reasonable person might accept as adequate to support a conclusion; it is more than a scintilla or permissible inference.

(14) Superintendent. - Includes the superintendent and the superintendent's designee.

(c) Notwithstanding the provisions of this Article, the policies and procedures for the discipline of students shall be consistent with the requirements of the Gun Free Schools Act, 20 U.S.C. § 7151, the Individuals with Disabilities Education Act (IDEA), 29 U.S.C. § 1400, et seq., section 504 of the Rehabilitation Act of 1973, 29 U.S.C. § 701, et seq., and with other federal laws and regulations. (2011-270, s. 1; 2011-282, s. 16; 2011-282, s. 2.)

§ 115C-390.2. Discipline policies.

(a) Local boards of education shall adopt policies to govern the conduct of students and establish procedures to be followed by school officials in disciplining students. These policies must be consistent with the provisions of this Article and the constitutions, statutes, and regulations of the United States and the State of North Carolina.

(b) Board policies shall include or provide for the development of a Code of Student Conduct that notifies students of the standards of behavior expected of them, conduct that may subject them to discipline, and the range of disciplinary measures that may be used by school officials.

(c) Board policies may authorize suspension for conduct not occurring on educational property, but only if the student's conduct otherwise violates the Code of Student Conduct and the conduct has or is reasonably expected to have a direct and immediate impact on the orderly and efficient operation of the schools or the safety of individuals in the school environment.

(d) Board policies shall not allow students to be long-term suspended or expelled from school solely for truancy or tardiness offenses and shall not allow short-term suspension of more than two days for such offenses.

(e) Board policies shall not impose mandatory long-term suspensions or expulsions for specific violations unless otherwise provided in State or federal law.

(f) Board policies shall minimize the use of long-term suspension and expulsion by restricting the availability of long-term suspension or expulsion to those violations deemed to be serious violations of the board's Code of Student Conduct that either threaten the safety of students, staff, or school visitors or threaten to substantially disrupt the educational environment. Examples of conduct that would not be deemed to be a serious violation include the use of inappropriate or disrespectful language, noncompliance with a staff directive, dress code violations, and minor physical altercations that do not involve weapons or injury. The principal may, however, in his or her discretion, determine that aggravating circumstances justify treating a minor violation as a serious violation.

(g)   Board policies shall not prohibit the superintendent and principals from considering the student's intent, disciplinary and academic history, the potential benefits to the student of alternatives to suspension, and other mitigating or aggravating factors when deciding whether to recommend or impose long-term suspension.

(h)   Board policies shall include the procedures to be followed by school officials in suspending, expelling, or administering corporal punishment to any student, which shall be consistent with this Article.

(i)   Each local board shall publish all policies, administrative procedures, or school rules mandated by this section and make them available to each student and his or her parent at the beginning of each school year and upon request.

(j)   Local boards of education are encouraged to include in their safe schools plans, adopted pursuant to G.S. 115C-105.47, research-based behavior management programs that take positive approaches to improving student behaviors.

(k)   School officials are encouraged to use a full range of responses to violations of disciplinary rules, such as conferences, counseling, peer mediation, behavior contracts, instruction in conflict resolution and anger management, detention, academic interventions, community service, and other similar tools that do not remove a student from the classroom or school building. (2011-282, s. 2.)

§ 115C-390.3. Reasonable force.

(a)   School personnel may use physical restraint only in accordance with G.S. 115C-391.1.

(b) School personnel may use reasonable force to control behavior or to remove a person from the scene in those situations when necessary for any of the following reasons:

(1) To correct students.

(2) To quell a disturbance threatening injury to others.

(3) To obtain possession of weapons or other dangerous objects on the person, or within the control, of a student.

(4) For self-defense.

(5) For the protection of persons or property.

(6) To maintain order on educational property, in the classroom, or at a school-related activity on or off educational property.

(c) Notwithstanding any other law, no officer or employee of the State Board of Education or of a local board of education shall be civilly liable for using reasonable force in conformity with State law, State or local rules, or State or local policies regarding the control, discipline, suspension, and expulsion of students. Furthermore, the burden of proof is on the claimant to show that the amount of force used was not reasonable.

(d) No school employee shall be reprimanded or dismissed for acting or failing to act to stop or intervene in an altercation between students if the employee's actions are consistent with local board policies. Local boards of education shall adopt policies, pursuant to their authority under G.S. 115C-47(18), which provide guidelines for an employee's response if the employee has personal knowledge or actual notice of an altercation between students. (2011-282, s. 2; 2012-149, s. 10.)

§ 115C-390.4. Corporal punishment.

(a) Each local board of education shall determine whether corporal punishment will be permitted in its school administrative unit. Notwithstanding a local board of education's prohibition on the use of corporal punishment, school personnel may use physical restraint in accordance with federal law and G.S. 115C-391.1 and reasonable force pursuant to G.S. 115C-390.3.

(b) To the extent that corporal punishment is permitted, the policies adopted for the administration of corporal punishment shall include at a minimum the following:

(1) Corporal punishment shall not be administered in a classroom with other students present.

(2) Only a teacher, principal, or assistant principal may administer corporal punishment and may do so only in the presence of a principal, assistant principal, or teacher who shall be informed beforehand and in the student's presence of the reason for the punishment.

(3) A school person shall provide the student's parent with notification that corporal punishment has been administered, and the person who administered the corporal punishment shall provide the student's parent a written explanation of the reasons and the name of the second person who was present.

(4) The school shall maintain records of each administration of corporal punishment and the reasons for its administration.

(5) In no event shall excessive force be used in the administration of corporal punishment. Excessive force includes force that results in injury to the child that requires medical attention beyond simple first aid.

(6) Corporal punishment shall not be administered on a student whose parent or guardian has stated in writing that corporal punishment shall not be administered to that student. Parents and guardians shall be given a form to make such an election at the beginning of the school year or when the student first enters the school during the year. The form shall advise the parent or guardian that the student may be subject to suspension, among other possible punishments, for offenses that would otherwise not require suspension if corporal punishment were available. If the parent or guardian does not return the form, corporal punishment may be administered on the student.

(c) Each local board of education shall report annually to the State Board of Education, in a manner prescribed by the State Board of Education, on the number of times that corporal punishment was administered. The report shall be in compliance with the federal Family Educational Rights and Privacy Act, 20 U.S.C. § 1232g, and shall include the following:

(1) The number of students who received corporal punishment.

(2) The number of students who received corporal punishment who were also students with disabilities and were eligible to receive special education and related services under the federal Individuals with Disabilities Education Act, 20 U.S.C. § 1400, et seq.

(3) The grade level of the students who received corporal punishment.

(4) The race, gender, and ethnicity of the students who received corporal punishment.

(5) The reason for the administration of the corporal punishment for each student who received corporal punishment. (2011-282, s. 2.)

§ 115C-390.5. Short-term suspension.

(a) The principal shall have authority to impose short-term suspension on a student who willfully engages in conduct that violates a provision of the Code of Student Conduct authorizing short-term suspension.

(b) If a student's short-term suspensions accumulate to more than 10 days in a semester, to the extent the principal has not already done so, he or she shall invoke the mechanisms provided for in the applicable safe schools plan adopted pursuant to G.S. 115C-105.47(b)(5) and (b)(6).

(c) A student subject to short-term suspension shall be provided the following:

(1) The opportunity to take textbooks home for the duration of the suspension.

(2) Upon request, the right to receive all missed assignments and, to the extent practicable, the materials distributed to students in connection with the assignment.

(3) The opportunity to take any quarterly, semester, or grading period examinations missed during the suspension period. (2011-282, s. 2.)

§ 115C-390.6. Short-term suspension procedures.

(a) Except as authorized in this section, no short-term suspension shall be imposed upon a student without first providing the student an opportunity for an informal hearing with the principal. The notice to the student of the charges may be oral or written, and the hearing may be held immediately after the notice is given. The student has the right to be present, to be informed of the charges and the basis for the accusations, and to make statements in defense or mitigation of the charges.

(b) The principal may impose a short-term suspension without providing the student an opportunity for a hearing if the presence of the student creates a direct and immediate threat to the safety of other students or staff, or substantially disrupts or interferes with the education of other students or the maintenance of discipline at the school. In such cases, the notice of the charges and informal hearing described in subsection (a) of this section shall occur as soon as practicable.

(c) The principal shall provide notice to the student's parent of any short-term suspension, including the reason for the suspension and a description of the alleged student conduct upon which the suspension is based. The notice shall be given by the end of the workday during which the suspension is imposed when reasonably possible, but in no event more than two days after the suspension is imposed. The notice shall be given by certified mail, telephone, facsimile, e-mail, or any other method reasonably designed to achieve actual notice.

(d) If English is the second language of the parent, the notice shall be provided in the parent's primary language, when the appropriate foreign language resources are readily available, and in English, and both versions shall be in plain language and shall be easily understandable.

(e) A student is not entitled to appeal the principal's decision to impose a short-term suspension to the superintendent or local board of education. Further, such a decision is not subject to judicial review. Notwithstanding this subsection, the local board of education, in its discretion, may provide students an opportunity for a review or appeal of a short-term suspension to the superintendent or local board of education. (2011-282, s. 2.)

§ 115C-390.7. Long-term suspension.

(a) A principal may recommend to the superintendent the long-term suspension of any student who willfully engages in conduct that violates a provision of the Code of Student Conduct that authorizes long-term suspension. Only the superintendent has the authority to long-term suspend a student.

(b) Before the superintendent's imposition of a long-term suspension, the student must be provided an opportunity for a hearing consistent with G.S. 115C-390.8.

(c) If the student recommended for long-term suspension declines the opportunity for a hearing, the superintendent shall review the circumstances of the recommended long-term suspension. Following such review, the superintendent (i) may impose the suspension if is it consistent with board policies and appropriate under the circumstances, (ii) may impose another appropriate penalty authorized by board policy, or (iii) may decline to impose any penalty.

(d) If a teacher is assaulted or injured by a student and as a result the student is long-term suspended or reassigned to alternative education services, the student shall not be returned to that teacher's classroom unless the teacher consents.

(e) Disciplinary reassignment of a student to a full-time educational program that meets the academic requirements of the standard course of study established by the State Board of Education as provided in G.S. 115C-12 and provides the student with the opportunity to make timely progress towards graduation and grade promotion is not a long-term suspension requiring the due process procedures described in G.S. 115C-390.8. (2011-282, s. 2.)

§ 115C-390.8. Long-term suspension procedures.

(a) When a student is recommended by the principal for long-term suspension, the principal shall give written notice to the student's parent. The notice shall be provided to the student's parent by the end of the workday during which the suspension was recommended when reasonably possible or as soon thereafter as practicable. The written notice shall provide at least the following information:

(1) A description of the incident and the student's conduct that led to the long-term suspension recommendation.

(2) A reference to the provisions of the Code of Student Conduct that the student is alleged to have violated.

(3) The specific process by which the parent may request a hearing to contest the decision, including the number of days within which the hearing must be requested.

(4) The process by which a hearing will be held, including, at a minimum, the procedures described in subsection (e) of this section.

(5) Notice that the parent is permitted to retain an attorney to represent the student in the hearing process.

(6) The extent to which the local board policy permits the parent to have an advocate, instead of an attorney, accompany the student to assist in the presentation of his or her appeal.

(7) Notice that the parent has the right to review and obtain copies of the student's educational records before the hearing.

(8) A reference to the local board policy on the expungement of discipline records as required by G.S. 115C-402.

(b) Written notice may be provided by certified mail, fax, e-mail, or any other written method reasonably designed to achieve actual notice of the recommendation for long-term suspension. When school personnel are aware that English is not the primary language of the parent or guardian, the notice shall be written in both English and in the primary language of the parent or guardian when the appropriate foreign language resources are readily available. All notices described in this section shall be written in plain English, and shall include the following information translated into the dominant non-English language used by residents within the local school administrative unit:

(1) The nature of the document, i.e., that it is a long-term suspension notice.

(2) The process by which the parent may request a hearing to contest the long-term suspension.

(3) The identity and phone number of a school employee that the parent may call to obtain assistance in understanding the English language information included in the document.

(c) No long-term suspension shall be imposed on a student until an opportunity for a formal hearing is provided to the student. If a hearing is timely requested, it shall be held and a decision issued before a long-term suspension is imposed, except as otherwise provided in this subsection. The student and parent shall be given reasonable notice of the time and place of the hearing.

(1) If no hearing is timely requested, the superintendent shall follow the procedures described in G.S. 115C-390.7(c).

(2) If the student or parent requests a postponement of the hearing, or if the hearing is requested beyond the time set for such request, the hearing shall be scheduled, but the student shall not have the right to return to school pending the hearing.

(3) If neither the student nor parent appears for the scheduled hearing, after having been given reasonable notice of the time and place of the hearing, the parent and student are deemed to have waived the right to a hearing and the superintendent shall conduct the review required by G.S. 115C-390.7(c).

(d) The formal hearing may be conducted by the local board of education, by the superintendent, or by a person or group of persons appointed by the local board or superintendent to serve as a hearing officer or hearing panel. Neither the board nor the superintendent shall appoint any individual to serve as a hearing officer or on a hearing panel who is under the direct supervision of the principal recommending suspension. If the hearing is conducted by an appointed hearing officer or hearing panel, such officer or panel shall determine the relevant facts and credibility of witnesses based on the evidence presented at the hearing. Following the hearing, the superintendent or local board shall make a final decision regarding the suspension. The superintendent or board shall adopt the hearing officer's or panel's factual determinations unless they are not supported by substantial evidence in the record.

(e) Long-term suspension hearings shall be conducted in accordance with policies adopted by the board of education. Such policies shall offer the student procedural due process including, but not limited to, the following:

(1)   The right to be represented at the hearing by counsel or, in the discretion of the local board, a non-attorney advocate.

(2)   The right to be present at the hearing, accompanied by his or her parents.

(3)   The right of the student, parent, and the student's representative to review before the hearing any audio or video recordings of the incident and, consistent with federal and State student records laws and regulations, the information supporting the suspension that may be presented as evidence at the hearing, including statements made by witnesses related to the charges consistent with subsection (h) of this section.

(4)   The right of the student, parent, or the student's representative to question witnesses appearing at the hearing.

(5)   The right to present evidence on his or her own behalf, which may include written statements or oral testimony, relating to the incident leading to the suspension, as well as any of the factors listed in G.S. 115C-390.2(g).

(6)   The right to have a record made of the hearing.

(7)   The right to make his or her own audio recording of the hearing.

(8)   The right to a written decision, based on substantial evidence presented at the hearing, either upholding, modifying, or rejecting the principal's recommendation of suspension and containing at least the following information:

a.   The basis for the decision, including a reference to any policy or rule that the student is determined to have violated.

b.   Notice of what information will be included in the student's official record pursuant to G.S. 115C-402.

c.   The student's right to appeal the decision and notice of the procedures for such appeal.

(f)   Following the issuance of the decision, the superintendent shall implement the decision by authorizing the student's return to school or by imposing the suspension reflected in the decision.

(g) Unless the decision was made by the local board, the student may appeal the decision to the local board in accordance with G.S. 115C-45(c) and policies adopted by the board. Notwithstanding the provisions of G.S. 115C-45(c), a student's appeal to the board of a decision upholding a long-term suspension shall be heard and a final written decision issued in not more than 30 calendar days following the request for such appeal.

(h) Nothing in this section shall compel school officials to release names or other information that could allow the student or his or her representative to identify witnesses when such identification could create a safety risk for the witness.

(i) A decision of the local board to uphold the long-term suspension of a student is subject to judicial review in accordance with Article 4 of Chapter 150B of the General Statutes. The action must be brought within 30 days of the local board's decision. A person seeking judicial review shall file a petition in the superior court of the county where the local board made its decision. Local rules notwithstanding, petitions for judicial review of a long-term suspension shall be set for hearing in the first succeeding term of superior court in the county following the filing of the certified copy of the official record. (2011-282, s. 2.)

§ 115C-390.9. Alternative education services.

(a) Students who are long-term suspended shall be offered alternative education services unless the superintendent provides a significant or important reason for declining to offer such services. The following may be significant or important reasons, depending on the circumstances and the nature and setting of the alternative education services:

(1) The student exhibits violent behavior.

(2) The student poses a threat to staff or other students.

(3) The student substantially disrupts the learning process.

(4) The student otherwise engaged in serious misconduct that makes the provision of alternative educational services not feasible.

(5) Educationally appropriate alternative education services are not available in the local school administrative unit due to limited resources.

(6) The student failed to comply with reasonable conditions for admittance into an alternative education program.

(b) If the superintendent declines to provide alternative education services to the suspended student, the student may seek review of such decision by the local board of education as permitted by G.S. 115C-45(c)(2). If the student seeks such review, the superintendent shall provide to the student and the local board, in advance of the board's review, a written explanation for the denial of services together with any documents or other information supporting the decision. (2011-282, s. 2.)

§ 115C-390.10. 365-day suspension for gun possession.

(a) All local boards of education shall develop and implement written policies and procedures, as required by the federal Gun Free Schools Act, 20 U.SC. § 7151, requiring suspension for 365 calendar days of any student who is determined to have brought or been in possession of a firearm or destructive device on educational property, or to a school-sponsored event off of educational property. A principal shall recommend to the superintendent the 365-day suspension of any student believed to have violated board policies regarding weapons. The superintendent has the authority to suspend for 365 days a student who has been recommended for such suspension by the principal when such recommendation is consistent with board policies. Notwithstanding the foregoing, the superintendent may modify, in writing, the required 365-day suspension for an individual student on a case-by-case basis. The superintendent shall not impose a 365-day suspension if the superintendent determines that the student took or received the firearm or destructive device from another person at school or found the firearm or destructive device at school, provided that the student delivered or reported the firearm or destructive device as soon as practicable to a law enforcement officer or a school employee and had no intent to use such firearm or destructive device in a harmful or threatening way.

(b) The principal must report all incidents of firearms or destructive devices on educational property or at a school-sponsored event as required by G.S. 115C-288(g) and State Board of Education policy.

(c) Nothing in this provision shall apply to a firearm that was brought onto educational property for activities approved and authorized by the local board of education, provided that the local board of education has adopted appropriate safeguards to protect student safety.

(d) At the time the student and parent receive notice that the student is suspended for 365 days under this section, the superintendent shall provide notice to the student and the student's parent of the right to petition the local board of education for readmission pursuant to G.S. 115C-390.12.

(e) The procedures described in G.S. 115C-390.8 apply to students facing a 365-day suspension pursuant to this section.

(f) Students who are suspended for 365 days pursuant to this section shall be considered for alternative educational services consistent with the provisions of G.S. 115C-390.9. (2011-282, s. 2.)

§ 115C-390.11. Expulsion.

(a) Upon recommendation of the superintendent, a local board of education may expel any student 14 years of age or older whose continued presence in school constitutes a clear threat to the safety of other students or school staff. Prior to the expulsion of any student, the local board shall conduct a hearing to determine whether the student's continued presence in school constitutes a clear threat to the safety of other students or school staff. The student shall be given reasonable notice of the recommendation in accordance with G.S. 115C-390.8(a) and (b), as well as reasonable notice of the time and place of the scheduled hearing.

(1) The procedures described in G.S. 115C-390.8(e)(1)-(8) apply to students facing expulsion pursuant to this section, except that the decision to expel a student by the local board of education shall be based on clear and convincing evidence that the student's continued presence in school constitutes a clear threat to the safety of other students and school staff.

(2) A local board of education may expel any student subject to G.S. 14-208.18 in accordance with the procedures of this section. Prior to ordering the expulsion of a student, the local board of education shall consider whether there are alternative education services that may be offered to the student. As provided by G.S. 14-208.18(f), if the local board of education determines that

the student shall be provided educational services on school property, the student shall be under the supervision of school personnel at all times.

(3) At the time a student is expelled under this section, the student shall be provided notice of the right to petition for readmission pursuant to G.S. 115C-390.12.

(b) During the expulsion, the student is not entitled to be present on any property of the local school administrative unit and is not considered a student of the local board of education. Nothing in this section shall prevent a local board of education from offering access to some type of alternative educational services that can be provided to the student in a manner that does not create safety risks to other students and school staff. (2011-282, s. 2.)

§ 115C-390.12. Request for readmission.

(a) All students suspended for 365 days or expelled may, after 180 calendar days from the date of the beginning of the student's suspension or expulsion, request in writing readmission to the local school administrative unit. The local board of education shall develop and publish written policies and procedures for the readmission of all students who have been expelled or suspended for 365 days, which shall provide, at a minimum, the following process:

(1) The process for 365-day suspended students.

a. At the local board's discretion, either the superintendent or the local board itself shall consider and decide on petitions for readmission. If the decision maker is the superintendent, the superintendent shall offer the student an opportunity for an in-person meeting. If the decision maker is the local board of education, the board may offer the student an in-person meeting or may make a determination based on the records submitted by the student and the superintendent.

b. The student shall be readmitted if the student demonstrates to the satisfaction of the board or superintendent that the student's presence in school no longer constitutes a threat to the safety of other students or staff.

c. A superintendent's decision not to readmit the student may be appealed to the local board of education pursuant to G.S. 115C-45(c). The superintendent shall notify the parents of the right to appeal.

d. There is no right to judicial review of the board's decision not to readmit a 365-day suspended student.

e. A decision on readmission under this subsection shall be issued within 30 days of the petition.

(2) The process for expelled students.

a. The board of education shall consider all petitions for readmission of expelled students, together with the recommendation of the superintendent on the matter, and shall rule on the request for readmission. The board shall consider the petition based on the records submitted by the student and the response by the administration and shall allow the parties to be heard in the same manner as provided by G.S. 115C-45(c).

b. The student shall be readmitted if the student demonstrates to the satisfaction of the board or superintendent that his or her presence in a school no longer constitutes a clear threat to the safety of other students or staff.

c. A decision by a board of education to deny readmission of an expelled student is not subject to judicial review.

d. An expelled student may subsequently request readmission not more often than every six months. The local board of education is not required to consider subsequent readmission petitions filed sooner than six months after the previous petition was filed.

e. A decision on readmission under this section shall be issued within 30 days of the petition.

(b) If a student is readmitted under this section, the board and the superintendent have the right to assign the student to any program within the school system and to place reasonable conditions on the readmission.

(c) If a teacher was assaulted or injured by a student, and as a result the student was expelled, the student shall not be returned to that teacher's classroom following readmission unless the teacher consents. (2011-282, s. 2.)

§ 115C-391: Repealed by Session Laws 2011-282, s. 1, effective June 23, 2011, and applicable beginning with the 2011-2012 school year.

§ 115C-391.1. Permissible use of seclusion and restraint.

(a) It is the policy of the State of North Carolina to:

(1) Promote safety and prevent harm to all students, staff, and visitors in the public schools.

(2) Treat all public school students with dignity and respect in the delivery of discipline, use of physical restraints or seclusion, and use of reasonable force as permitted by law.

(3) Provide school staff with clear guidelines about what constitutes use of reasonable force permissible in North Carolina public schools.

(4) Improve student achievement, attendance, promotion, and graduation rates by employing positive behavioral interventions to address student behavior in a positive and safe manner.

(5) Promote retention of valuable teachers and other school personnel by providing appropriate training in prescribed procedures, which address student behavior in a positive and safe manner.

(b) The following definitions apply in this section:

(1) "Assistive technology device" means any item, piece of equipment, or product system that is used to increase, maintain, or improve the functional capacities of a child with a disability.

(2) "Aversive procedure" means a systematic physical or sensory intervention program for modifying the behavior of a student with a disability which causes or reasonably may be expected to cause one or more of the following:

a. Significant physical harm, such as tissue damage, physical illness, or death.

b. Serious, foreseeable long-term psychological impairment.

c. Obvious repulsion on the part of observers who cannot reconcile extreme procedures with acceptable, standard practice, for example: electric shock applied to the body; extremely loud auditory stimuli; forcible introduction of foul substances to the mouth, eyes, ears, nose, or skin; placement in a tub of cold water or shower; slapping, pinching, hitting, or pulling hair; blindfolding or other forms of visual blocking; unreasonable withholding of meals; eating one's own vomit; or denial of reasonable access to toileting facilities.

(3) "Behavioral intervention" means the implementation of strategies to address behavior that is dangerous, disruptive, or otherwise impedes the learning of a student or others.

(4) "IEP" means a student's Individualized Education Plan.

(5) "Isolation" means a behavior management technique in which a student is placed alone in an enclosed space from which the student is not prevented from leaving.

(6) "Law enforcement officer" means a sworn law enforcement officer with the power to arrest.

(7) "Mechanical restraint" means the use of any device or material attached or adjacent to a student's body that restricts freedom of movement or normal access to any portion of the student's body and that the student cannot easily remove.

(8) "Physical restraint" means the use of physical force to restrict the free movement of all or a portion of a student's body.

(9) "School personnel" means:

a. Employees of a local board of education.

b. Any person working on school grounds or at a school function under a contract or written agreement with the public school system to provide educational or related services to students.

c. Any person working on school grounds or at a school function for another agency providing educational or related services to students.

(10) "Seclusion" means the confinement of a student alone in an enclosed space from which the student is:

a. Physically prevented from leaving by locking hardware or other means.

b. Not capable of leaving due to physical or intellectual incapacity.

(11) "Time-out" means a behavior management technique in which a student is separated from other students for a limited period of time in a monitored setting.

(c) Physical Restraint:

(1) Physical restraint of students by school personnel shall be considered a reasonable use of force when used in the following circumstances:

a. As reasonably needed to obtain possession of a weapon or other dangerous objects on a person or within the control of a person.

b. As reasonably needed to maintain order or prevent or break up a fight.

c. As reasonably needed for self-defense.

d. As reasonably needed to ensure the safety of any student, school employee, volunteer, or other person present, to teach a skill, to calm or comfort a student, or to prevent self-injurious behavior.

e. As reasonably needed to escort a student safely from one area to another.

f. If used as provided for in a student's IEP or Section 504 plan or behavior intervention plan.

g. As reasonably needed to prevent imminent destruction to school or another person's property.

(2) Except as set forth in subdivision (1) of this subsection, physical restraint of students shall not be considered a reasonable use of force, and its use is prohibited.

(3) Physical restraint shall not be considered a reasonable use of force when used solely as a disciplinary consequence.

(4) Nothing in this subsection shall be construed to prevent the use of force by law enforcement officers in the lawful exercise of their law enforcement duties.

(d) Mechanical Restraint:

(1) Mechanical restraint of students by school personnel is permissible only in the following circumstances:

a. When properly used as an assistive technology device included in the student's IEP or Section 504 plan or behavior intervention plan or as otherwise prescribed for the student by a medical or related service provider.

b. When using seat belts or other safety restraints to secure students during transportation.

c. As reasonably needed to obtain possession of a weapon or other dangerous objects on a person or within the control of a person.

d. As reasonably needed for self-defense.

e. As reasonably needed to ensure the safety of any student, school employee, volunteer, or other person present.

(2) Except as set forth in subdivision (1) of this subsection, mechanical restraint, including the tying, taping, or strapping down of a student, shall not be considered a reasonable use of force, and its use is prohibited.

(3) Nothing in this subsection shall be construed to prevent the use of mechanical restraint devices such as handcuffs by law enforcement officers in the lawful exercise of their law enforcement duties.

(e) Seclusion:

(1) Seclusion of students by school personnel may be used in the following circumstances:

a. As reasonably needed to respond to a person in control of a weapon or other dangerous object.

b. As reasonably needed to maintain order or prevent or break up a fight.

c. As reasonably needed for self-defense.

d. As reasonably needed when a student's behavior poses a threat of imminent physical harm to self or others or imminent substantial destruction of school or another person's property.

e. When used as specified in the student's IEP, Section 504 plan, or behavior intervention plan; and

1. The student is monitored while in seclusion by an adult in close proximity who is able to see and hear the student at all times.

2. The student is released from seclusion upon cessation of the behaviors that led to the seclusion or as otherwise specified in the student's IEP or Section 504 plan.

3. The space in which the student is confined has been approved for such use by the local education agency.

4. The space is appropriately lighted.

5. The space is appropriately ventilated and heated or cooled.

6. The space is free of objects that unreasonably expose the student or others to harm.

(2) Except as set forth in subdivision (1) of this subsection, the use of seclusion is not considered reasonable force, and its use is not permitted.

(3) Seclusion shall not be considered a reasonable use of force when used solely as a disciplinary consequence.

(4) Nothing in this subsection shall be construed to prevent the use of seclusion by law enforcement officers in the lawful exercise of their law enforcement duties.

(f) Isolation. - Isolation is permitted as a behavior management technique provided that:

(1) The space used for isolation is appropriately lighted, ventilated, and heated or cooled.

(2) The duration of the isolation is reasonable in light of the purpose of the isolation.

(3) The student is reasonably monitored while in isolation.

(4) The isolation space is free of objects that unreasonably expose the student or others to harm.

(g) Time-Out. - Nothing in this section is intended to prohibit or regulate the use of time-out as defined in this section.

(h) Aversive Procedures. - The use of aversive procedures as defined in this section is prohibited in public schools.

(i) Nothing in this section modifies the rights of school personnel to use reasonable force as permitted under G.S. 115C-390.3 or modifies the rules and procedures governing discipline under G.S. 115C-390.1 through G.S. 115C-390.12.

(j) Notice, Reporting, and Documentation.

(1) Notice of procedures. - Each local board of education shall provide copies of this section and all local board policies developed to implement this section to school personnel and parents or guardians at the beginning of each school year.

(2) Notice of specified incidents:

a. School personnel shall promptly notify the principal or principal's designee of:

1. Any use of aversive procedures.

2. Any prohibited use of mechanical restraint.

3. Any use of physical restraint resulting in observable physical injury to a student.

4. Any prohibited use of seclusion or seclusion that exceeds 10 minutes or the amount of time specified on a student's behavior intervention plan.

b. When a principal or principal's designee has personal knowledge or actual notice of any of the events described in this subdivision, the principal or principal's designee shall promptly notify the student's parent or guardian and will provide the name of a school employee the parent or guardian can contact regarding the incident.

(3) As used in subdivision (2) of this subsection, "promptly notify" means by the end of the workday during which the incident occurred when reasonably possible, but in no event later than the end of following workday.

(4) The parent or guardian of the student shall be provided with a written incident report for any incident reported under this section within a reasonable period of time, but in no event later than 30 days after the incident. The written incident report shall include:

a. The date, time of day, location, duration, and description of the incident and interventions.

b. The events or events that led up to the incident.

c. The nature and extent of any injury to the student.

d. The name of a school employee the parent or guardian can contact regarding the incident.

(5) No local board of education or employee of a local board of education shall discharge, threaten, or otherwise retaliate against another employee of the board regarding that employee's compensation, terms, conditions, location, or privileges of employment because the employee makes a report alleging a prohibited use of physical restraint, mechanical restraint, aversive procedure, or seclusion, unless the employee knew or should have known that the report was false.

(k) Nothing in this section shall be construed to create a private cause of action against any local board of education, its agents or employees, or any institutions of teacher education or their agents or employees or to create a criminal offense. (2005-205, s. 2; 2006-264, s. 58; 2011-282, s. 3.)

§ 115C-392. Appeal of disciplinary measures.

Appeals of disciplinary measures are subject to the provisions of G.S. 115C-45(c). (1981, c. 423, s. 1.)

§§ 115C-393 through 115C-397. Reserved for future codification purposes.

Article 27A.

Management and Placement of Disruptive Students.

§ 115C-397.1. Management and placement of disruptive students.

If, after a teacher has requested assistance from the principal two or more times due to a student's disruptive behavior, the teacher finds that the student's disruptive behavior continues to interfere with the academic achievement of that student or other students in the class, then the teacher may refer the matter to a school-based committee. The teacher may request that additional classroom teachers participate in the committee's proceedings. For the purposes of this section, the committee shall notify the student's parent, guardian, or legal custodian and shall encourage that person's participation in the proceedings of the committee concerning the student. Nothing in this section requires a student to be screened, evaluated, or identified as a child with a disability under Article 9 of this Chapter. The committee shall review the matter and shall take one or more of the following actions: (i) advise the teacher on managing the student's behavior more effectively, (ii) recommend to the principal the transfer of the student to another class within the school, (iii) recommend to the principal a multidisciplinary evaluation of the student, (iv) recommend to the principal that the student be assigned to an alternative learning program, or (v) recommend to the principal that the student receive any additional services that the school or the school unit has the resources to provide for the student. If the principal does not follow the recommendation of the committee, the principal shall provide a written explanation to the committee, the teacher who referred the matter to the committee, and the superintendent, of any actions taken to resolve the matter and of the reason the principal did not follow the recommendation of the committee.

This section shall be in addition to the supplemental to disciplinary action taken in accordance with any other law. The recommendation of the committee is final and shall not be appealed under G.S. 115C-45(c). Nothing in this section shall authorize a student to refer a disciplinary matter to this committee or to have the matter of the student's behavior referred to this committee before any discipline is imposed on the student. (1997-443, s. 8.29(b); 2006-69, s. 3(m).)

Article 28.

Student Liability.

§ 115C-398. Damage to school buildings, furnishings, textbooks.

Students and their parents or legal guardians may be liable for damage to school buildings, furnishings and textbooks pursuant to the provisions of G.S. 115C-523, 115C-100 and 14-132. (1981, c. 423, s. 1; 1985, c. 581, s. 3.)

§ 115C-399. Trespass on or damage to school bus.

Any person who willfully trespasses upon or damages a school bus may be liable pursuant to the provisions of G.S. 14-132.2. (1981, c. 423, s. 1.)

Article 29.

Protective Provisions and Maintenance of Student Records.

§ 115C-400. School personnel to report child abuse.

Any person who has cause to suspect child abuse or neglect has a duty to report the case of the child to the Director of Social Services of the county, as provided in Article 3 of Chapter 7B of the General Statutes. (1981, c. 423, s. 1; 1998-202, s. 13(bb).)

§ 115C-401. School counseling inadmissible evidence.

Information given to a school counselor to enable him to render counseling services may be privileged as provided in G.S. 8-53.4. (1981, c. 423, s. 1.)

§ 115C-401.1. Prohibition on the disclosure of information about students.

(a)   It is unlawful for a person who enters into a contract with a local board of education or its designee to sell any personally identifiable information that is obtained from a student as a result of the person's performance under the contract. This prohibition does not apply if the person obtains the prior written authorization of the student's parent or guardian. This authorization shall include the parent's or guardian's original signature. The person shall not solicit this authorization and signature through the school's personnel or equipment or on school grounds.

(b)   The following definitions apply in this section:

(1)   "Contract" means a contract for the provision of goods or services.

(2)   "Personally identifiable information" means any information directly related to a student, including the student's name, birthdate, address, social security number, individual purchasing behavior or preferences, parents' names, telephone number, or any other information or identification number that would provide information about a specific student.

(3)   "Sell" means sell or otherwise use for a business or marketing purpose.

(c)   A violation of subsection (a) of this section shall be punished as a Class 2 misdemeanor, and when the defendant is an organization as defined in G.S. 15A-773(c) the fine shall be five thousand dollars ($5,000) for the first violation, ten thousand dollars ($10,000) for a second violation, and twenty-five thousand dollars ($25,000) for a third or subsequent violation.

(d)   Nothing in this section shall preclude the enforcement of civil remedies as otherwise provided by law.

(e) Nothing in this section prohibits the identification and disclosure of directory information in compliance with federal law and local board of education policy or procedure. (2001-500, s. 1.)

§ 115C-402. Student records; maintenance; contents; confidentiality.

(a) The official record of each student enrolled in North Carolina public schools shall be permanently maintained in the files of the appropriate school after the student graduates, or should have graduated, from high school unless the local board determines that such files may be filed in the central office or other location designated by the local board for that purpose.

(b) The official record shall contain, as a minimum, adequate identification data including date of birth, attendance data, grading and promotion data, and such other factual information as may be deemed appropriate by the local board of education having jurisdiction over the school wherein the record is maintained. Each student's official record also shall include notice of any long-term suspension or expulsion imposed pursuant to G.S. 115C-390.7 through G.S. 115C-390.11 and the conduct for which the student was suspended or expelled. The superintendent or the superintendent's designee shall expunge from the record the notice of suspension or expulsion if the following criteria are met:

(1) One of the following persons makes a request for expungement:

a. The student's parent, legal guardian, or custodian.

b. The student, if the student is at least 16 years old or is emancipated.

(2) The student either graduates from high school or is not expelled or suspended again during the two-year period commencing on the date of the student's return to school after the expulsion or suspension.

(3) The superintendent or the superintendent's designee determines that the maintenance of the record is no longer needed to maintain safe and orderly schools.

(4) The superintendent or the superintendent's designee determines that the maintenance of the record is no longer needed to adequately serve the child.

(c) Notwithstanding subdivision (b)(1) of this section, a superintendent or the superintendent's designee may expunge from a student's official record any notice of suspension or expulsion provided all other criteria under subsection (b) are met.

(d) Each local board's policy on student records shall include information on the procedure for expungement under subsection (b) of this section.

(e) The official record of each student is not a public record as the term "public record" is defined by G.S. 132-1. The official record shall not be subject to inspection and examination as authorized by G.S. 132-6.

(f) The actual address and telephone number of a student who is a participant in the Address Confidentiality Program established pursuant to Chapter 15C of the General Statutes or a student with a parent who is a participant in the Address Confidentiality Program established pursuant to Chapter 15C of the General Statutes shall be kept confidential from the public and shall not be disclosed except as provided in Chapter 15C of the General Statutes. (1975, c. 624, ss. 1, 2; 1981, c. 423, s. 1; 1985, c. 268; c. 416; 1997-443, s. 8.29(s); 2001-195, s. 1; 2002-171, s. 6; 2011-282, s. 13.)

§ 115C-403. Flagging and verification of student records; notification of law enforcement agencies.

(a) Upon notification by a law enforcement agency or the North Carolina Center for Missing Persons of a child's disappearance, the superintendent of a local school administrative unit or his designee shall flag or mark the record of any child who is currently or was previously enrolled in a school of that unit and who is reported as missing. The flag or mark shall be made in such a manner that when a copy of or information regarding the record is requested, school personnel are alerted to the fact that the record is that of a missing child.

Before providing a copy of the school record or other information concerning the child whose record is flagged pursuant to this section, the superintendent or his designee shall notify the agency that requested that the record be flagged of every inquiry made concerning the flagged record, and shall provide a copy to the agency of any written request for information concerning the flagged record.

(b) When any child transfers from one school system to another school system, the receiving school shall, within 30 days of the child's enrollment, obtain the child's record from the school from which the child is transferring. If the child's parent, custodian, or guardian provides a copy of the child's record from the school from which the child is transferring, the receiving school shall, within 30 days of the child's enrollment, request written verification of the school record by contacting the school or institution named on the transferring child's record. Upon receipt of a request, the principal or the principal's designee of the school from which the child is transferring shall not withhold the record or verification for any reason, except as is authorized under the Family Educational Rights and Privacy Act. Any information received indicating that the transferring child is a missing child shall be reported to the North Carolina Center for Missing Persons. (1989, c. 331, s. 1; 1998-220, s. 12.)

§ 115C-404. Use of juvenile court information.

(a) Written notifications received in accordance with G.S. 7B-3101 and information gained from examination of juvenile records in accordance with G.S. 7B-3100 are confidential records, are not public records as defined under G.S. 132-1, and shall not be made part of the student's official record under G.S. 115C-402. Immediately upon receipt, the principal shall maintain these documents in a safe, locked record storage that is separate from the student's other school records. The principal shall shred, burn, or otherwise destroy documents received in accordance with G.S. 7B-3100 to protect the confidentiality of the information when the principal receives notification that the court dismissed the petition under G.S. 7B-2411, the court transferred jurisdiction over the student to superior court under G.S. 7B-2200, or the court granted the student's petition for expunction of the records. The principal shall shred, burn, or otherwise destroy all information gained from examination of juvenile records in accordance with G.S. 7B-3100 when the principal finds that the school no longer needs the information to protect the safety of or to improve the educational opportunities for the student or others. In no case shall the principal make a copy of these documents.

(b) (Effective until July 1, 2014) Documents received under this section shall be used only to protect the safety of or to improve the education opportunities for the student or others. Information gained in accordance with G.S. 7B-3100 shall not be the sole basis for a decision to suspend or expel a student. Upon receipt of each document, the principal shall share the document with those individuals who have (i) direct guidance, teaching, or supervisory responsibility for the student, and (ii) a specific need to know in order to protect the safety of the student or others. Those individuals shall indicate in writing that they have read the document and that they agree to maintain its confidentiality. Failure to maintain the confidentiality of these documents as required by this section is grounds for the dismissal of an employee who is not a career employee and is grounds for dismissal of an employee who is a career employee, in accordance with G.S. 115C-325(e)(1)i.

(b) (Effective July 1, 2014, until June 30, 2018) Documents received under this section shall be used only to protect the safety of or to improve the education opportunities for the student or others. Information gained in accordance with G.S. 7B-3100 shall not be the sole basis for a decision to suspend or expel a student. Upon receipt of each document, the principal shall share the document with those individuals who have (i) direct guidance, teaching, or supervisory responsibility for the student, and (ii) a specific need to know in order to protect the safety of the student or others. Those individuals shall indicate in writing that they have read the document and that they agree to maintain its confidentiality. Failure to maintain the confidentiality of these documents as required by this section is grounds for the dismissal of an employee who is not employed on contract, grounds for dismissal of an employee on contract in accordance with G.S. 115C-325.4(a)(9), and grounds for dismissal of an employee who is a career teacher in accordance with G.S. 115C-325(e)(1)i.

(b) (Effective June 30, 2018) Documents received under this section shall be used only to protect the safety of or to improve the education opportunities for the student or others. Information gained in accordance with G.S. 7B-3100 shall not be the sole basis for a decision to suspend or expel a student. Upon receipt of each document, the principal shall share the document with those individuals who have (i) direct guidance, teaching, or supervisory responsibility for the student, and (ii) a specific need to know in order to protect the safety of the student or others. Those individuals shall indicate in writing that they have read the document and that they agree to maintain its confidentiality. Failure to maintain the confidentiality of these documents as required by this section is grounds for the dismissal of an employee who is not employed on contract and grounds for dismissal of an employee on contract in accordance with G.S. 115C-325.4(a)(9).

(c) If the student graduates, withdraws from school, is suspended for the remainder of the school year, is expelled, or transfers to another school, the principal shall return all documents not destroyed in accordance with subsection (a) of this section to the juvenile court counselor and, if applicable, shall provide the counselor with the name and address of the school to which the student is transferring. (1997-443, s. 8.29(f); 1998-202, ss. 8, 13(cc); 1998-217, s. 12; 2000-140, s. 25; 2013-360, s. 9.7(l), (v).)

§ 115C-405. Reserved for future codification purposes.

§ 115C-406. Reserved for future codification purposes.

Article 29A.

Policy Prohibiting Use of Tobacco Products.

§ 115C-407. Policy prohibiting tobacco use in school buildings, grounds, and at school-sponsored events.

(a) Not later than August 1, 2008, local boards of education shall adopt, implement, and enforce a written policy prohibiting at all times the use of any tobacco product by any person in school buildings, in school facilities, on school campuses, and in or on any other school property owned or operated by the local school administrative unit. The policy shall further prohibit the use of all tobacco products by persons attending a school-sponsored event at a location not listed in this subsection when in the presence of students or school personnel or in an area where smoking is otherwise prohibited by law.

(b) The policy shall include at least all of the following elements:

(1) Adequate notice to students, parents, the public, and school personnel of the policy.

(2) Posting of signs prohibiting at all times the use of tobacco products by any person in and on school property.

(3) Requirements that school personnel enforce the policy.

(c) The policy may permit tobacco products to be included in instructional or research activities in public school buildings if the activity is conducted or supervised by the faculty member overseeing the instruction or research and the activity does not include smoking, chewing, or otherwise ingesting the tobacco product.

(d) The North Carolina Health and Wellness Trust Fund Commission shall work with local boards of education to provide assistance with the implementation of this policy including providing information regarding smoking cessation and prevention resources. Nothing in this section, G.S. 143-595 through G.S. 143-601, or any other section prohibits a local board of education from adopting and enforcing a more restrictive policy on the use of tobacco in school buildings, in school facilities, on school campuses, or at school-related or school-sponsored events, and in or on other school property. (2003-421, s. 1; 2007-236, s. 1.)

§ 115C-407.1: Reserved for future codification purposes.

§ 115C-407.2: Reserved for future codification purposes.

§ 115C-407.3: Reserved for future codification purposes.

§ 115C-407.4: Reserved for future codification purposes.

Article 29B.

Interstate Compact on Educational Opportunity for Military Children.

§ 115C-407.5. Interstate Compact on Educational Opportunity for Military Children.

The Interstate Compact on Educational Opportunity for Military Children is hereby enacted into law and entered into with all jurisdictions legally joining therein in the form substantially as follows:

ARTICLE I.

PURPOSE.

It is the purpose of this compact to remove barriers to educational success imposed on children of military families because of frequent moves and deployment of their parents by:

A. Facilitating the timely enrollment of children of military families and ensuring that they are not placed at a disadvantage due to difficulty in the transfer of education records from the previous school district(s) or variations in entrance/age requirements.

B. Facilitating the student placement process through which children of military families are not disadvantaged by variations in attendance requirements, scheduling, sequencing, grading, course content or assessment.

C. Facilitating the qualification and eligibility for enrollment, educational programs, and participation in extracurricular academic, athletic, and social activities.

D. Facilitating the on-time graduation of children of military families.

E. Providing for the promulgation and enforcement of administrative rules implementing the provisions of this compact.

F. Providing for the uniform collection and sharing of information between and among member states, schools and military families under this compact.

G. Promoting coordination between this compact and other compacts affecting military children.

H. Promoting flexibility and cooperation between the educational system, parents and the student in order to achieve educational success for the student.

ARTICLE II.

DEFINITIONS.

As used in this compact, unless the context clearly requires a different construction:

A. "Active duty" means: full-time duty status in the active uniformed service of the United States, including members of the National Guard and Reserve on active duty orders pursuant to 10 U.S.C. § 12301, et. seq. and 10 U.S.C. § 12401, et. seq.

B. "Children of military families" means: a school-aged child(ren), enrolled in Kindergarten through Twelfth (12th) grade, in the household of an active duty member.

C. "Compact commissioner" means: the voting representative of each compacting state appointed pursuant to Article VIII of this compact.

D. "Deployment" means: the period one (1) month prior to the service members' departure from their home station on military orders though six (6) months after return to their home station.

E. "Education(al) records" means: those official records, files, and data directly related to a student and maintained by the school or local education agency, including but not limited to records encompassing all the material kept in the student's cumulative folder such as general identifying data, records of attendance and of academic work completed, records of achievement and results of evaluative tests, health data, disciplinary status, test protocols, and individualized education programs.

F. "Extracurricular activities" means: a voluntary activity sponsored by the school or local education agency or an organization sanctioned by the local education agency. Extracurricular activities include, but are not limited to, preparation for and involvement in public performances, contests, athletic competitions, demonstrations, displays, and club activities.

G. "Interstate Commission on Educational Opportunity for Military Children" means: the commission that is created under Article IX of this compact, which is generally referred to as Interstate Commission.

H. "Local education agency" means: a public authority legally constituted by the state as an administrative agency to provide control of and direction for Kindergarten through Twelfth (12th) grade public educational institutions.

I. "Member state" means: a state that has enacted this compact.

J. "Military installation" means: a base, camp, post, station, yard, center, homeport facility for any ship, or other activity under the jurisdiction of the Department of Defense, including any leased facility, which is located within any of the several States, the District of Columbia, the Commonwealth of Puerto Rico, the U.S. Virgin Islands, Guam, American Samoa, the Northern Marianas Islands and any other U.S. Territory. Such term does not include any facility used primarily for civil works, rivers and harbors projects, or flood control projects.

K. "Non-member state" means: a state that has not enacted this compact.

L. "Receiving state" means: the state to which a child of a military family is sent, brought, or caused to be sent or brought.

M. "Rule" means: a written statement by the Interstate Commission promulgated pursuant to Article XII of this compact that is of general applicability, implements, interprets or prescribes a policy or provision of the Compact, or an organizational, procedural, or practice requirement of the Interstate Commission, and has the force and effect of rules promulgated under the Administrative Procedures Act as found in Chapter 150B of the North Carolina General Statutes, and includes the amendment, repeal, or suspension of an existing rule.

N. "Sending state" means: the state from which a child of a military family is sent, brought, or caused to be sent or brought.

O. "State" means: a state of the United States, the District of Columbia, the Commonwealth of Puerto Rico, the U.S. Virgin Islands, Guam, American Samoa, the Northern Marianas Islands and any other U.S. Territory.

P. "Student" means: the child of a military family for whom the local education agency receives public funding and who is formally enrolled in Kindergarten through Twelfth (12th) grade.

Q. "Transition" means: 1) the formal and physical process of transferring from school to school or 2) the period of time in which a student moves from one school in the sending state to another school in the receiving state.

R. "Uniformed service(s)" means: the Army, Navy, Air Force, Marine Corps, Coast Guard as well as the Commissioned Corps of the National Oceanic and Atmospheric Administration, and Public Health Services.

S. "Veteran" means: a person who served in the uniformed services and who was discharged or released there from under conditions other than dishonorable.

ARTICLE III.

APPLICABILITY.

A. Except as otherwise provided in Section B, this compact shall apply to the children of:

1. active duty members of the uniformed services as defined in this compact, including members of the National Guard and Reserve on active duty orders pursuant to 10 U.S.C. § 12301, et. seq. and 10 U.S.C. § 12401, et. seq.;

2. members or veterans of the uniformed services who are severely injured and medically discharged or retired for a period of one (1) year after medical discharge or retirement; and

3. members of the uniformed services who die on active duty or as a result of injuries sustained on active duty for a period of one (1) year after death.

B. The provisions of this interstate compact shall only apply to local education agencies as defined in this compact.

C. The provisions of this compact shall not apply to the children of:

1. inactive members of the National Guard and military reserves;

2. members of the uniformed services now retired, except as provided in Section A;

3. veterans of the uniformed services, except as provided in Section A; and other U.S. Dept. of Defense personnel and other federal agency civilian and contract employees not defined as active duty members of the uniformed services.

ARTICLE IV.

EDUCATIONAL RECORDS & ENROLLMENT.

A. Unofficial or "hand-carried" education records - In the event that official education records cannot be released to the parents for the purpose of transfer, the custodian of the records in the sending state shall prepare and furnish to the parent a complete set of unofficial educational records containing uniform information as determined by the Interstate Commission. Upon receipt of the unofficial education records by a school in the receiving state, the school shall enroll and appropriately place the student based on the information provided in the unofficial records pending validation by the official records, as quickly as possible.

B.   Official education records/transcripts - Simultaneous with the enrollment and conditional placement of the student, the school in the receiving state shall request the student's official education record from the school in the sending state. Upon receipt of this request, the school in the sending state will process and furnish the official education records to the school in the receiving state within ten (10) days or within such time as is reasonably determined under the rules promulgated by the Interstate Commission.

C.   Immunizations - Compacting states shall give thirty (30) days from the date of enrollment or within such time as is reasonably determined under the rules promulgated by the Interstate Commission, for students to obtain any immunization(s) required by the receiving state. For a series of immunizations, initial vaccinations must be obtained within thirty (30) days or within such time as is reasonably determined under the rules promulgated by the Interstate Commission.

D.   Kindergarten and First grade entrance age - Students shall be allowed to continue their enrollment at grade level in the receiving state commensurate with their grade level (including Kindergarten) from a local education agency in the sending state at the time of transition, regardless of age. A student that has satisfactorily completed the prerequisite grade level in the local education agency in the sending state shall be eligible for enrollment in the next highest grade level in the receiving state, regardless of age. A student transferring after the start of the school year in the receiving state shall enter the school in the receiving state on their validated level from an accredited school in the sending state.

ARTICLE V.

PLACEMENT & ATTENDANCE.

A.   Course placement - When the student transfers before or during the school year, the receiving state school shall initially honor placement of the student in educational courses based on the student's enrollment in the sending state school and/or educational assessments conducted at the school in the sending state if the courses are offered. Course placement includes but is not limited to Honors, International Baccalaureate, Advanced Placement, vocational, technical and career pathways courses. Continuing the student's academic program from the previous school and promoting placement in academically and career challenging courses should be paramount when considering placement. This does not preclude the school in the receiving state from performing subsequent evaluations to ensure appropriate placement and continued enrollment of the student in the course(s).

B.   Educational program placement - The receiving state school shall initially honor placement of the student in educational programs based on current educational assessments conducted at the school in the sending state or participation/placement in like programs in the sending state. Such programs include, but are not limited to: 1) gifted and talented programs; and 2) English as a second language (ESL). This does not preclude the school in the receiving state from performing subsequent evaluations to ensure appropriate placement of the student.

C.   Special education services - 1) In compliance with the federal requirements of the Individuals with Disabilities Education Act (IDEA), 20 U.S.C. § 1400 et seq., the receiving state shall initially provide comparable services to a student with disabilities based on his/her current Individualized Education Program (IEP); and 2) In compliance with the requirements of Section 504 of the Rehabilitation Act, 29 U.S.C. § 794, and with Title II of the Americans with Disabilities Act, 42 U.S.C. §§ 12131-12165, the receiving state shall make reasonable accommodations and modifications to address the needs of incoming students with disabilities, subject to an existing 504 or Title II Plan, to provide the student with equal access to education. This does not preclude the school in the receiving state from performing subsequent evaluations to ensure appropriate placement of the student.

D.   Placement flexibility - Local education agency administrative officials shall have flexibility in waiving course/program prerequisites, or other preconditions for placement in courses/programs offered under the jurisdiction of the local education agency.

E.   Absence as related to deployment activities - A student whose parent or legal guardian is an active duty member of the uniformed services, as defined by the compact, and has been called to duty for, is on leave from, or immediately returned from deployment to a combat zone or combat support posting, shall be granted additional excused absences at the discretion of the local education agency superintendent to visit with his or her parent or legal guardian relative to such leave or deployment of the parent or guardian.

ARTICLE VI.

ELIGIBILITY.

A. Eligibility for enrollment - Children of military families shall be eligible for enrollment in the public schools of North Carolina pursuant to the provisions of G.S. 115C-366, including the provisions of G.S. 115C-366(a3) that provides for admission, without the payment of tuition, of children of military families not domiciled within the school district, provided that the affidavits provided for in that section and other specified conditions are met.

B. Eligibility for extracurricular participation - State and local education agencies shall facilitate the opportunity for transitioning military children's inclusion in extracurricular activities, regardless of application deadlines, to the extent they are otherwise qualified.

ARTICLE VII.

GRADUATION.

In order to facilitate the on-time graduation of children of military families, states and local education agencies shall incorporate the following procedures:

A. Waiver requirements - Local education agency administrative officials shall waive specific courses required for graduation if similar course work has been satisfactorily completed in another local education agency or shall provide reasonable justification for denial. Should a waiver not be granted to a student who would qualify to graduate from the sending school, the local education agency shall provide an alternative means of acquiring required coursework so that graduation may occur on time.

B. Exit exams - States shall accept: 1) exit or end-of-course exams required for graduation from the sending state; or 2) national norm-referenced achievement tests or 3) alternative testing, in lieu of testing requirements for graduation in the receiving state. In the event the above alternatives cannot be accommodated by the receiving state for a student transferring in his or her Senior year, then the provisions of Article VII, Section C shall apply.

C. Transfers during Senior year - Should a military student transferring at the beginning or during his or her Senior year be ineligible to graduate from the receiving local education agency after all alternatives have been considered, the sending and receiving local education agencies shall ensure the receipt of a diploma from the sending local education agency, if the student meets the graduation requirements of the sending local education agency. In the event that one of the states in question is not a member of this compact, the member state shall use best efforts to facilitate the on-time graduation of the student in accordance with Sections A and B of this Article.

ARTICLE VIII.

STATE COORDINATION.

A. Each member state shall, through the creation of a State Council or use of an existing body or board, provide for the coordination among its agencies of government, local education agencies and military installations concerning the state's participation in, and compliance with, this compact and Interstate Commission activities. While each member state may determine the membership of its own State Council, its membership must include at least: the state superintendent of education, superintendent of a school district with a high concentration of military children, representative from a military installation, one representative each from the legislative and executive branches of government, and other offices and stakeholder groups the State Council deems appropriate. A member state that does not have a school district deemed to contain a high concentration of military children may appoint a superintendent from another school district to represent local education agencies on the State Council.

B. The State Council of each member state shall appoint or designate a military family education liaison to assist military families and the state in facilitating the implementation of this compact.

C. The compact commissioner responsible for the administration and management of the state's participation in the compact shall be appointed by the Governor or as otherwise determined by each member state.

D. The compact commissioner and the military family education liaison designated herein shall be ex-officio members of the State Council, unless either is already a full voting member of the State Council.

ARTICLE IX

INTERSTATE COMMISSION ON EDUCATIONAL OPPORTUNITY FOR MILITARY CHILDREN

The member states hereby create the "Interstate Commission on Educational Opportunity for Military Children." The activities of the Interstate Commission are the formation of public policy and are a discretionary state function. The Interstate Commission shall:

A. Be a body corporate and joint agency of the member states and shall have all the responsibilities, powers and duties set forth herein, and such additional powers as may be conferred upon it by a subsequent concurrent action of the respective legislatures of the member states in accordance with the terms of this compact.

B. Consist of one Interstate Commission voting representative from each member state who shall be that state's compact commissioner.

1. Each member state represented at a meeting of the Interstate Commission is entitled to one vote.

2. A majority of the total member states shall constitute a quorum for the transaction of business, unless a larger quorum is required by the bylaws of the Interstate Commission.

3. A representative shall not delegate a vote to another member state. In the event the compact commissioner is unable to attend a meeting of the Interstate Commission, the Governor or State Council may delegate voting authority to another person from their state for a specified meeting.

4. The bylaws may provide for meetings of the Interstate Commission to be conducted by telecommunication or electronic communication.

C. Consist of ex-officio, non-voting representatives who are members of interested organizations. Such ex-officio members, as defined in the bylaws, may include but not be limited to, members of the representative organizations of military family advocates, local education agency officials, parent and teacher groups, the U.S. Department of Defense, the Education Commission of the States, the Interstate Agreement on the Qualification of Educational Personnel and other interstate compacts affecting the education of children of military members.

D. Meet at least once each calendar year. The chairperson may call additional meetings and, upon the request of a simple majority of the member states, shall call additional meetings.

E. Establish an executive committee, whose members shall include the officers of the Interstate Commission and such other members of the Interstate Commission as determined by the bylaws. Members of the executive committee shall serve a one year term. Members of the executive committee shall be entitled to one vote each. The executive committee shall have the power to act on behalf of the Interstate Commission, with the exception of rulemaking, during periods when the Interstate Commission is not in session. The executive committee shall oversee the day-to-day activities of the administration of the compact including enforcement and compliance with the provisions of the compact, its bylaws and rules, and other such duties as deemed necessary. The U.S. Dept. of Defense shall serve as an ex-officio, nonvoting member of the executive committee.

F. Establish bylaws and rules that provide for conditions and procedures under which the Interstate Commission shall make its information and official records available to the public for inspection or copying. The Interstate Commission may exempt from disclosure information or official records to the extent they would adversely affect personal privacy rights or proprietary interests.

G. Give public notice of all meetings and all meetings shall be open to the public, except as set forth in the rules or as otherwise provided in the compact. The Interstate Commission and its committees may close a meeting, or portion thereof, where it determines by two-thirds vote that an open meeting would be likely to:

1. Relate solely to the Interstate Commission's internal personnel practices and procedures;

2. Disclose matters specifically exempted from disclosure by federal and state statute;

3. Disclose trade secrets or commercial or financial information which is privileged or confidential;

4. Involve accusing a person of a crime, or formally censuring a person;

5. Disclose information of a personal nature where disclosure would constitute a clearly unwarranted invasion of personal privacy;

6. Disclose investigative records compiled for law enforcement purposes; or

7. Specifically relate to the Interstate Commission's participation in a civil action or other legal proceeding.

H. Shall cause its legal counsel or designee to certify that a meeting may be closed and shall reference each relevant exemptible provision for any meeting, or portion of a meeting, which is closed pursuant to this provision. The Interstate Commission shall keep minutes which shall fully and clearly describe all matters discussed in a meeting and shall provide a full and accurate summary of actions taken, and the reasons therefore, including a description of the views expressed and the record of a roll call vote. All documents considered in connection with an action shall be identified in such minutes. All minutes and documents of a closed meeting shall remain under seal, subject to release by a majority vote of the Interstate Commission.

I. Shall collect standardized data concerning the educational transition of the children of military families under this compact as directed through its rules which shall specify the data to be collected, the means of collection and data exchange and reporting requirements. Such methods of data collection, exchange and reporting shall, in so far as is reasonably possible, conform to current technology and coordinate its information functions with the appropriate custodian of records as identified in the bylaws and rules.

J. Shall create a process that permits military officials, education officials and parents to inform the Interstate Commission if and when there are alleged violations of the compact or its rules or when issues subject to the jurisdiction of the compact or its rules are not addressed by the state or local education agency. This section shall not be construed to create a private right of action against the Interstate Commission, any member state, or any local education agency.

ARTICLE X.

POWERS AND DUTIES OF THE INTERSTATE COMMISSION.

The Interstate Commission shall have the following powers:

A. To provide for dispute resolution among member states.

B. To promulgate rules and take all necessary actions to effect the goals, purposes and obligations as enumerated in this compact. The rules shall have the force and effect of rules promulgated under the Administrative Procedures Act as found in Chapter 150B of the North Carolina General Statutes and shall be binding in the compact states to the extent and in the manner provided in this compact.

C. To issue, upon request of a member state, advisory opinions concerning the meaning or interpretation of the interstate compact, its bylaws, rules and actions.

D. To enforce compliance with the compact provisions, the rules promulgated by the Interstate Commission, and the bylaws, using all necessary and proper means, including but not limited to the use of judicial process. Any action to enforce compliance with the compact provisions by the Interstate Commission shall be brought against a member state only.

E. To establish and maintain offices which shall be located within one or more of the member states.

F. To purchase and maintain insurance and bonds.

G. To borrow, accept, hire or contract for services of personnel.

H. To establish and appoint committees including, but not limited to, an executive committee as required by Article IX, Section E, which shall have the power to act on behalf of the Interstate Commission in carrying out its powers and duties hereunder.

I. To elect or appoint such officers, attorneys, employees, agents, or consultants, and to fix their compensation, define their duties and determine their qualifications; and to establish the Interstate Commission's personnel policies and programs relating to conflicts of interest, rates of compensation, and qualifications of personnel.

J. To accept any and all donations and grants of money, equipment, supplies, materials, and services, and to receive, utilize, and dispose of it.

K. To lease, purchase, accept contributions or donations of, or otherwise to own, hold, improve or use any property, real, personal, or mixed.

L. To sell, convey, mortgage, pledge, lease, exchange, abandon, or otherwise dispose of any property, real, personal or mixed.

M. To establish a budget and make expenditures.

N. To adopt a seal and bylaws governing the management and operation of the Interstate Commission.

O. To report annually to the legislatures, governors, judiciary, and state councils of the member states concerning the activities of the Interstate Commission during the preceding year. Such reports shall also include any recommendations that may have been adopted by the Interstate Commission.

P. To coordinate education, training and public awareness regarding the compact, its implementation and operation for officials and parents involved in such activity.

Q. To establish uniform standards for the reporting, collecting and exchanging of data.

R. To maintain corporate books and records in accordance with the bylaws.

S. To perform such functions as may be necessary or appropriate to achieve the purposes of this compact.

T. To provide for the uniform collection and sharing of information between and among member states, schools and military families under this compact.

ARTICLE XI.

ORGANIZATION AND OPERATION OF THE INTERSTATE COMMISSION

A. The Interstate Commission shall, by a majority of the members present and voting, within 12 months after the first Interstate Commission meeting, adopt bylaws to govern its conduct as may be necessary or appropriate to carry out the purposes of the compact, including, but not limited to:

1. Establishing the fiscal year of the Interstate Commission;

2. Establishing an executive committee, and such other committees as may be necessary;

3. Providing for the establishment of committees and for governing any general or specific delegation of authority or function of the Interstate Commission;

4. Providing reasonable procedures for calling and conducting meetings of the Interstate Commission, and ensuring reasonable notice of each such meeting;

5. Establishing the titles and responsibilities of the officers and staff of the Interstate Commission;

6. Providing a mechanism for concluding the operations of the Interstate Commission and the return of surplus funds that may exist upon the termination of the compact after the payment and reserving of all of its debts and obligations.

7. Providing "start up" rules for initial administration of the compact.

B. The Interstate Commission shall, by a majority of the members, elect annually from among its members a chairperson, a vice-chairperson, and a treasurer, each of whom shall have such authority and duties as may be specified in the bylaws. The chairperson or, in the chairperson's absence or disability, the vice-chairperson, shall preside at all meetings of the Interstate Commission. The officers so elected shall serve without compensation or remuneration from the Interstate Commission; provided that, subject to the availability of budgeted funds, the officers shall be reimbursed for ordinary and necessary costs and expenses incurred by them in the performance of their responsibilities as officers of the Interstate Commission.

C. Executive Committee, Officers and Personnel

1. The executive committee shall have such authority and duties as may be set forth in the bylaws, including but not limited to:

a. Managing the affairs of the Interstate Commission in a manner consistent with the bylaws and purposes of the Interstate Commission;

b. Overseeing an organizational structure within, and appropriate procedures for the Interstate Commission to provide for the creation of rules, operating procedures, and administrative and technical support functions; and

c. Planning, implementing, and coordinating communications and activities with other state, federal and local government organizations in order to advance the goals of the Interstate Commission.

2. The executive committee may, subject to the approval of the Interstate Commission, appoint or retain an executive director for such period, upon such terms and conditions and for such compensation, as the Interstate Commission may deem appropriate. The executive director shall serve as secretary to the Interstate Commission, but shall not be a Member of the Interstate Commission. The executive director shall hire and supervise such other persons as may be authorized by the Interstate Commission.

D. The Interstate Commission's executive director and its employees shall be immune from suit and liability, either personally or in their official capacity, for a claim for damage to or loss of property or personal injury or other civil liability caused or arising out of or relating to an actual or alleged act, error, or omission that occurred, or that such person had a reasonable basis for believing occurred, within the scope of Interstate Commission employment, duties, or responsibilities; provided, that such person shall not be protected from suit or liability for damage, loss, injury, or liability caused by the intentional or willful and wanton misconduct of such person.

1. The liability of the Interstate Commission's executive director and employees or Interstate Commission representatives, acting within the scope of such person's employment or duties for acts, errors, or omissions occurring within such person's state may not exceed the limits of liability set forth under the Constitution and laws of that state for state officials, employees, and agents. The Interstate Commission is considered to be an instrumentality of the states for the purposes of any such action. Nothing in this subsection shall be construed to protect such person from suit or liability for damage, loss, injury, or liability caused by the intentional or willful and wanton misconduct of such person.

2. The Interstate Commission shall defend the executive director and its employees and, subject to the approval of the Attorney General or other appropriate legal counsel of the member state represented by an Interstate Commission representative, shall defend such Interstate Commission representative in any civil action seeking to impose liability arising out of an actual or alleged act, error or omission that occurred within the scope of Interstate Commission employment, duties or responsibilities, or that the defendant had a reasonable basis for believing occurred within the scope of

Interstate Commission employment, duties, or responsibilities, provided that the actual or alleged act, error, or omission did not result from intentional or willful and wanton misconduct on the part of such person.

3. To the extent not covered by the state involved, member state, or the Interstate Commission, the representatives or employees of the Interstate Commission shall be held harmless in the amount of a settlement or judgment, including attorney's fees and costs, obtained against such persons arising out of an actual or alleged act, error, or omission that occurred within the scope of Interstate Commission employment, duties, or responsibilities, or that such persons had a reasonable basis for believing occurred within the scope of Interstate Commission employment, duties, or responsibilities, provided that the actual or alleged act, error, or omission did not result from intentional or willful and wanton misconduct on the part of such persons.

ARTICLE XII.

RULEMAKING FUNCTIONS OF THE INTERSTATE COMMISSION

A. Rulemaking Authority - The Interstate Commission shall promulgate reasonable rules in order to effectively and efficiently achieve the purposes of this Compact. Notwithstanding the foregoing, in the event the Interstate Commission exercises its rulemaking authority in a manner that is beyond the scope of the purposes of this Act, or the powers granted hereunder, then such an action by the Interstate Commission shall be invalid and have no force or effect.

B. Rulemaking Procedure - Rules shall be made pursuant to a rulemaking process that substantially conforms to the "Model State Administrative Procedure Act," of 1981 Act, Uniform Laws Annotated, Vol. 15, p.1 (2000) as amended, as may be appropriate to the operations of the Interstate Commission.

C. Not later than thirty (30) days after a rule is promulgated, any person may file a petition for judicial review of the rule; provided, that the filing of such a petition shall not stay or otherwise prevent the rule from becoming effective unless the court finds that the petitioner has a substantial likelihood of success. The court shall give deference to the actions of the Interstate Commission consistent with applicable law and shall not find the rule to be unlawful if the rule represents a reasonable exercise of the Interstate Commission's authority.

D. If a majority of the legislatures of the compacting states rejects a Rule by enactment of a statute or resolution in the same manner used to adopt the compact, then such rule shall have no further force and effect in any compacting state.

ARTICLE XIII.

OVERSIGHT, ENFORCEMENT, AND DISPUTE RESOLUTION

A. Oversight

1. The executive, legislative and judicial branches of state government in each member state shall enforce this compact and shall take all actions necessary and appropriate to effectuate the compact's purposes and intent. The provisions of this compact and the rules promulgated hereunder shall have standing as rules promulgated under the Administrative Procedures Act as found in Chapter 150B of the North Carolina General Statutes.

2. All courts shall take judicial notice of the compact and the rules in any judicial or administrative proceeding in a member state pertaining to the subject matter of this compact which may affect the powers, responsibilities or actions of the Interstate Commission.

3. The Interstate Commission shall be entitled to receive all service of process in any such proceeding, and shall have standing to intervene in the proceeding for all purposes. Failure to provide service of process to the Interstate Commission shall render a judgment or order void as to the Interstate Commission, this compact or promulgated rules.

B. Default, Technical Assistance, Suspension and Termination - If the Interstate Commission determines that a member state has defaulted in the performance of its obligations or responsibilities under this compact, or the bylaws or promulgated rules, the Interstate Commission shall:

1. Provide written notice to the defaulting state and other member states, of the nature of the default, the means of curing the default and any action taken by the Interstate Commission. The Interstate Commission shall specify the conditions by which the defaulting state must cure its default.

2. Provide remedial training and specific technical assistance regarding the default.

3. If the defaulting state fails to cure the default, the defaulting state shall be terminated from the compact upon an affirmative vote of a majority of the member states and all rights, privileges and benefits conferred by this compact shall be terminated from the effective date of termination. A cure of the default does not relieve the offending state of obligations or liabilities incurred during the period of the default.

4. Suspension or termination of membership in the compact shall be imposed only after all other means of securing compliance have been exhausted. Notice of intent to suspend or terminate shall be given by the Interstate Commission to the Governor, the majority and minority leaders of the defaulting state's legislature, and each of the member states.

5. The state which has been suspended or terminated is responsible for all assessments, obligations and liabilities incurred through the effective date of suspension or termination including obligations, the performance of which extends beyond the effective date of suspension or termination.

6. The Interstate Commission shall not bear any costs relating to any state that has been found to be in default or which has been suspended or terminated from the compact, unless otherwise mutually agreed upon in writing between the Interstate Commission and the defaulting state.

7. The defaulting state may appeal the action of the Interstate Commission by petitioning the U.S. District Court for the District of Columbia or the federal district where the Interstate Commission has its principal offices. The prevailing party shall be awarded all costs of such litigation including reasonable attorney's fees.

C. Dispute Resolution

1. The Interstate Commission shall attempt, upon the request of a member state, to resolve disputes which are subject to the compact and which may arise among member states and between member and non-member states.

2. The Interstate Commission shall promulgate a rule providing for both mediation and binding dispute resolution for disputes as appropriate.

D. Enforcement

1. The Interstate Commission, in the reasonable exercise of its discretion, shall enforce the provisions and rules of this compact.

2. The Interstate Commission, may by majority vote of the members, initiate legal action in the United States District Court for the District of Columbia or, at the discretion of the Interstate Commission, in the federal district where the Interstate Commission has its principal offices, to enforce compliance with the provisions of the compact, its promulgated rules and bylaws, against a member state in default. The relief sought may include both injunctive relief and damages. In the event judicial enforcement is necessary the prevailing party shall be awarded all costs of such litigation including reasonable attorney's fees.

3. The remedies herein shall not be the exclusive remedies of the Interstate Commission. The Interstate Commission may avail itself of any other remedies available under state law or the regulation of a profession.

ARTICLE XIV.

FINANCING OF THE INTERSTATE COMMISSION

A. The Interstate Commission shall pay, or provide for the payment of the reasonable expenses of its establishment, organization and ongoing activities.

B. The Interstate Commission may levy on and collect an annual assessment from each member state to cover the cost of the operations and activities of the Interstate Commission and its staff which must be in a total amount sufficient to cover the Interstate Commission's annual budget as approved each year. The aggregate annual assessment amount shall be allocated based upon a formula to be determined by the Interstate Commission, which shall promulgate a rule binding upon all member states.

C. The Interstate Commission shall not incur obligations of any kind prior to securing the funds adequate to meet the same; nor shall the Interstate Commission pledge the credit of any of the member states, except by and with the authority of the member state.

D. The Interstate Commission shall keep accurate accounts of all receipts and disbursements. The receipts and disbursements of the Interstate Commission shall be subject to the audit and accounting procedures established under its bylaws. However, all receipts and disbursements of funds handled by the Interstate Commission shall be audited yearly by a certified or licensed public accountant and the report of the audit shall be included in and become part of the annual report of the Interstate Commission.

ARTICLE XV.

MEMBER STATES, EFFECTIVE DATE AND AMENDMENT

A. Any state is eligible to become a member state.

B. The compact shall become effective and binding upon legislative enactment of the compact into law by no less than ten (10) of the states. The effective date shall be no earlier than December 1, 2007. Thereafter it shall become effective and binding as to any other member state upon enactment of the compact into law by that state. The governors of non-member states or their designees shall be invited to participate in the activities of the Interstate Commission on a nonvoting basis prior to adoption of the compact by all states.

C. The Interstate Commission may propose amendments to the compact for enactment by the member states. No amendment shall become effective and binding upon the Interstate Commission and the member states unless and until it is enacted into law by unanimous consent of the member states.

ARTICLE XVI.

WITHDRAWAL AND DISSOLUTION

A. Withdrawal

1. Once effective, the compact shall continue in force and remain binding upon each and every member state; provided that a member state may withdraw from the compact by specifically repealing the statute, which enacted the compact into law.

2. Withdrawal from this compact shall be by the enactment of a statute repealing the same, but shall not take effect until one (1) year after the effective date of such statute and until written notice of the withdrawal has been given by the withdrawing state to the Governor of each other member jurisdiction.

3. The withdrawing state shall immediately notify the chairperson of the Interstate Commission in writing upon the introduction of legislation repealing this compact in the withdrawing state. The Interstate Commission shall notify the

other member states of the withdrawing state's intent to withdraw within sixty (60) days of its receipt thereof.

4. The withdrawing state is responsible for all assessments, obligations and liabilities incurred through the effective date of withdrawal, including obligations, the performance of which extend beyond the effective date of withdrawal.

5. Reinstatement following withdrawal of a member state shall occur upon the withdrawing state reenacting the compact or upon such later date as determined by the Interstate Commission.

B. Dissolution of Compact

1. This compact shall dissolve effective upon the date of the withdrawal or default of the member state which reduces the membership in the compact to one (1) member state.

2. Upon the dissolution of this compact, the compact becomes null and void and shall be of no further force or effect, and the business and affairs of the Interstate Commission shall be concluded and surplus funds shall be distributed in accordance with the bylaws.

ARTICLE XVII.

SEVERABILITY AND CONSTRUCTION

A. The provisions of this compact shall be severable, and if any phrase, clause, sentence or provision is deemed unenforceable, the remaining provisions of the compact shall be enforceable.

B. The provisions of this compact shall be liberally construed to effectuate its purposes.

C. Nothing in this compact shall be construed to prohibit the applicability of other interstate compacts to which the states are members.

ARTICLE XVIII.

BINDING EFFECT OF COMPACT AND OTHER LAWS

A. Other Laws

1. Nothing herein prevents the enforcement of any other law of a member state that is not inconsistent with this compact.

2. All member states' laws conflicting with this compact are superseded to the extent of the conflict.

B. Binding Effect of the Compact

1. All lawful actions of the Interstate Commission, including all rules and bylaws promulgated by the Interstate Commission, are binding upon the member states.

2. All agreements between the Interstate Commission and the member states are binding in accordance with their terms.

3. In the event any provision of this compact exceeds the constitutional limits imposed on the legislature of any member state, such provision shall be ineffective to the extent of the conflict with the constitutional provision in question in that member state. (2008-185, s. 1; 2009-281, s. 1.)

§ 115C-407.6. Creation of a State Council.

The State Board of Education shall establish a State Council, as required by Article VIII of the compact. The membership of the State Council shall include, at a minimum, the Superintendent of Public Instruction, a superintendent of a local school administrative unit with a high concentration of military children, a representative from a military installation, a representative of the executive branch of government, a representative of the North Carolina School Boards Association, a representative of the North Carolina Association of School Administrators, a member appointed by the General Assembly upon the recommendation of the President Pro Tempore of the Senate, and a member appointed by the General Assembly upon the recommendation of the Speaker of the House of Representatives. (2008-185, s. 1.)

§ 115C-407.7. Appointment of compact commissioner.

As required by Article VIII of the compact, the Governor shall appoint as compact commissioner a licensed North Carolina attorney who represents at least one local board of education, with preference given to an attorney representing a local board of education with a high concentration of military children or an attorney familiar with military issues. The compact commissioner shall be responsible for the administration and management of the State's participation in the compact. (2008-185, s. 1.)

§ 115C-407.8. Effective date of compact.

This Article becomes effective July 1, 2008, or upon enactment of the compact into law by nine other states, whichever date occurs later. (2008-185, s. 1.)

§ 115C-407.9: Reserved for future codification purposes.

§ 115C-407.10: Reserved for future codification purposes.

§ 115C-407.11: Reserved for future codification purposes.

§ 115C-407.12: Reserved for future codification purposes.

§ 115C-407.13: Reserved for future codification purposes.

§ 115C-407.14: Reserved for future codification purposes.

Article 29C.

School Violence Prevention.

§ 115C-407.15. Bullying and harassing behavior.

(a) As used in this Article, "bullying or harassing behavior" is any pattern of gestures or written, electronic, or verbal communications, or any physical act or any threatening communication, that takes place on school property, at any school-sponsored function, or on a school bus, and that:

(1) Places a student or school employee in actual and reasonable fear of harm to his or her person or damage to his or her property; or

(2) Creates or is certain to create a hostile environment by substantially interfering with or impairing a student's educational performance, opportunities, or benefits. For purposes of this section, "hostile environment" means that the victim subjectively views the conduct as bullying or harassing behavior and the conduct is objectively severe or pervasive enough that a reasonable person would agree that it is bullying or harassing behavior.

Bullying or harassing behavior includes, but is not limited to, acts reasonably perceived as being motivated by any actual or perceived differentiating characteristic, such as race, color, religion, ancestry, national origin, gender, socioeconomic status, academic status, gender identity, physical appearance, sexual orientation, or mental, physical, developmental, or sensory disability, or by association with a person who has or is perceived to have one or more of these characteristics.

(b) No student or school employee shall be subjected to bullying or harassing behavior by school employees or students.

(c) No person shall engage in any act of reprisal or retaliation against a victim, witness, or a person with reliable information about an act of bullying or harassing behavior.

(d) A school employee who has witnessed or has reliable information that a student or school employee has been subject to any act of bullying or harassing behavior shall report the incident to the appropriate school official.

(e) A student or volunteer who has witnessed or has reliable information that a student or school employee has been subject to any act of bullying or harassing behavior should report the incident to the appropriate school official. (2009-212, s. 1; 2009-570, s. 39.)

§ 115C-407.16. Policy against bullying or harassing behavior.

(a) Before December 31, 2009, each local school administrative unit shall adopt a policy prohibiting bullying or harassing behavior.

(b) The policy shall contain, at a minimum, the following components:

(1) A statement prohibiting bullying or harassing behavior.

(2) A definition of bullying or harassing behavior no less inclusive than that set forth in this Article.

(3) A description of the type of behavior expected for each student and school employee.

(4) Consequences and appropriate remedial action for a person who commits an act of bullying or harassment.

(5) A procedure for reporting an act of bullying or harassment, including a provision that permits a person to report such an act anonymously. This shall not be construed to permit formal disciplinary action solely on the basis of an anonymous report.

(6) A procedure for prompt investigation of reports of serious violations and complaints of any act of bullying or harassment, identifying either the principal or the principal's designee as the person responsible for the investigation.

(7) A statement that prohibits reprisal or retaliation against any person who reports an act of bullying or harassment, and the consequence and appropriate remedial action for a person who engages in reprisal or retaliation.

(8) A statement of how the policy is to be disseminated and publicized, including notice that the policy applies to participation in school-sponsored functions.

(c) Nothing in this Article shall prohibit a local school administrative unit from adopting a policy that includes components beyond the minimum components provided in this section or that is more inclusive than the requirements of this Article.

(d) Notice of the local policy shall appear in any school unit publication that sets forth the comprehensive rules, procedures, and standards of conduct for schools within the school unit and in any student and school employee handbook.

(e) Information regarding the local policy against bullying or harassing behavior shall be incorporated into a school's employee training program.

(f) To the extent funds are appropriated for these purposes, a local school administrative unit shall, by March 1, 2010, provide training on the local policy to school employees and volunteers who have significant contact with students. (2009-212, s. 1; 2009-570, s. 39.)

§ 115C-407.17. Prevention of school violence.

Schools shall develop and implement methods and strategies for promoting school environments that are free of bullying or harassing behavior. (2009-212, s. 1; 2009-570, s. 39.)

§ 115C-407.18. Construction of this Article.

(a) This Article shall not be construed to permit school officials to punish student expression or speech based on an undifferentiated fear or apprehension of disturbance or out of a desire to avoid the discomfort and unpleasantness that always accompany an unpopular viewpoint.

(b) This Article shall not be interpreted to prevent a victim of bullying or harassing behavior from seeking redress under any other available law, either civil or criminal.

(c) Nothing in this Article shall be construed to require an exhaustion of the administrative complaint process before civil or criminal law remedies may be pursued regarding bullying or harassing behavior.

(d) The provisions of this Article are severable, and if any provision of this Article is held invalid by a court of competent jurisdiction, the invalidity shall not affect other provisions of this Article which can be given effect without the invalid provision.

(e) The provisions of this Article shall be liberally construed to give effect to its purposes.

(f) Nothing in this act shall be construed to create any classification, protected class, suspect category, or preference beyond those existing in present statute or case law. (2009-212, s. 1; 2009-570, s. 39.)

Subchapter VII. Fiscal Affairs.

Article 30

Financial Powers of the State Board of Education.

§ 115C-408. Funds under control of the State Board of Education.

(a) It is the policy of the State of North Carolina to create a public school system that graduates good citizens with the skills demanded in the marketplace, and the skills necessary to cope with contemporary society, using State, local and other funds in the most cost-effective manner. The Board shall have general supervision and administration of the educational funds provided by the State and federal governments, except those mentioned in Section 7 of Article IX of the State Constitution, and also excepting such local funds as may be provided by a county, city, or district.

(b) To insure a quality education for every child in North Carolina, and to assure that the necessary resources are provided, it is the policy of the State of North Carolina to provide from State revenue sources the instructional expenses for current operations of the public school system as defined in the standard course of study.

It is the policy of the State of North Carolina that the facilities requirements for a public education system will be met by county governments.

It is the intent of the 1983 General Assembly to further clarify and delineate the specific financial responsibilities for the public schools to be borne by State and local governments. (1955, c. 1372, art. 2, s. 2; 1957, c. 541, s. 11; 1961, c. 969; 1963, c. 448, ss. 24, 27; c. 688, ss. 1, 2; c. 1223, s. 1; 1965, c. 1185, s. 2; 1967, c. 643, s. 1; 1969, c. 517, s. 1; 1971, c. 704, s. 4; c. 745; 1973, c. 476, s. 138; c. 675; 1975, c. 699, s. 2; c. 975; 1979, c. 300, s. 1; c. 935; 1981, c. 423, s. 1; 1983 (Reg. Sess., 1984), c. 1103, s. 12.)

§ 115C-409. Power to accept federal funds and aid.

(a) The Board is authorized to accept, receive, use or reallocate to local school administrative units any federal funds, or aids, that may be appropriated now or hereafter by the federal government for the encouragement and improvement of any phase of the free public school program which, in the judgment of the Board, will be beneficial to the operation of the schools. However, the Board is not authorized to accept any such funds upon any condition that the public schools of this State shall be operated contrary to any provisions of the Constitution or statutes of this State.

(b) The State Board of Education or any other State agency designated by the Governor shall have the power and authority to provide library resources, textbooks, and other instructional materials purchased from federal funds appropriated for the funding of the Elementary and Secondary Education Act of 1965 (Public Law 89-10, 89th Congress, HR 2362, effective April 11, 1965) or other acts of Congress for the use of children and teachers in private elementary and secondary schools in the State as required by acts of Congress and rules and regulations promulgated thereunder. (1955, c. 1372, art. 2, s. 2; 1957, c. 541, s. 11; 1961, c. 969; 1963, c. 448, ss. 24, 27; c. 688, ss. 1, 2; c. 1223, s. 1; 1965, c. 1185, s. 2; 1967, c. 643, s. 1; 1969, c. 517, s. 1; 1971, c. 704, s. 4; c. 745; 1973, c. 476, s. 138; c. 675; 1975, c. 699, s. 2; c. 975; 1979, c. 300, s. 1; c. 935; 1981, c. 423, s. 1.)

§ 115C-410. Power to accept gifts and grants.

The Board is authorized to accept, receive, use, or reallocate to local school administrative units any gifts, donations, grants, devises, or other forms of voluntary contributions. (1955, c. 1372, art. 2, s. 2; 1957, c. 541, s. 11; 1961, c. 969; 1963, c. 448, ss. 24, 27; c. 688, ss. 1, 2; c. 1223, s. 1; 1965, c. 1185, s. 2; 1967, c. 643, s. 1; 1969, c. 517, s. 1; 1971, c. 704, s. 4; c. 745; 1973, c. 476, s. 138; c. 675; 1975, c. 699, s. 2; c. 975; 1979, c. 300, s. 1; c. 935; 1981, c. 423, s. 1; 2011-284, s. 76.)

§ 115C-411. Authority to invest school funds.

The Board is authorized to direct the State Treasurer to invest in interest-bearing securities any funds which may come into its possession, and which it deems expedient to invest, as other funds of the State are now or may be hereafter invested. (1955, c. 1372, art. 2, s. 2; 1957, c. 541, s. 11; 1961, c. 969; 1963, c. 448, ss. 24, 27; c. 688, ss. 1, 2; c. 1223, s. 1; 1965, c. 1185, s. 2; 1967, c. 643, s. 1; 1969, c. 517, s. 1; 1971, c. 704, s. 4; c. 745; 1973, c. 476, s. 138; c. 675; 1975, c. 699, s. 2; c. 975; 1979, c. 300, s. 1; c. 935; 1981, c. 423, s. 1.)

§ 115C-412. Power to purchase at mortgage sales.

The State Board of Education is authorized to purchase at public sale any land upon which it has a mortgage or deed of trust securing the purchase price, or any part thereof, and when any land so sold and purchased by the said Board of Education is a part of a drainage district theretofore constituted, upon which said land assessments have been levied for the maintenance thereof, such assessments shall be paid by the said State Board of Education, as if said land had been purchased or owned by an individual. (1955, c. 1372, art. 2, s. 2; 1957, c. 541, s. 11; 1961, c. 969; 1963, c. 448, ss. 24, 27; c. 688, ss. 1, 2; c. 1223, s. 1; 1965, c. 1185, s. 2; 1967, c. 643, s. 1; 1969, c. 517, s. 1; 1971, c. 704, s. 4; c. 745; 1973, c. 476, s. 138; c. 675; 1975, c. 699, s. 2; c. 975; 1979, c. 300, s. 1; c. 935; 1981, c. 423, s. 1.)

§ 115C-413. Power to adjust debts.

The State Board of Education is hereby authorized and empowered to settle, compromise or otherwise adjust any indebtedness due it upon the purchase price of any land or property sold by it, or to cancel and surrender the notes, mortgages, trust deeds, or other evidence of indebtedness without payment, when, in the discretion of said Board, it appears that it is proper to do so. The Board of Education is further authorized and empowered to sell or otherwise dispose of any such notes, mortgages, trust deeds, or other evidence of indebtedness. (1955, c. 1372, art. 2, s. 2; 1957, c. 541, s. 11; 1961, c. 969; 1963, c. 448, ss. 24, 27; c. 688, ss. 1, 2; c. 1223, s. 1; 1965, c. 1185, s. 2; 1967, c. 643, s. 1; 1969, c. 517, s. 1; 1971, c. 704, s. 4; c. 745; 1973, c. 476, s. 138; c. 675; 1975, c. 699, s. 2; c. 975; 1979, c. 300, s 1; c. 935; 1981, c. 423, s. 1.)

§ 115C-414. State Board as successor to powers of abolished commissions and boards.

The Board shall succeed to all the powers and trusts of the president and directors of the Literary Fund of North Carolina; and to all the powers, functions, duties, and property of all abolished commissions and boards including the State School Commission, the State Textbook Commission, the Department of Health and Human Services, and the State Board of Commercial Education, including the power to take, hold and convey property, both real and personal, to the same extent that any corporation might take, hold and convey the same under the laws of this State. (1955, c. 1372, art. 2, s. 2; 1957, c. 541, s. 11; 1961, c. 969; 1963, c. 448, ss. 24, 27; c. 688, ss. 1, 2; c. 1223, s. 1; 1965, c. 1185, s. 2; 1967, c. 643, s. 1; 1969, c. 517, s. 1; 1971, c. 704, s. 4; c. 745; 1973, c. 476, s. 138; c. 675; 1975, c. 699, s. 2; c. 975; 1979, c. 300, s. 1; c. 935; 1981, c. 423, s. 1; 1997-443, s. 11A.122.)

§ 115C-415: Repealed by Session Laws 1997-18, s. 15(l).

§ 115C-416. Power to allot funds for teachers and other personnel.

The Board shall have power to provide for the enrichment and strengthening of educational opportunities for the children of the State, and when sufficient State funds are available to provide first for the allotment of such a number of teachers as to prevent the teacher loan from being too great in any school, the Board is authorized, in its discretion, to make an additional allotment of teaching personnel to local school administrative units of the State to be used either jointly or separately, as the Board may prescribe. Such additional teaching personnel may be used in the local school administrative units as librarians, special teachers, or supervisors of instruction and for other special instructional services such as art, music, physical education, adult education, special education, or industrial arts as may be authorized and approved by the Board. The salary of all such personnel shall be determined in accordance with the State salary schedule adopted by the Board.

In addition, the Board is authorized and empowered in its discretion, to make allotments of funds for clerical assistants for classified principals and for school social workers.

The Board is further authorized, in its discretion, to allot teaching personnel to local school administrative units for experimental programs and purposes.

The Board may also allot teaching and other positions, within funds available, to local school administrative units to allow local units to place personnel occupying those positions in private hospitals and treatment facilities for the limited purpose of providing education to students confined to those institutions. The Board shall adopt rules to ensure that any such placements do not contribute to the profitability of private institutions and that they are otherwise in accordance with State and federal law. (1955, c. 1372, art. 2, s. 2; 1957, c. 541,

s. 11; 1961, c. 969; 1963, c. 448, ss. 24, 27; c. 688, ss. 1, 2; c. 1223, s. 1; 1965, c. 1185, s. 2; 1967, c. 643, s. 1; 1969, c. 517, s. 1; 1971, c. 704, s. 4; c. 745; 1973, c. 476, s. 138; c. 675; 1975, c. 699, s. 2; c. 975; 1979, c. 300, s. 1; c. 935; 1981, c. 423, s. 1; 1985, c. 686, s. 1; 1989 (Reg. Sess., 1990), c. 1066, s. 92.)

§ 115C-417. Availability of funds allocated for staff development.

Funds allocated by the State Board of Education for staff development at the local level shall become available for expenditure on July 1 of each fiscal year and shall remain available for expenditure until December 31 of the subsequent fiscal year. (1991 (Reg. Sess., 1992), c. 900, s. 63(c); 1997-443, s. 8.21.)

§ 115C-418: Repealed by Session Laws 1995, c. 450, s. 23.

§§ 115C-419 through 115C-421. Reserved for future codification purposes.

Article 31.

The School Budget and Fiscal Control Act.

Part 1. General Provisions.

§ 115C-422. Short title.

This Article may be cited as "The School Budget and Fiscal Control Act." (1975, c. 437, s. 1; 1981, c. 423, s. 1.)

§ 115C-423. Definitions.

The words and phrases defined in this section have the meanings indicated when used in this Article, unless the context clearly requires another meaning:

(1) "Budget" is a plan proposed by a board of education for raising and spending money for specified school programs, functions, activities, or objectives during a fiscal year.

(2) "Budget resolution" is a resolution adopted by a board of education that appropriates revenues for specified school programs, functions, activities, or objectives during a fiscal year.

(3) "Budget year" is the fiscal year for which a budget is proposed and a budget resolution is adopted.

(4) "Fiscal year" is the annual period for the compilation of fiscal operations. The fiscal year begins on July 1 and ends on June 30.

(5) "Fund" is an independent fiscal and accounting entity consisting of cash and other resources together with all related liabilities, obligations, reserves, and equities which are segregated by appropriate accounting techniques for the purpose of carrying on specific activities or attaining certain objectives in accordance with established legal regulations, restrictions or limitations.

(6) "Vending facilities" has the same meaning as it does in G.S. 111-42(d), but also means any mechanical or electronic device dispensing items or something of value or entertainment or services for a fee, regardless of the method of activation, and regardless of the means of payment, whether by coin, currency, tokens, or other means. (1975, c. 437, s. 1; 1981, c. 423, s. 1; 1983 (Reg. Sess., 1984), c. 1034, s. 167; 2006-203, s. 34.)

§ 115C-424. Uniform system; conflicting laws and local acts superseded.

It is the intent of the General Assembly by enactment of this Article to prescribe for the public schools a uniform system of budgeting and fiscal control. To this end, all provisions of general laws and local acts in effect as of July 1, 1976, and in conflict with the provisions of this Article are repealed except local acts providing for the levy or for the levy and collection of school supplemental taxes. No local act enacted or taking effect after July 1, 1976, may be construed to modify, amend, or repeal any portion of this Article unless it expressly so provides by specific reference to the appropriate section. (1975, c. 437, s. 1; 1981, c. 423, s. 1.)

Part 2. Budget.

§ 115C-425. Annual balanced budget resolution.

(a) Each local school administrative unit shall operate under an annual balanced budget resolution adopted and administered in accordance with this Article. A budget resolution is balanced when the sum of estimated net revenues and appropriated fund balances is equal to appropriations. Appropriated fund balance in any fund shall not exceed the sum of cash and investments minus the sum of liabilities, encumbrances, and deferred revenues arising from cash receipts, as those figures stand at the close of the fiscal year next preceding the budget year. The budget resolution shall cover one fiscal year.

(b) It is the intent of this Article that all moneys received and expended by a local school administrative unit should be included in the school budget resolution. Therefore, notwithstanding any other provisions of law, after July 1, 1976, no local school administrative unit may expend any moneys, regardless of their source (including moneys derived from federal, State, or private sources), except in accordance with a budget resolution adopted pursuant to this Article.

(c) Subsection (b) of this section does not apply to funds of individual schools, as defined in G.S. 115C-448. (1975, c. 437, s. 1; 1981, c. 423, s. 1; 1993, c. 179, s. 1.)

§ 115C-426. Uniform budget format.

(a) The State Board of Education, in cooperation with the Local Government Commission, shall cause to be prepared and promulgated a standard budget format for use by local school administrative units throughout the State.

(b) The uniform budget format shall be organized so as to facilitate accomplishment of the following objectives: (i) to enable the board of education and the board of county commissioners to make the local educational and local fiscal policies embodied therein; (ii) to control and facilitate the fiscal management of the local school administrative unit during the fiscal year; and (iii) to facilitate the gathering of accurate and reliable fiscal data on the operation of the public school system throughout the State.

(c) The uniform budget format shall require the following funds:

(1) The State Public School Fund.

(2) The local current expense fund.

(3) The capital outlay fund.

In addition, other funds may be used to account for reimbursements, including indirect costs, fees for actual costs, tuition, sales tax revenues distributed using the ad valorem method pursuant to G.S. 105-472(b)(2), sales tax refunds, gifts and grants restricted as to use, trust funds, federal appropriations made directly to local school administrative units, and funds received for prekindergarten programs. In addition, the appropriation or use of fund balance or interest income by a local school administrative unit shall not be construed as a local current expense appropriation included as a part of the local current expense fund.

Each local school administrative unit shall maintain those funds shown in the uniform budget format that are applicable to its operations.

(d) The State Public School Fund shall include appropriations for the current operating expenses of the public school system from moneys made available to the local school administrative unit by the State Board of Education.

(e) The local current expense fund shall include appropriations sufficient, when added to appropriations from the State Public School Fund, for the current operating expense of the public school system in conformity with the educational goals and policies of the State and the local board of education, within the financial resources and consistent with the fiscal policies of the board of county commissioners. These appropriations shall be funded by revenues accruing to the local school administrative unit by virtue of Article IX, Sec. 7 of the Constitution, moneys made available to the local school administrative unit by the board of county commissioners, supplemental taxes levied by or on behalf of the local school administrative unit pursuant to a local act or G.S. 115C-501 to 115C-511, State money disbursed directly to the local school administrative unit, and other moneys made available or accruing to the local school administrative unit for the current operating expenses of the public school system.

(f) The capital outlay fund shall include appropriations for:

(1) The acquisition of real property for school purposes, including but not limited to school sites, playgrounds, athletic fields, administrative headquarters, and garages.

(2) The acquisition, construction, reconstruction, enlargement, renovation, or replacement of buildings and other structures, including but not limited to buildings for classrooms and laboratories, physical and vocational educational purposes, libraries, auditoriums, gymnasiums, administrative offices, storage, and vehicle maintenance.

(3) The acquisition or replacement of furniture and furnishings, instructional apparatus, data-processing equipment, business machines, and similar items of furnishings and equipment.

(4) The acquisition of school buses as additions to the fleet.

(5) The acquisition of activity buses and other motor vehicles.

(6) Such other objects of expenditure as may be assigned to the capital outlay fund by the uniform budget format.

The cost of acquiring or constructing a new building, or reconstructing, enlarging, or renovating an existing building, shall include the cost of all real property and interests in real property, and all plants, works, appurtenances, structures, facilities, furnishings, machinery, and equipment necessary or useful in connection therewith; financing charges; the cost of plans, specifications, studies, reports, and surveys; legal expenses; and all other costs necessary or incidental to the construction, reconstruction, enlargement, or renovation.

No contract for the purchase of a site shall be executed nor any funds expended therefor without the approval of the board of county commissioners as to the amount to be spent for the site; and in case of a disagreement between a board of education and a board of county commissioners as to the amount to be spent for the site, the procedure provided in G.S. 115C-431 shall, insofar as the same may be applicable, be used to settle the disagreement.

Appropriations in the capital outlay fund shall be funded by revenues made available for capital outlay purposes by the State Board of Education and the board of county commissioners, supplemental taxes levied by or on behalf of the local school administrative unit pursuant to a local act or G.S. 115C-501 to

115C-511, the proceeds of the sale of capital assets, the proceeds of claims against fire and casualty insurance policies, and other sources.

(g)   Other funds shall include appropriations for such purposes funded from such sources as may be prescribed by the uniform budget format. (1975, c. 437, s. 1; 1981, c. 423, s. 1; 2010-31, s. 7.17(a); 2013-355, s. 2(a).)

§ 115C-426.1. Vending facilities.

Moneys received by a local school administrative unit on account of operation of vending facilities shall be deposited, budgeted, appropriated, and expended in accordance with the provisions of this Article. (1983 (Reg. Sess., 1984), c. 1034, s. 168.)

§ 115C-426.2. Joint planning.

In order to promote greater mutual understanding of immediate and long-term budgetary issues and constraints affecting public schools and county governments, local boards of education and boards of county commissioners are strongly encouraged to conduct periodic joint meetings during each fiscal year. In particular, the boards are encouraged to assess the school capital outlay needs, to develop and update a joint five-year plan for meeting those needs, and to consider this plan in the preparation and approval of each year's budget under this Article. (1995 (Reg. Sess., 1996), c. 666, s. 2.)

§ 115C-427. Preparation and submission of budget and budget message.

(a)   Before the close of each fiscal year, the superintendent shall prepare a budget for the ensuing year for consideration by the board of education. The budget shall comply in all respects with the limitations imposed by G.S. 115C-432.

(b)   The budget, together with a budget message, shall be submitted to the board of education not later than May 1. The budget and budget message should, but need not, be submitted at a formal meeting of the board. The budget message should contain a concise explanation of the educational goals fixed by the budget for the budget year, should set forth the reasons for stated changes from the previous year in program goals, programs, and appropriation levels, and should explain any major changes in educational or fiscal policy. (1975, c. 437, s. 1; 1981, c. 423, s. 1.)

§ 115C-428. Filing and publication of the budget; budget hearing.

(a) On the same day that he submits the budget to the board of education, the superintendent shall file a copy of it in his office where it shall remain available for public inspection until the budget resolution is adopted. He may also publish a statement in a newspaper qualified under G.S. 1-597 to publish legal advertisements in the county that the budget has been submitted to the board of education, and is available for public inspection in the office of the superintendent of schools. The statement should also give notice of the time and place of the budget hearing authorized by subsection (b) of this section.

(b) Before submitting the budget to the board of county commissioners, the board of education may hold a public hearing at which time any persons who wish to be heard on the school budget may appear. (1975, c. 437, s. 1; 1981, c. 423, s. 1.)

§ 115C-429. Approval of budget; submission to county commissioners; commissioners' action on budget.

(a) Upon receiving the budget from the superintendent and following the public hearing authorized by G.S. 115C-428(b), if one is held, the board of education shall consider the budget, make such changes therein as it deems advisable, and submit the entire budget as approved by the board of education to the board of county commissioners not later than May 15, or such later date as may be fixed by the board of county commissioners.

(b) The board of county commissioners shall complete its action on the school budget on or before July 1, or such later date as may be agreeable to the board of education. The commissioners shall determine the amount of county revenues to be appropriated in the county budget ordinance to the local school administrative unit for the budget year. The board of county commissioners may, in its discretion, allocate part or all of its appropriation by purpose, function, or project as defined in the uniform budget format.

(c) The board of county commissioners shall have full authority to call for, and the board of education shall have the duty to make available to the board of county commissioners, upon request, all books, records, audit reports, and other information bearing on the financial operation of the local school administrative unit.

(d) Nothing in this Article shall be construed to place a duty on the board of commissioners to fund a deficit incurred by a local school administrative unit through failure of the unit to comply with the provisions of this Article or rules and regulations issued pursuant hereto, or to provide moneys lost through misapplication of moneys by a bonded officer, employee or agent of the local school administrative unit when the amount of the fidelity bond required by the board of education was manifestly insufficient. (1975, c. 437, s. 1; 1981, c. 423, s. 1.)

§ 115C-430. Apportionment of county appropriations among local school administrative units.

If there is more than one local school administrative unit in a county, all appropriations by the county to the local current expense funds of the units, except appropriations funded by supplemental taxes levied less than countywide pursuant to a local act of G.S. 115C-501 to 115C-511, must be apportioned according to the membership of each unit. County appropriations are properly apportioned when the dollar amount obtained by dividing the amount so appropriated to each unit by the total membership of the unit is the same for each unit. The total membership of the local school administrative unit is the unit's average daily membership for the budget year to be determined by and certified to the unit and the board of county commissioners by the State Board of Education. (1975, c. 437, s. 1; 1981, c. 423, s. 1; 1985 (Reg. Sess., 1986), c. 1014, s. 78.)

§ 115C-431. Procedure for resolution of dispute between board of education and board of county commissioners.

(a) If the board of education determines that the amount of money appropriated to the local current expense fund, or the capital outlay fund, or both, by the board of county commissioners is not sufficient to support a system of free public schools, the chairman of the board of education and the chairman of the board of county commissioners shall arrange a joint meeting of the two boards to be held within seven days after the day of the county commissioners' decision on the school appropriations.

Prior to the joint meeting, the Senior Resident Superior Court Judge shall appoint a mediator unless the boards agree to jointly select a mediator. The mediator shall preside at the joint meeting and shall act as a neutral facilitator of disclosures of factual information, statements of positions and contentions, and efforts to negotiate an agreement settling the boards' differences.

At the joint meeting, the entire school budget shall be considered carefully and judiciously, and the two boards shall make a good-faith attempt to resolve the differences that have arisen between them.

(b) If no agreement is reached at the joint meeting of the two boards, the mediator shall, at the request of either board, commence a mediation immediately or within a reasonable period of time. The mediation shall be held in accordance with rules and standards of conduct adopted under Chapter 7A of the General Statutes governing mediated settlement conferences but modified as appropriate and suitable to the resolution of the particular issues in disagreement.

Unless otherwise agreed upon by both boards, the following individuals shall constitute the two working groups empowered to represent their respective boards during the mediation:

(1) The chair of each board or the chair's designee;

(2) The superintendent of the local school administrative unit and the county manager or either's designee;

(3) The finance officer of each board; and

(4) The attorney for each board.

Members of both boards, their chairs, and representatives shall cooperate with and respond to all reasonable requests of the mediator to participate in the mediation. Notwithstanding Article 33C of Chapter 143 of the General Statutes, the mediation proceedings involving the two working groups shall be conducted in private. Evidence of statements made and conduct occurring in a mediation are not subject to discovery and are inadmissible in any court action. However, no evidence otherwise discoverable is inadmissible merely because it is presented or discussed in a mediation. The mediator shall not be compelled to testify or produce evidence concerning statements made and conduct occurring in a mediation in any civil proceeding for any purpose, except disciplinary hearings before the State Bar or any agency established to enforce standards of conduct for mediators. Reports by members of either working group to their respective boards shall be made in compliance with Article 33C of Chapter 143 of the General Statutes.

Unless both boards agree otherwise, or unless the boards have already resolved their dispute, the mediation shall end no later than August 1. The mediator shall have the authority to determine that an impasse exists and to discontinue the mediation. The mediation may continue beyond August 1 provided both boards agree. If both boards agree to continue the mediation beyond August 1, the board of county commissioners shall appropriate to the local school administrative unit for deposit in the local current expense fund a sum of money sufficient to equal the local contribution to this fund for the previous year.

If the working groups reach a proposed agreement, the terms and conditions must be approved by each board. If no agreement is reached, the mediator shall announce that fact to the chairs of both boards, the Senior Resident Superior Court Judge, and the public. The mediator shall not disclose any other information about the mediation. The mediator shall not make any recommendations or public statement of findings or conclusions.

The local board of education and the board of county commissioners shall share equally the mediator's compensation and expenses. The mediator's compensation shall be determined according to rules adopted under Chapter 7A of the General Statutes.

(c) Within five days after an announcement of no agreement by the mediator, the local board of education may file an action in the superior court division of the General Court of Justice. Either board has the right to have the issues of fact tried by a jury. When a jury trial is demanded, the cause shall be set for the first succeeding term of the superior court in the county, and shall take precedence over all other business of the court. However, if the judge presiding certifies to the Chief Justice of the Supreme Court, either before or during the term, that because of the accumulation of other business, the public interest will be best served by not trying the cause at the term next succeeding the filing of the action, the Chief Justice shall immediately call a special term of the superior court for the county, to convene as soon as possible, and assign a judge of the superior court or an emergency judge to hold the court, and the cause shall be tried at this special term. The judge shall find, or if the issue is submitted to the jury, the jury shall find the facts as to the following in order to maintain a system of free public schools as defined by State law and State Board of Education policy: (i) the amount of money legally necessary from all sources and (ii) the amount of money legally necessary from the board of county commissioners. In making the finding, the judge or the jury shall consider the educational goals and policies of the State and the local board of education, the budgetary request of the local board of education, the financial resources of the county and the local board of education, and the fiscal policies of the board of county commissioners and the local board of education.

All findings of fact in the superior court, whether found by the judge or a jury, shall be conclusive. When the facts have been found, the court shall give judgment ordering the board of county commissioners to appropriate a sum certain to the local school administrative unit, and to levy such taxes on property as may be necessary to make up this sum when added to other revenues available for the purpose.

(d) An appeal may be taken to the appellate division of the General Court of Justice, and notice of appeal shall be given in writing within 10 days after entry of the judgment. All papers and records relating to the case shall be considered a part of the record on appeal. The conclusion of the school or fiscal year shall not be deemed to resolve the question in controversy between the parties while an appeal is still pending. Any final judgment shall be legally binding on the parties at the conclusion of the appellate process. The payment of any final judgment by the county in favor of the local school administrative unit shall not be considered, or used in any manner, to deny or reduce appropriations to the local school administrative unit by the county in fiscal years subsequent to the one at issue to offset such payment of a final judgment.

(e) If, in an action filed under this section, the final judgment of the General Court of Justice is rendered after the due date prescribed by law for property taxes, the board of county commissioners is authorized to levy such supplementary taxes as may be required by the judgment, notwithstanding any other provisions of law with respect to the time for doing acts necessary to a property tax levy. Upon making a supplementary levy under this subsection, the board of county commissioners shall designate the person who is to compute and prepare the supplementary tax receipts and records for all such taxes. Upon delivering the supplementary tax receipts to the tax collector, the board of county commissioners shall proceed as provided in G.S. 105-321.

The due date of supplementary taxes levied under this subsection is the date of the levy, and the taxes may be paid at par or face amount at any time before the one hundred and twentieth day after the due date. On or after the one hundred and twentieth day and before the one hundred and fiftieth day from the due date there shall be added to the taxes interest at the rate of two percent (2%). On or after the one hundred and fiftieth day from the due date, there shall be added to the taxes, in addition to the two percent (2%) provided above, interest at the rate of three-fourths of one percent (3/4 of 1%) per 30 days or fraction thereof until the taxes plus interest have been paid. No discounts for prepayment of supplementary taxes levied under this subsection shall be allowed. (1975, c. 437, s. 1; 1981, c. 423, s. 1; 1989, c. 493, s. 2; 1995 (Reg. Sess., 1996), c. 666, s. 3; 1997-222, s. 1; 2007-92, s. 1; 2013-141, s. 1.)

§ 115C-432. The budget resolution; adoption; limitations; tax levy; filing.

(a) After the board of county commissioners has made its appropriations to the local school administrative unit, or after the appeal procedure set out in G.S. 115C-431 has been concluded, the board of education shall adopt a budget resolution making appropriations for the budget year in such sums as the board may deem sufficient and proper. The budget resolution shall conform to the uniform budget format established by the State Board of Education.

(b) The following directions and limitations shall bind the board of education in adopting the budget resolution:

(1) If the county budget ordinance allocates appropriations to the local school administrative unit pursuant to G.S. 115C-429(b), the school budget resolution shall conform to that allocation. The budget resolution may be amended to change allocated appropriations only in accordance with G.S. 115C-433.

(2) Subject to the provisions of G.S. 115C-429(d), the full amount of any lawful deficit from the prior fiscal year shall be appropriated.

(3) Contingency appropriations in a fund may not exceed five percent (5%) of the total of all other appropriations in that fund. Each expenditure to be charged against a contingency appropriation shall be authorized by resolution of the board of education, which resolution shall be deemed an amendment to the budget resolution, not subject to G.S. 115C-429(b) and 115C-433(b), setting up or increasing an appropriation for the object of expenditure authorized. The board of education may authorize the superintendent to authorize expenditures from contingency appropriations subject to such limitations and procedures as it may prescribe. Any such expenditure shall be reported to the board of education at its next regular meeting and recorded in the minutes.

(4) Sufficient funds to meet the amounts to be paid during the fiscal year under continuing contracts previously entered into shall be appropriated.

(5) The sum of estimated net revenues and appropriated fund balances in each fund shall be equal to appropriations in that fund.

(6) No appropriation may be made that would require the levy of supplemental taxes pursuant to a local act or G.S. 115C-501 to 115C-511 in excess of the rate of tax approved by the voters, or the expenditure of revenues for purposes not permitted by law.

(7) In estimating revenues to be realized from the levy of school supplemental taxes pursuant to a local act or G.S. 115C-501 to 115C-511, the estimated percentage of collection may not exceed the percentage of that tax actually realized in cash during the preceding fiscal year, or if the tax was not levied in the preceding fiscal year, the percentage of the general county tax levy actually realized in cash during the preceding fiscal year.

(8) Amounts to be realized from collection of supplemental taxes levied in prior fiscal years shall be included in estimated revenues.

(9) No appropriation may be made to or from the capital outlay fund to or from any other fund, except as permitted by G.S. 115C-433(d).

(c) If the local school administrative unit levies its own supplemental taxes pursuant to a local act, the budget resolution shall make the appropriate tax levy in accordance with the local act, and the board of education shall notify the county or city that collects the levy in accordance with G.S. 159-14.

(d) The budget resolution shall be entered in the minutes of the board of education, and within five days after adoption, copies thereof shall be filed with the superintendent, the school finance officer and the county finance officer. (1975, c. 437, s. 1; 1981, c. 423, s. 1; 1987 (Reg. Sess., 1988), c. 1025, s. 13; 1993, c. 57, s. 1.)

§ 115C-433. Amendments to the budget resolution; budget transfers.

(a) Subject to the provisions of subsection (b) of this section, the board of education may amend the budget resolution at any time after its adoption, in any manner, so long as the resolution as amended continues to satisfy the requirements of G.S. 115C-425 and 115C-432.

(b) If the board of county commissioners allocates part or all of its appropriations pursuant to G.S. 115C-429(b), the board of education must obtain the approval of the board of county commissioners for an amendment to the budget that (i) increases or decreases expenditures from the capital outlay fund for projects listed in G.S. 115C-426(f)(1) or (2), or (ii) increases or decreases the amount of county appropriation allocated to a purpose or function by twenty-five percent (25%) or more from the amount contained in the budget ordinance adopted by the board of county commissioners: Provided, that at its discretion, the board may in its budget ordinance specify a lesser percentage, so long as such percentage is not less than ten percent (10%).

(c) The board of education may by appropriate resolution authorize the superintendent to transfer moneys from one appropriation to another within the same fund, subject to such limitations and procedures as may be prescribed by the board of education or State or federal law or regulations. Any such transfers shall be reported to the board of education at its next regular meeting and shall be entered in the minutes.

(d) The board of education may amend the budget to transfer money to or from the capital outlay fund to or from any other fund, with the approval of the board of county commissioners, to meet emergencies unforeseen and unforeseeable at the time the budget resolution was adopted. When such an emergency arises, the board of education may adopt a resolution requesting approval from the board of commissioners for the transfer of a specified amount of money to or from the capital outlay fund to or from some other fund. The resolution shall state the nature of the emergency, why the emergency was not foreseen and was not foreseeable when the budget resolution was adopted, what specific objects of expenditure will be added or increased as a result of the transfer, and what objects of expenditure will be eliminated or reduced as a result of the transfer. A certified copy of this resolution shall be transmitted to the board of county commissioners for (its) approval and to the boards of education of all other local school administrative units in the county for their information. The board of commissioners shall act upon the request within 30 days after it is received by the clerk to the board of commissioners or the chairman of the board of commissioners, after having afforded the boards of education of all other local school administrative units in the county an opportunity to comment on the request. The board of commissioners may either approve or disapprove the request as presented. Upon either approving or disapproving the request, the board of commissioners shall forthwith so notify the board of education making the request and any other board of education that exercised its right to comment thereon. Upon receiving such notification, the board of education may proceed to amend the budget resolution in the manner indicated in the request. Failure of the board of county commissioners to act within the time allowed for approval or disapproval shall be deemed approval of the request. The time limit for action by the board of county commissioners may be extended by mutual agreement of the board of county commissioners and the board of education making the request. A budget resolution amended in accordance with this subsection need not comply with G.S. 115C-430. (1975, c. 437, s. 1; 1981, c. 423, s. 1.)

§ 115C-434. Interim budget.

In case the adoption of the budget resolution is delayed until after July 1, the board of education shall make interim appropriations for the purpose of paying salaries and the usual ordinary expenses of the local school administrative unit for the interval between the beginning of the fiscal year and the adoption of the budget resolution. Interim appropriations so made and expended shall be charged to the proper appropriations in the budget resolution. (1975, c. 437, s. 1; 1981, c. 423, s. 1.)

Part 3. Fiscal Control.

§ 115C-435. School finance officer.

Each local school administrative unit shall have a school finance officer who shall be appointed or designated by the superintendent of schools and approved by the board of education, with the school finance officer serving at the pleasure of the superintendent. The duties of school finance officer may be conferred on any officer or employee of the local school administrative unit or, upon request of the superintendent, with approval by the board of education and the board of county commissioners, on the county finance officer. In counties where there is more than one local school administrative unit, the duties of finance officer may be conferred on any one officer or employee of the several local school administrative units by agreement between the affected superintendents with the concurrence of the affected board of education and the board of county commissioners. The position of school finance officer is hereby declared to be an office that may be held concurrently with other appointive, but not elective, offices pursuant to Article VI, Sec. 9, of the Constitution. (1975, c. 437, s. 1; 1981, c. 423, s. 1.)

§ 115C-436. Duties of school finance officer.

(a) The school finance officer shall be responsible to the superintendent for:

(1) Keeping the accounts of the local school administrative unit in accordance with generally accepted principles of governmental accounting, the rules and regulations of the State Board of Education, and the rules and regulations of the Local Government Commission.

(2) Giving the preaudit certificate required by G.S. 115C-441.

(3) Signing and issuing all checks, drafts, and State warrants by the local school administrative unit, investing idle cash, and receiving and depositing all moneys accruing to the local school administrative unit.

(4) Preparing and filing a statement of the financial condition of the local school administrative unit as often as requested by the superintendent, and when requested in writing, with copy to the superintendent, by the board of education or the board of county commissioners.

(5) Performing such other duties as may be assigned to him by law, by the superintendent, or by rules and regulations of the State Board of Education and the Local Government Commission.

All references in other portions of the General Statutes or local acts to school treasurers, county treasurers, or other officials performing any of the duties conferred by this section on the school finance officer shall be deemed to refer to the school finance officer.

(b) The State Board of Education has authority to issue rules and regulations having the force of law governing procedures for the disbursement of money allocated to the local school administrative unit by or through the State. The Local Government Commission has authority to issue rules and regulations having the force of law governing procedures for the disbursement of all other moneys allocated or accruing to the local school administrative unit. The State Board of Education and the Local Government Commission may inquire into and investigate the internal control procedures of a local school administrative unit with respect to moneys under their respective jurisdictions and may require any modifications in internal control procedures which may be necessary or desirable to prevent embezzlements or mishandling of public moneys. (1975, c. 437, s. 1; 1981, c. 423, s. 1.)

§ 115C-437. Allocation of revenues to the local school administrative unit by the county.

Revenues accruing to the local school administrative unit by virtue of Article IX, Sec. 7, of the Constitution and taxes levied by or on behalf of the local school administrative unit pursuant to a local act or G.S. 115C-501 to 115C-511 shall be remitted to the school finance officer by the officer having custody thereof within 10 days after the close of the calendar month in which the revenues were received or collected. The clear proceeds of all penalties and forfeitures and of all fines collected for any breach of the penal laws of the State, as referred to in Article IX, Sec. 7 of the Constitution, shall include the full amount of all penalties, forfeitures or fines collected under authority conferred by the State, diminished only by the actual costs of collection, not to exceed ten percent (10%) of the amount collected. Revenues appropriated to the local school administrative unit by the board of county commissioners from general county revenues shall be made available to the school finance officer by such procedures as may be mutually agreeable to the board of education and the board of county commissioners, but if no such agreement is reached, these funds shall be remitted to the school finance officer by the county finance officer in monthly installments sufficient to meet its lawful expenditures from the county appropriation until the county appropriation to the local school administrative unit is exhausted. Each installment shall be paid not later than 10 days after the close of each calendar month. When revenue has been appropriated to the local school administrative unit by the board of county commissioners from funds which carry specific restrictions binding upon the county as recipient, the board of commissioners must inform the local school administrative unit in writing of those restrictions. (1975, c. 437, s. 1; 1981, c. 423, s. 1; 1985, c. 779.)

§ 115C-438. Provision for disbursement of State money.

The deposit of money in the State treasury to the credit of local school administrative units shall be made in monthly installments, and additionally as necessary, at such time and in such a manner as may be most convenient for the operation of the public school system. Before an installment is credited, the school finance officer shall certify to the State Board of Education the expenditures to be made by the local school administrative unit from the State Public School Fund during the month. This certification shall be filed on or before the fifth day following the end of the month preceding the period in which the expenditures will be made. The State Board of Education shall determine whether the moneys requisitioned are due the local school administrative unit, and upon determining the amount due, shall cause the requisite amount to be credited to the local school administrative unit. Upon receiving notice from the State Treasurer of the amount placed to the credit of the local school administrative unit, the finance officer may issue State warrants up to the amount so certified.

The State Board of Education may withhold money for payment of salaries for administrative officers of local school administrative units if any report required to be filed with State school authorities is more than 30 days overdue. The State Board of Education shall withhold money for payment of salaries for the superintendent, finance officer, and all other administrative officers charged with providing payroll information pursuant to G.S. 115C-12(18), if the local school administrative unit fails to provide the payroll information to the State Board in a timely fashion and substantially in accordance with the standards set by the State Board. The State Board of Education shall also withhold money used for payment of salaries for the superintendent, transportation director, and all other administrative officers or employees charged by the local board of education or the local superintendent with implementing the Transportation Information Management System, pursuant to G.S. 115C-240(d), if the State Board finds that a local school administrative unit is not progressing in good faith and is not using its best efforts to implement the Transportation Information Management System.

Money in the State Public School Fund and State bond moneys shall be released only on warrants drawn on the State Treasurer, signed by such local official as may be required by the State Board of Education. (1975, c. 437, s. 1; 1981, c. 423, s. 1; 1987, c. 414, s. 14; 1987 (Reg. Sess., 1988), c. 1025, s. 15; 1989 (Reg. Sess., 1990), c. 1066, s. 106; 1991, c. 689, s. 39.2; 1991 (Reg. Sess., 1992), c. 900, s. 77(b).)

§ 115C-439. Facsimile signatures.

The board of education may provide by appropriate resolution for the use of facsimile signature machines, signature stamps, or similar devices in signing checks and drafts and in signing the preaudit certificate on contracts or purchase orders. The board shall charge the finance officer or some other bonded officer or employee with the custody of the necessary machines, stamps, plates, or other devices, and that person and the sureties on his official bond are liable for any illegal, improper, or unauthorized use of them. (1975, c. 437, s. 1; 1981, c. 423, s. 1.)

§ 115C-440. Accounting system.

(a) System Required. - Each local school administrative unit shall establish and maintain an accounting system designed to show in detail its assets, liabilities, equities, revenues, and expenditures. The system shall also be designed to show appropriations and estimated revenues as established in the budget resolution as originally adopted and subsequently amended.

(b) Basis of Accounting. - Local school administrative units shall use the modified accrual basis of accounting in recording transactions.

(c) Encumbrance Systems. - Except as otherwise provided in this subsection, no local school administrative unit is required to record or show encumbrances in its accounting system. The Local Government Commission, in consultation with the State Board of Education, shall establish regulations, based on total membership of the local school administrative unit or some other appropriate criterion, setting forth which units are required to maintain an accounting system that records and shows the encumbrances outstanding against each category of expenditure appropriated in the budget resolution. Any other local school administrative unit may record and show encumbrances in its accounting system.

(d) Commission Regulations. - The Local Government Commission, in consultation with the State Board of Education, may prescribe rules and regulations having the force of law as to:

(1) Features of accounting systems to be maintained by local school administrative units.

(2) Bases of accounting, including identifying in detail the characteristics of a modified accrual basis and identifying what revenues are susceptible to accrual.

(3) Definitions of terms not clearly defined in this Article.

These rules and regulations may be varied according to the size of the local school administrative unit, or according to any other criteria reasonably related to the purpose or complexity of the financial operations involved. (1975, c. 437, s. 1; 1981, c. 423, s. 1.)

§ 115C-440.1. Report on county spending on public capital outlay.

(a) It is the purpose of Article 42 of Chapter 105 of the General Statutes for counties to appropriate funds generated under that Article to increase the level of county spending for public elementary and secondary school capital outlay (including retirement of indebtedness incurred by the county for this purpose) above and beyond the level of spending prior to the levy of the additional tax authorized under that Article.

(b) On or before May 1 of each year the Local Government Commission shall furnish to the General Assembly a report of the level of each county's appropriations for public school capital outlay, including appropriations to the public school capital outlay fund, funds expended by counties on behalf of and for the benefit of public schools for capital outlay, monies reserved for future years' retirement of debt incurred or capital outlay, and any other information the Local Government Commission considers relevant. For purposes of this subsection, the term "public schools" includes charter schools, if authorized. The Local Government Commission shall develop and implement by May 1, 1997, a uniform reporting system whereby counties are able to report all county expenditures under this subsection.

(c) Any local board of education may petition the Local Government Commission to make a finding that the funds provided by a county for public school capital outlay purposes are, within the financial resources available and consistent with the fiscal policies of the Board of County Commissioners, inadequate to meet the public school capital outlay needs within that county and that the Board of County Commissioners has not complied with the requirements or intent of this Article. The petition shall be in the form prescribed by the Commission. In making its finding, the Commission shall consider the facts it is required to report under subsection (b) of this section, as well as any other information it deems necessary. The Commission shall report its findings on such petition, together with any recommendations it deems appropriate, to the Joint Legislative Commission on Governmental Operations. (1985 (Reg. Sess., 1986), c. 906, s. 1; 1995, c. 507, s. 17.5; 1995 (Reg. Sess., 1996), c. 666, ss. 4, 5.)

§ 115C-441. Budgetary accounting for appropriations.

(a) Incurring Obligations. - Except as set forth below, no obligation may be incurred by a local school administrative unit unless the budget resolution includes an appropriation authorizing the obligation and an unencumbered balance remains in the appropriation sufficient to pay in the current fiscal year the sums obligated by the transaction for the current fiscal year. If an obligation is evidenced by a contract or agreement requiring the payment of money or by a purchase order for supplies and materials, the contract, agreement, or purchase order shall include on its face a certificate stating that the instrument has been preaudited to assure compliance with this section. The certificate, which shall be signed by the finance officer, shall take substantially the following form:

"This instrument has been preaudited in the manner required by the School Budget and Fiscal Control Act.

(Date)

(Signature of finance officer)"

An obligation incurred in violation of this section is invalid and may not be enforced. The finance officer shall establish procedures to assure compliance with this section.

(b) Disbursements. - When a bill, invoice, or other claim against a local school administrative unit is presented, the finance officer shall either approve or disapprove the necessary disbursement. The finance officer may approve the claim only if he determines the amount to be payable, the budget resolution includes an appropriation authorizing the expenditure and either (i) an encumbrance has been previously created for the transaction or (ii) an unencumbered balance remains in the appropriation sufficient to pay the amount to be disbursed. A bill, invoice, or other claim may not be paid unless it has been approved by the finance officer or, under subsection (c) of this section, by the board of education.

(c) Board of Education Approval of Bills, Invoices, or Claims. - The board of education may, as permitted by this subsection, approve a bill, invoice, or other claim against the local school administrative unit that has been disapproved by the finance officer. It may not approve a claim for which no appropriation appears in the budget resolution, or for which the appropriation contains no encumbrance and the unencumbered balance is less than the amount to be paid. The board of education shall approve payment by formal resolution stating the board's reasons for allowing the bill, invoice, or other claim. The resolution shall be entered in the minutes together with the names of those voting in the affirmative. The chairman of the board or some other member designated for this purpose shall sign the certificate on the check or draft given in payment of the bill, invoice, or other claim. If payment results in a violation of law, each member of the board voting to allow payment is jointly and severally liable for the full amount of the check or draft given in payment.

(c1) Continuing Contracts for Capital Outlay. - An administrative unit may enter into a contract for capital outlay expenditures, some portion or all of which is to be performed and/or paid in ensuing fiscal years, without the budget resolution including an appropriation for the entire obligation, provided:

a. The budget resolution includes an appropriation authorizing the current fiscal year's portion of the obligation;

b. An unencumbered balance remains in the appropriation sufficient to pay in the current fiscal year the sums obligated by the transaction for the current fiscal year; and

c. Contracts for capital outlay expenditures are approved by a resolution adopted by the board of county commissioners, which resolution when adopted shall bind the board of county commissioners to appropriate sufficient funds in ensuing fiscal years to meet the amounts to be paid under the contract in those years.

(d) Payment. - A local school administrative unit may not pay a bill, invoice, salary, or other claim except by a check or draft on an official depository, by a bank wire transfer from an official depository, or by a warrant on the State Treasurer. Except as provided in this subsection each check or draft on an official depository shall bear on its face a certificate signed by the finance officer or signed by the chairman or some other member of the board pursuant to subsection (c) of this section. The certificate shall take substantially the following form:

"This disbursement has been approved as required by the School Budget and Fiscal Control Act.

_____

(Signature of finance officer)"

No certificate is required on payroll checks or drafts or on State warrants.

(e) Penalties. - If an officer or employee of a local school administrative unit incurs an obligation or pays out or causes to be paid out any funds in violation of this section, he and the sureties on his official bond are liable for any sums so committed or disbursed. If the finance officer gives a false certificate to any contract, agreement, purchase order, check, draft, or other document, he and the sureties on his official bond are liable for any sums illegally committed or disbursed thereby. (1975, c. 437, s. 1; 1981, c. 423, s. 1; 1985, c. 783, ss. 1, 2; 1997-456, s. 27.)

§ 115C-441.1. Dependent care assistance program.

The State Board of Education is authorized to provide eligible employees of local school administrative units a program of dependent care assistance as available under Section 129 and related sections of the Internal Revenue Code of 1986, as amended. The State Board may authorize local school administrative units to enter into annual agreements with employees who elect to participate in the program to provide for a reduction in salary. Should the State Board decide to contract with a third party to administer the terms and conditions of a program of dependent care assistance, it may select a contractor only upon a thorough and completely competitive procurement process. (1989, c. 458, s. 1; 1991 (Reg. Sess., 1992), c. 1044, s. 14(b); 1993, c. 561, s. 42; 1993 (Reg. Sess, 1994), c. 769, s. 7.28A; 1997-443, s. 33.20(a); 1999-237, s. 28.27(a).)

§ 115C-442. Fidelity bonds.

(a) The finance officer shall give a true accounting and faithful performance bond with sufficient sureties in an amount to be fixed by the board of education, not less than fifty thousand dollars ($50,000). This bond shall cover the faithful performance of all duties placed on the finance officer by or pursuant to law and the faithful accounting for all funds in his custody except State funds placed to the credit of the local school administrative unit by the State Treasurer. The premium on the bond shall be paid by the local school administrative unit.

(b) The State Board of Education shall provide for adequate and appropriate bonding of school finance officers and such other employees as it deems appropriate with respect to the disbursement of State funds. When it requires such bonds, the State Board of Education is authorized to place the bonds and pay the premiums thereon.

(c) The treasurer of each individual school and all other officers, employees and agents of each local school administrative unit who have custody of public school money in the normal course of their employment or agency shall give a true accounting bond with sufficient sureties in an amount to be fixed by the board of education. The premiums on these bonds shall be paid by the local school administrative unit. Instead of individual bonds, a local school administrative unit may provide for a blanket bond to cover all officers, employees, and agents of the local school administrative unit required to be bonded, except the finance officer. The finance officer may be included within the blanket bond if the blanket bond protects against risks not protected against by the individual bond. (1975, c. 437, s. 1; 1981, c. 423, s. 1; 2007-85, s. 1.)

§ 115C-443. Investment of idle cash.

(a) A local school administrative unit may deposit at interest or invest all or part of the cash balance of any fund. The finance officer shall manage investments subject to whatever restrictions and directions the board of education may impose. The finance officer shall have the power to purchase, sell, and exchange securities on behalf of the board of education. The investment program shall be so managed that investments and deposits can be converted into cash when needed.

(b) Moneys may be deposited at interest at any bank, savings and loan association, or trust company in this State in the form of certificates of deposit or such other forms of time deposit as the Local Government Commission may approve. Investment deposits shall be secured as provided in G.S. 115C-444(b).

(c) Moneys may be invested in the following classes of securities, and no others:

(1) Obligations of the United States of America.

(2) Obligations of any agency or instrumentality of the United States of America if the payment of interest and principal of such obligations is fully guaranteed by the United States of America.

(3) Obligations of the State of North Carolina.

(4) Bonds and notes of any North Carolina local government or public authority, subject to such restrictions as the Secretary of the Local Government Commission may impose.

(5) Shares of any savings and loan association organized under the laws of this State and shares of any federal savings and loan association having its principal office in this State, to the extent that the investment in such shares is fully insured by the United States of America or an agency thereof or by any mutual deposit guaranty association authorized by the Commissioner of Insurance of North Carolina to do business in North Carolina pursuant to Article 7A of Chapter 54 of the General Statutes.

(6) Obligations maturing no later than 18 months after the date of purchase of the Federal Intermediate Credit Banks, the Federal Home Loan Banks, Fannie Mae, the Banks for Cooperatives, and the Federal Land Banks.

(7) Any form of investment allowed by law to the State Treasurer.

(8) Any form of investment allowed by G.S. 159-30 to local governments and public authorities.

(d) Investment securities may be bought, sold, and traded by private negotiation, and local school administrative units may pay all incidental costs thereof and all reasonable cost of administering the investment and deposit program. Securities and deposit certificates shall be in the custody of the finance officer who shall be responsible for their safekeeping and for keeping accurate investment accounts and records.

(e) Interest earned on deposits and investments shall be credited to the fund whose cash is deposited or invested. Cash of several funds may be combined for deposit or investment if not otherwise prohibited by law; and when such joint deposits or investments are made, interest earned shall be prorated and credited to the various funds on the basis of the amounts thereof invested, figured according to an average periodic balance or some other sound accounting principle. Interest earned on the deposit or investment of bond funds shall be deemed a part of the bond proceeds.

(f) Registered securities acquired for investment may be released from registration and transferred by signature of the finance officer.

(g) It is the intent of this Article that the foregoing provisions of this section shall apply only to those funds received by the local school administrative unit as required by G.S. 115C-437. The county finance officer shall be responsible for the investment of all county funds allocated to the local school administrative unit prior to such county funds actually being remitted to the school finance officer as provided by G.S. 115C-437. (1975, c. 437, s. 1; 1981, c. 423, s. 1; 1985, c. 246, s. 1; 2001-487, s. 14(h).)

§ 115C-444. Selection of depository; deposits to be secured.

(a) Each board of education shall designate as the official depositories of the local school administrative unit one or more banks, savings and loan associations, or trust companies in this State. It shall be unlawful for any money belonging to a local school administrative unit or an individual school to be deposited in any place, bank, or trust company other than an official depository, except as permitted by G.S. 115C-443(b); however, moneys belonging to an administrative unit or an individual school may be deposited in official depositories in Negotiable Order of Withdrawal (NOW) accounts.

(b) Money on deposit in an official depository or deposited at interest pursuant to G.S. 115C-443(b) shall be secured by deposit insurance, surety bonds, or investment securities of such nature, in a sufficient amount to protect the administrative unit or an individual school on account of deposit of moneys made therein, and in such manner, as may be prescribed by rule or regulation of the Local Government Commission. When deposits are secured in accordance with this subsection, no public officer or employee may be held liable for any losses sustained by a local school administrative unit because of the default or insolvency of the depository. (1975, c. 437, s. 1; 1981, c. 423, s. 1; c. 682, s. 23; c. 866, ss. 1, 2; 1985, c. 246, s. 2.)

§ 115C-445. Daily deposits.

Except as otherwise provided by law, all moneys collected or received by an officer, employee or agent of a local school administrative unit or an individual school shall be deposited in accordance with this section. Each officer, employee and agent of a local school administrative unit or individual school whose duty it is to collect or receive any taxes or other moneys shall deposit his collections and receipts daily. If the board of education gives its approval, deposits shall be required only when the moneys on hand amount to as much as two hundred fifty dollars ($250.00), but in any event a deposit shall be made on the last business day of the month. All deposits shall be made with the finance officer or in an official depository. Deposits in an official depository shall be immediately reported to the finance officer or individual school treasurer by means of a duplicate deposit ticket. The finance officer may at any time audit the accounts of any officer, employee or agent collecting or receiving any taxes or other moneys, and may prescribe the form and detail of these accounts. The accounts of such an officer, employee or agent shall be audited at least annually. (1975, c. 437, s. 1; 1981, c. 423, s. 1.)

§ 115C-446. Semiannual reports on status of deposits and investments.

Each school finance officer shall report to the Secretary of the Local Government Commission on January 1 and July 1 of each year, or such other dates as the Secretary may prescribe, the amounts of money then in his custody and in the custody of treasurers of individual schools within the local school administrative unit, the amount of deposits of such money in depositories, a list of all investment securities and time deposits held by the local school administrative unit and individual schools therein. In like manner, each bank or trust company acting as the official depository of any administrative unit or individual school may be required to report to the Secretary a description of the surety bonds or investment securities securing such public deposits. If the Secretary finds at any time that any moneys of a local school administrative unit or an individual school are not properly deposited or secured, or are invested in securities not eligible for investment, he shall notify the officer in charge of the moneys of the failure to comply with law. Upon such notification, the officer shall comply with the law within 30 days, except as to the sale of securities not eligible for investment which shall be sold within nine months at a price to be approved by the Secretary. The Local Government Commission may extend the time for sale of ineligible securities, but no one extension may cover a period of more than one year. (1975, c. 437, s. 1; 1981, c. 423, s. 1; c. 866, s. 3.)

§ 115C-447. Annual independent audit.

(a) Each local school administrative unit shall have its accounts and the accounts of individual schools therein audited as soon as possible after the close of each fiscal year by a certified public accountant or by an accountant certified by the Local Government Commission as cualified to audit local government accounts. The auditor who audits the accounts of a local school administrative unit shall also audit the accounts of its individual schools. The auditor shall be selected by and shall report directly to the board of education. The audit contract shall be in writing, shall include all its terms and conditions, and shall be submitted to the Secretary of the Local Government Commission for his approval as to form, terms and conditions. The terms and conditions of the audit contract shall include the scope of the audit, and the requirement that upon completion of the examination the auditor shall prepare a typewritten or printed report embodying financial statements and his opinion and comments relating thereto. The financial statements accompanying the auditor's report shall be prepared in conformity with generally accepted accounting principles. The auditor shall file a copy of the audit report with the Secretary of the Local Government Commission, the State Board of Education, the board of education and the board of county commissioners, and shall submit all bills or claims for audit fees and costs to the Secretary of the Local Government Commission for his approval. It shall be unlawful for any local school administrative unit to pay or permit the payment of such bills or claims without this approval. Each officer, employee and agent of the local school administrative unit having custody of public money or responsibility for keeping records of public financial or fiscal affairs shall produce all books and records requested by the auditor and shall divulge such information relating to fiscal affairs as he may request. If any member of a board of education or any other public officer, employee or agent shall conceal, falsify, or refuse to deliver or divulge any books, records, or information, with an intent thereby to mislead the auditor or impede or interfere with the audit, he is guilty of a Class 1 misdemeanor.

The State Auditor shall have authority to prescribe the manner in which funds disbursed by administrative units by warrants on the State Treasurer shall be audited.

(b)   When the State Board of Education finds that incidents of fraud, embezzlement, theft, or management failures in a local school administrative unit make it appropriate to review the internal control procedures of the unit, the State Board of Education shall so notify the unit. If the incidents were discovered by the firm performing the audit under subsection (a) of this section, the board of the local school administrative unit shall submit the audit together with a plan for any corrective actions relative to its internal control procedures to the State Board of Education and the Local Government Commission for approval and shall implement the approved changes prior to the next annual audit. Where the firm preparing the audit under subsection (a) of this section identifies significant problems with internal control procedures the local school administrative unit shall submit the audit together with a plan for any corrective actions relative to its internal control procedures to the State Board of Education and the Local Government Commission for approval and shall implement the approved changes prior to the next annual audit.

If the incidents were not discovered by the firm performing the audit under subsection (a) of this section, the State Board of Education and the Local Government Commission shall employ an audit firm to review the internal control procedures of that local school administrative unit. Upon completion of this review, the audit firm shall report publicly to the State Board of Education, the Local Government Commission, and the board of the local school administrative unit. If the State Board of Education determines that significant changes are needed in the internal control procedures of the local school administrative unit, the local board shall submit a plan of corrective actions to the State Board of Education and the Local Government Commission for approval and shall implement the approved changes prior to the next annual audit. The local school administrative unit shall pay the cost of this audit. (1975, c. 437, s. 1; 1981, c. 423, s. 1; 1983, c. 913, s. 17; 1987 (Reg. Sess., 1988), c. 1025, s. 14; 1993, c. 539, s. 891; 1994, Ex. Sess., c. 24, s. 14(c); 2005-276, s. 7.58.)

§ 115C-448. Special funds of individual schools.

(a) The board of education shall appoint a treasurer for each school within the local school administrative unit that handles special funds. The treasurer shall keep a complete record of all moneys in his charge in such form and detail as may be prescribed by the finance officer of the local school administrative unit, and shall make such reports to the superintendent and finance officer of the local school administrative unit as they or the board of education may prescribe. Special funds of individual schools shall be deposited in an official depository of the local school administrative unit in special accounts to the credit of the individual school, and shall be paid only on checks or drafts signed by the principal of the school and the treasurer. The board of education may, in its discretion, waive the requirements of this section for any school which handles less than three hundred dollars ($300.00) in any school year.

(b) Nothing in this section shall prevent the board of education from requiring that all funds of individual schools be deposited with and accounted for by the school finance officer. If this is done, these moneys shall be disbursed and accounted for in the same manner as other school funds except that the check or draft shall not bear the certificate of preaudit.

(c) For the purposes of this section, "special funds of individual schools" includes by way of illustration and not limitation funds realized from gate receipts of interscholastic athletic competition, sale of school annuals and newspapers, and dues of student organizations.

(d) Special funds of individual schools shall not be included as part of the local current expense fund of a local school administrative unit for the purposes of determining the per pupil share of the local current expense fund transferred to a charter school pursuant to G.S. 115C-238.29H(b). (1975, c. 437, s. 1; 1981, c. 423, s. 1; 2013-355, s. 2(b).)

§ 115C-449. Proceeds of insurance claims.

Moneys paid to a local school administrative unit pursuant to contracts of insurance against loss of capital assets through fire or casualty shall be used to repair or replace the damaged asset, or if the asset is not repaired or replaced, placed to the credit of the capital outlay fund for appropriation at some future time. (1975, c. 437, s. 1; 1981, c. 423, s. 1.)

§ 115C-450. School food services.

(a) School food services shall be included in the budget of each local school administrative unit and the State Board of Education shall provide for school food services in the uniform budget format required by G.S. 115C-426.

(b) No local school administrative unit shall assess indirect costs to a child nutrition program unless the program has a minimum of one month's operating balance. One month's operating balance shall be derived from net cash resources divided by one month's operating costs. "Net cash resources" means all monies, as determined in accordance with the State agency's established accounting system, that are available to or have accrued to a school food authority's nonprofit child nutrition account at any given time, less cash payables and other liabilities. When calculating the average month's operating balance, the Department of Public Instruction shall use the complete and final figures obtained from the annual financial report from each child nutrition program's operation. An average month's operating balance shall be calculated and published by the Department of Public Instruction for each child nutrition program and shall be equal to the average of the three prior fiscal years' monthly operating balances. If complete and final financial reports for a given year are not yet available for a child nutrition program, the Department of Public Instruction may use projected figures but shall update the published average month's operating balance once complete and final financial reports become available. As used in this subsection, the term "indirect costs" is as defined in the United States Office of Budget and Management Circular A-87, as revised, and the term "net cash resources" is as defined in 7 C.F.R. § 210.2. (1975, c. 437, s. 1; 1981, c. 423, s. 1; 2013-235, s. 1.)

§ 115C-451. Reports to State Board of Education; failure to comply with School Budget Act.

(a) The State Board of Education shall have authority to require local school administrative units to make such reports as it may deem advisable with respect to the financial operation of the public schools.

(b) The State Board of Education shall be responsible for assuring that local boards of education comply with State laws and regulations regarding the budgeting, management, and expenditure of funds. When a local board of education willfully or negligently fails or refuses to comply with these laws and regulations, the State Board of Education shall issue a warning to the local board of education and direct it to take remedial action. In addition, the State Board may suspend the flexibility given to the local board under G.S. 115C-105.21A and may require the local board to use funds during the term of suspension only for the purposes for which they were allotted or for other purposes with the specific approval from the State Board.

(c) If the local board of education, after warning, persists in willfully or negligently failing or refusing to comply with these laws and regulations, the State Board of Education shall by resolution assume control of the financial affairs of the local board of education and shall appoint an administrator to exercise the powers assumed. The adoption of a resolution shall have the effect of divesting the local board of education of its powers as to the adoption of budgets, expenditure of money, and all other financial powers conferred upon the local board of education by law. (1975, c. 437, s. 1; 1981, c. 423, s. 1; 1991, c. 529, s. 5; 1997-443, s. 8.7.)

§ 115C-452. Fines and forfeitures.

The clear proceeds of all penalties and forfeitures and of all fines collected in the General Court of Justice in each county shall be remitted by the clerk of the superior court to the county finance officer, who shall forthwith determine what portion of the total is due to each local school administrative unit in the county and remit the appropriate portion of the amount to the finance officer of each local school administrative unit. Fines and forfeitures shall be apportioned according to the projected average daily membership of each local school administrative unit as determined by and certified to the local school administrative units and the board of county commissioners by the State Board of Education pursuant to G.S. 115C-430. (1975, c. 437, s. 1; 1981, c. 423, s. 1.)

§§ 115C-453 through 115C-457. Reserved for future codification purposes.

Article 31A.

Civil Penalty and Forfeiture Fund.

§ 115C-457.1. Creation of Fund; administration.

(a) There is created the Civil Penalty and Forfeiture Fund. The Fund shall consist of the clear proceeds of all civil penalties, civil forfeitures, and civil fines that are collected by a State agency and that the General Assembly is authorized to place in a State fund pursuant to Article IX, Section 7(b) of the Constitution.

(b) The Fund shall be administered by the Office of State Budget and Management. The Fund and all interest accruing to the Fund shall be faithfully used exclusively for maintaining free public schools. (1997-443, s. 8.20; 2000-140, s. 93.1(a); 2001-424, s. 12.2(b); 2003-423, s. 2.)

§ 115C-457.2. Remittance of moneys to the Fund.

The clear proceeds of all civil penalties, civil forfeitures, and civil fines that are collected by a State agency and that the General Assembly is authorized to place in a State fund pursuant to Article IX, Section 7(b) of the Constitution shall be remitted to the Office of State Budget and Management by the officer having custody of the funds within 10 days after the close of the calendar month in which the revenues were received or collected. Notwithstanding any other law, all such funds shall be deposited in the Civil Penalty and Forfeiture Fund. The clear proceeds of these funds include the full amount of all civil penalties, civil forfeitures, and civil fines collected under authority conferred by the State, diminished only by the actual costs of collection, not to exceed twenty percent (20%) of the amount collected. The collection cost percentage to be used by a State agency shall be established and approved by the Office of State Budget and Management on an annual basis based upon the computation of actual collection costs by each agency for the prior fiscal year. (1997-443, s. 8.20; 2000-140, s. 93.1(a); 2001-424, s. 12.2(b); 2003-423, s. 3; 2005-276, s. 6.37(v); 2006-66, s. 6.9(c).)

§ 115C-457.3. Appropriation of moneys in the Fund.

(a) The General Assembly shall appropriate moneys in the Civil Penalty and Forfeiture Fund in the Current Operations Appropriations Act. These appropriations shall be made to the State Public School Fund for allotment by the State Board of Education, on behalf of the counties, to local school administrative units on a per pupil basis in accordance with Article IX, Section 7(b) of the North Carolina Constitution.

(b) In accordance with subsection (a) of this section, the State Board of Education shall allocate these funds according to the allotted average daily membership of each local school administrative unit as determined by and certified to the local school administrative units and the board of county commissioners by the State Board pursuant to G.S. 115C-430. (1997-443, s. 8.20; 2000-140, s. 93.1(a); 2001-424, s. 12.2(b); 2003-423, s. 3.2; 2005-276, s. 6.37(g).)

Article 32.

State Literary Fund.

§ 115C-458. State Literary Fund.

The State Literary Fund includes all funds derived from the sources enumerated in Sec. 6, Article IX, of the Constitution, and all funds that may be hereafter so derived, together with any interest that may accrue thereon. This Fund shall be separate and distinct from other funds of the State.

The State Literary Fund shall be faithfully appropriated and used exclusively for establishing and maintaining a uniform system of free public schools. (1955, c. 1372, art. 11, s. 1; 1971, c. 704, s. 11; c. 1096; 1981, c. 423, s. 1; 2009-451, s. 7.37(a).)

§ 115C-459. Terms of loans.

Loans made under the provisions of this Article shall be payable in 10 installments, shall bear interest at a uniform rate determined by the State Board of Education not to exceed eight percent (8%), payable annually, and shall be evidenced by the note of the county, executed by the chairman, the clerk of the board of county commissioners, and the chairman and secretary of the local board of education, and deposited with the State Treasurer. The first installment of such loan, together with the interest on the whole amount then due, shall be paid by the local board on the tenth day of February after the tenth day of August subsequent to the making of such loan, and the remaining installments, together with the interest, shall be paid on the tenth day of February of each subsequent year until all shall have been paid. (1955, c. 1372, art. 11, s. 2; 1971, c. 1094; 1981, c. 423, s. 1; 1983, c. 477.)

§ 115C-460: Repealed by Session Laws 2009-451, s. 7.37(c), effective July 1, 2009.

§ 115C-461: Repealed by Session Laws 2009-451, s. 7.37(c), effective July 1, 2009.

§ 115C-462: Repealed by Session Laws 2009-451, s. 7.37(c), effective July 1, 2009.

§ 115C-463: Repealed by Session Laws 2009-451, s. 7.37(c), effective July 1, 2009.

§ 115C-464: Repealed by Session Laws 2009-451, s. 7.37(c), effective July 1, 2009.

§ 115C-465: Repealed by Session Laws 2009-451, s. 7.37(c), effective July 1, 2009.

§ 115C-466: Repealed by Session Laws 2009-451, s. 7.37(c), effective July 1, 2009.

§ 115C-467: Repealed by Session Laws 2009-451, s. 7.37(c), effective July 1, 2009.

Article 32A.

Scholarship Loan Fund for Prospective Teachers.

§ 115C-468: Recodified as G.S. 116-209.33 by Session Laws 2005-276, s. 9.17(b), effective January 1, 2006, and applicable to scholarship loans awarded on or after that date.

§§ 115C-469, 115C-470: Repealed by Session Laws 2005-276, s. 9.17(b), effective January 1, 2006, and applicable to scholarship loans awarded on or after that date.

§ 115C-471: Recodified as G.S. 116-209.34 by Session Laws 2005-276, s. 9.17(b), effective January 1, 2006, and applicable to scholarship loans awarded on or after that date.

§ 115C-472: Repealed by Session Laws 1997-18, s. 11.

§ 115C-472.1: Repealed by Session Laws 2005-276, s. 9.17(b), effective January 1, 2006, and applicable to scholarship loans awarded on or after that date.

Article 32B.

Computer Loan Revolving Fund.

§ 115C-472.5: Repealed by Session Laws 2009-451, s. 7.36(a), effective July 1, 2009.

§§ 115C-472.6 through 115C-472.9. Reserved for future codification purposes.

Article 32C.

Fund for the Reduction of Class Size in Public Schools.

§ 115C-472.10. Establishment of the Fund for the Reduction of Class Size in Public Schools.

(a) There is established under the control and direction of the State Board of Education the Fund for the Reduction of Class Size in Public Schools. This fund shall be a nonreverting special revenue fund consisting of moneys credited to it under G.S. 20-81.12(b12) from the sale of special registration plates to support the public schools.

(b) The State Board of Education shall allocate funds in the Fund for the Reduction of Class Size in Public Schools to local school administrative units to reduce class size in public schools. (2000-159, s. 8.)

§ 115C-472.11: Reserved for future codification purposes.

§ 115C-472.12: Reserved for future codification purposes.

§ 115C-472.13: Reserved for future codification purposes.

§ 115C-472.14: Reserved for future codification purposes.

Article 32D.

Fund for Special Education and Related Services.

§ 115C-472.15: Repealed by Session Laws 2013-364, s. 6(a), effective July 1, 2013.

Article 33.

Assumption of School District Indebtedness by Counties.

§ 115C-473. Method of assumption; validation of proceedings.

The county board of education, with the approval of the board of commissioners, and when the assumption of such indebtedness is approved at an election as hereinafter provided, if such election is required by the Constitution, may include in the debt service fund in the school budget all outstanding indebtedness for school purposes of every city, town, school district, school taxing district, township, city administrative unit or other political subdivision in the county, hereinafter collectively called "local districts," lawfully incurred in erecting and equipping school buildings necessary for the school term. The election on the question of assuming such indebtedness shall be called and held in accordance with the provisions of Chapter 159 of the General Statutes, known as "The Local Government Finance Act," insofar as the same may be made applicable, and the returns of such election shall be canvassed and a statement of the result thereof prepared, filed and published as provided in the Local Government Finance Act. No right of action or defense founded upon the invalidity of the election shall be asserted, nor shall the validity of the election be open to question in any court upon any ground whatever, except in an action or proceeding commenced within 30 days after the publication of such statement of result. When such indebtedness is taken over for payment by the county as a whole and the local districts are relieved of their annual payments, the county funds provided for such purpose shall be deducted from the debt service fund prior to the division of such fund among the schools of the county as provided in Article 31 of this Chapter.

The assumption, as herein provided, by any county, at any time prior to the 28th day of February, 1951, of the indebtedness of local districts for school purposes and all proceedings had in connection therewith are hereby in all respects ratified, approved, confirmed, and validated: Provided, that nothing herein shall prevent counties and local taxing districts from levying taxes to provide for the payment of their debt service requirements if they have not been otherwise provided for. (1955, c. 1372, art. 12, s. 1; 1981, c. 423, s. 1.)

§ 115C-474. Taxes levied and collected for bonds assumed to be paid into school debt service fund of county; discharge of sinking fund custodian.

In any county where the bonds of a local district have been assumed under the provisions of this Article, all taxes levied and collected for the purpose of paying the principal of and interest on said bonds, or for creating a sinking fund for the retirement of said bonds, shall be deposited in the school debt service fund of the county. The custodian of all moneys and other assets of a sinking fund created for the retirement of said bonds is hereby authorized to turn over such moneys and assets to the county treasurer, the county sinking fund commissioner or other county officer charged with the custodianship of sinking funds, and such custodian shall thereby be discharged from further responsibility for administration of and accounting for such sinking fund. (1955, c. 1372, art. 12, s. 2; 1981, c. 423, s. 1.)

§ 115C-475. Allocation to district bonds of taxes collected.

The collections of taxes levied for debt service on all taxable property of a county in which local district bonds have been assumed shall be proportionately allocated to each issue of such bonds. (1955, c. 1372, art. 12, s. 3; 1981, c. 423, s. 1.)

§§ 115C-476 through 115C-480. Reserved for future codification purposes.

Article 34.

Refunding and Funding Bonds of School Districts.

§ 115C-481. School district defined.

The term "school district" as used in this Article shall be deemed to include any special school taxing district, local tax district, special charter district, city administrative unit or other political subdivision of a county by which or on behalf of which bonds have been issued for erecting and equipping school buildings, or for refunding the same, and such bonds are outstanding. (1955, c. 1372, art. 13, s. 1; 1981, c. 423, s. 1.)

§ 115C-482. Continuance of district until bonds are paid.

Notwithstanding the provisions of any law which affect the continued existence of a school district or the levy of taxes therein for the payment of its bonds, such school district shall continue in existence with its boundaries unchanged from those established at the time of issuance of its bonds, unless such boundaries shall have been extended and thereby embrace additional territory subject to the levy of such taxes, until all of its outstanding bonds, together with the interest thereon, shall be paid. (1955, c. 1372, art. 13, s. 2; 1981, c. 423, s. 1.)

§ 115C-483. Funding and refunding of bonds authorized; issuance and sale or exchange; tax levy for repayment.

The board of commissioners of the county in which any such school district is located is hereby authorized to issue bonds at one time or from time to time for the purpose of refunding or funding the principal or interest of any bonds of such school district then outstanding. Such refunding or funding bonds shall be issued in the name of the school district and they may be sold or delivered in exchange for or upon the extinguishment of the obligations or indebtedness refunded or funded. Except as otherwise provided in this Article, such refunding and funding bonds shall be issued in accordance with the provisions of Chapter 159 of the General Statutes, the Local Government Finance Act. The tax-levying body or bodies authorized by law to levy taxes for the payment of the bonds, the principal or interest of which shall be refunded or funded, shall levy annually a special tax on all taxable property in such school district sufficient to pay the principal and interest of said refunding or funding bonds as the same become due. (1955, c. 1372, art. 13, s. 3; 1981, c. 423, s. 1.)

§ 115C-484. Issuance of bonds by cities and towns; debt statement; tax levy for repayment.

In case the governing body of any city or town is the body authorized by law to levy taxes for the payment of the bonds of such district, whether the territory embraced in such district lies wholly or partly within the corporate limits of such city or town, such governing body of such city or town is hereby authorized to issue bonds at the time or from time to time for the purpose of refunding or funding the principal or interest of any bonds then outstanding which were issued by or on behalf of such school district. Except as otherwise provided in this Article, such refunding and funding bonds shall be issued in accordance with the provisions of the Local Government Bond Act, relating to the issuance of refunding and funding bonds under that act, and the provisions of the Local Government Finance Act, except in the following respects:

(1) The bonds shall be issued in the name and on behalf of the school district by the governing body of such city or town.

(2) It shall not be necessary to include in the ordinance authorizing the bonds, or in the notice required to be published after the passage of the ordinance, any statement concerning the filing of a debt statement, and, as applied to said bonds, G.S. 159-54 and G.S. 159-55 (the Local Government Bond Act,) shall be read and understood as if they contained no requirements in respect to such matters.

(3) The governing body of such city or town shall annually levy and collect a tax ad valorem upon all the taxable property in such school district sufficient to pay the principal and interest of such refunding or funding bonds as the same become due. (1955, c. 1372, art. 13, s. 4; 1981, c. 423, s. 1.)

§§ 115C-485 through 115C-489. Reserved for future codification purposes.

Article 34A.

Critical School Facility Needs Fund.

§ 115C-489.1, 115C-489.2: Repealed by Session Laws 1995 (Reg. Sess., 1996), c. 631, s. 14, effective 30 days after the last school administrative unit on the priority list established in 1988 by the Commission on School Facility Needs is funded.

§ 115C-489.2. Repealed by Session Laws 1995 (Reg. Sess., 1996), c. 631, s. 14, effective 30 days after the last school administrative unit on the priority list established in 1988 by the Commission on School Facility Needs is funded.

§§ 115C-489.3 through 115C-489.4: Repealed by Session Laws 1995 (Regular Session, 1996), c. 631, s. 13.

Article 34B.

Qualified Zone Academy Bonds and Qualified School Construction Bonds.

§ 115C-489.5. Qualified zone academy bonds and qualified school construction bonds; findings.

The General Assembly finds:

(1) Section 226 of the Taxpayer Relief Act of 1997, as codified at 26 U.S.C. § 54E, provides funds for school improvements through taxable qualified zone academy bonds. Ninety-five percent (95%) or more of the proceeds of a qualified zone academy bond issue must be used for a qualified purpose with respect to a qualified zone academy established by an eligible local education agency.

(2) Partnerships between private entities and local schools are promoted through the use of qualified zone academy bonds. Issuers must certify that they have received written commitments from one or more private entities to make qualified contributions valued at ten percent (10%) of the proceeds of the issue.

(2a) Section 1521, et seq., of the American Recovery and Reinvestment Tax Act of 2009 (ARRTA), enacted as 26 U.S.C. § 54F, provides a new source of funds for construction, rehabilitation, or repair of public school facilities or for acquisition of land for public school facilities through the issuance of qualified school construction bonds.

(3) Eligible taxpayers may receive federal tax credits for holding the qualified zone academy bonds or qualified school construction bonds. It is intended that the qualified zone academy bonds and qualified school construction bonds be sold at a price so that the tax credits received produce the economic equivalent of interest that otherwise would have been paid on the bonds. Therefore, issuers of qualified zone academy bonds or qualified school

construction bonds are obligated to repay the principal amount of the qualified zone academy bonds or qualified school construction bonds but need not make interest payments.

(4) Applicable federal law limits the amount of qualified zone academy bonds and qualified school construction bonds that may be issued in North Carolina in a calendar year. The amount of qualified school construction bonds that may be issued in the State is divided between amounts specifically designated for identified local school districts pursuant to ARRTA ("local allocation") and amounts allocated to the entire State for use throughout the State ("statewide allocation"). (2000-69, s. 1; 2009-140, s. 1.)

§ 115C-489.6. Administration; consultation; issuance of bonds.

(a) QZAB Program. - The State Board of Education is designated the State education agency responsible for administering the qualified zone academy bond program in North Carolina for the purposes of 26 U.S.C. § 54E. The State Board of Education shall perform all activities required to implement and carry out the qualified zone activity bond program in North Carolina. Those activities include:

(1) Defining those areas and schools that are eligible under federal law to participate in the qualified zone academy bond program in North Carolina.

(2) Designing an application process under which proposals may be solicited from qualified zone academies.

(3) Determining the eligibility of an applicant to be a participating qualified zone academy.

(4) Awarding the State's allocation of total funds among selected applicants and establishing conditions upon the usage of the allocation. These conditions must include:

a. Requiring that the bond proceeds be used only for rehabilitating or repairing the public school facility in which the qualified zone academy is located, which may include (i) wiring and other infrastructure improvements related to providing technology and (ii) equipment related to the rehabilitation or repair, but not personal computers or similar technology equipment.

b.   Conditions designed to assure that the allocation is used in a timely manner.

(5)   Confirming that the terms of any qualified zone academy bonds issued in accordance with this program are consistent with the terms of the federal program.

(a1)   Qualified School Construction Bond Program. - The State Board of Education is designated the State education agency responsible for administering the statewide allocation of authority to issue qualified school construction bonds under 26 U.S.C. § 54F. The State Board of Education shall perform all activities required to implement and carry out the statewide allocation for the qualified school construction bond program in North Carolina. Those activities include:

(1)   Designing an application process under which proposals may be solicited from issuers wishing to issue qualified school construction bonds pursuant to the statewide allocation.

(2)   Awarding the State's allocation of total funds among selected applicants and establishing conditions upon the usage of the allocation. These conditions may include:

a.   Requiring that the bond proceeds be used for purposes permitted under 26 U.S.C. § 54F.

b.   Conditions designed to assure that the allocation is used in a timely manner and that the allocations are made in accordance with the requirements of federal statutes, regulations, and rulings.

(3)   Confirming that the terms of any qualified school construction bonds issued in accordance with this program are consistent with the terms of the federal program.

(4)   Acting as the State entity designated to receive notice from any local school district that it will not utilize its local allocation so that the unused resource will become part of the statewide allocation. Local school districts receiving a local allocation are hereby directed to coordinate the use of such allocation with the State Board of Education so that any local allocation that will not be used by the local school district becomes eligible for use as part of the statewide allocation.

(b) Assistance. - The Department of Public Instruction shall provide the State Board of Education any support it requires in carrying out this section.

(c) Consultation. - In reviewing applications and awarding allocations, the State Board of Education shall consult with the Local Government Commission to determine whether a prospective issuer of qualified zone academy bonds or qualified school construction bonds is able to issue or incur marketable obligations.

(d) Issuance of Bonds. - Any qualified zone academy bonds or qualified school construction bonds may be issued pursuant to the applicable provisions of and in compliance with the Local Government Bond Act, Article 4 of Chapter 159 of the General Statutes, or pursuant to the applicable provisions of and in compliance with G.S. 160A-20, to the extent authorized by G.S. 153A-158.1. As provided in G.S. 159-123(b), qualified zone academy bonds or qualified school construction bonds to be issued pursuant to the Local Government Bond Act may be sold by the Local Government Commission at private sale. (2000-69, s. 1; 2009-140, s. 1.)

Article 35.

Voluntary Endowment Fund for Public Schools.

§ 115C-490. Creation of endowment funds; administration.

Any local board of education is hereby authorized and empowered upon the passage of a resolution to create and establish a permanent endowment fund which shall be financed by gifts, donations, devises, or other forms of voluntary contributions. Any endowment fund established under the provisions of this Article shall be administered by the members of such board of education who, ex officio, shall constitute and be known as "The Board of Trustees of the Endowment Fund of the Public Schools of _____ County or _____ City or Town" (in which shall be inserted the name of the county, city or town). The board of trustees so established shall determine its own organization and methods of procedure. (1961, c. 970; 1981, c. 423, s. 1; 2011-284, s. 77.)

§ 115C-491. Boards of trustees public corporations; powers and authority generally; investments.

Any board of trustees created and organized under this Article shall be a body politic, public corporation and instrumentality of government and as such may sue and be sued in matters relating to the endowment fund and shall have the power and authority to acquire, hold, purchase and invest in all forms of property, both real and personal, including, but not by way of limitation, all types of stocks, bonds, securities, mortgages and all types, kinds and subjects of investments of any nature and description. The board of trustees of said endowment fund may receive pledges, gifts, donations, devises, and may in its discretion retain such in the form in which they are made, and may use the same as a permanent endowment fund. The board of trustees of any endowment fund created hereunder shall have the power to sell any property, real, personal or choses in action, of the endowment fund, at either public or private sale. The board of trustees shall be responsible for the prudent investment of any funds or monies belonging to the endowment fund in the exercise of its sound discretion without regard to any statute or rule of law relating to the investment of funds by fiduciaries. (1961, c. 970; 1981, c. 423, s. 1; 2011-284, s. 78.)

§ 115C-492. Expenditure of funds; pledges.

It is not the intent that such endowment fund created hereunder shall take the place of State appropriations or any regular appropriations, tax funds or other funds made available by counties, cities, towns or local school administrative units for the normal operation of the public schools. Any endowment fund created hereunder, or the income from same, shall be used for the benefit of the public schools of the county, city or town involved and to supplement regular and normal appropriations to the end that the public schools may improve and increase their functions, may enlarge their areas of service and may become more useful to a greater number of people. The board of trustees in its discretion shall determine the objects and purposes for which the endowment fund shall be spent. Nothing herein shall be construed to prevent the board of trustees of any such endowment fund established hereunder from receiving pledges, gifts, donations, and devises and from using the same for such lawful school purposes as the donor or donors designate: Provided, always, that the administration of any such pledges, gifts, donations, and devises, or the expenditure of funds from same, will not impose any financial burden or obligation on the State of North Carolina or any subdivisions of government of the State. The board of trustees may, with the consent of the donor of any pledges, transfer and assign such pledges as security for loans. This consent by the donor may be made at the time of the pledge or at any time before said pledges are paid off in full. It is the purpose of this provision to enable the board of trustees to have the immediate use of funds which the donor may desire to pledge as payable over a period of years. (1961, c. 970; 1981, c. 423, s. 1; 2011-284, s. 79.)

§ 115C-493. When only income from fund expended.

Where the donor of said pledges, gifts, donations, and devises so provides, the board of trustees shall keep the principal of such gift or gifts intact and only the income therefrom may be expended. (1961, c. 970; 1981, c. 423, s. 1; 2011-284, s. 80.)

§ 115C-494. Property and income of board of trustees exempt from State taxation.

All property received, purchased, contributed or donated to the board of trustees for the benefit of any endowment fund created hereunder and all donations, gifts and devises received or otherwise administered for the benefit of said endowment fund, as well as the principal and income from said endowment fund, shall at all times be free from taxation, of any nature whatsoever, within the State. (1961, c. 970; 1981, c. 423, s. 1; 2011-284, s. 81.)

§§ 115C-495 through 115C-499. Reserved for future codification purposes.

Article 35A.

College Scholarships.

§ 115C-499.1. Definitions.

The following definitions apply to this Article:

(1) Academic year. - A period of time in which a student is expected to complete the equivalent of at least two semesters' or three quarters' academic work.

(2) Authority. - The State Education Assistance Authority created by Article 23 of Chapter 116 of the General Statutes.

(3) Eligible postsecondary institution. - A school that is:

a. A constituent institution of The University of North Carolina as defined in G.S. 116-2(4); or

b. A community college as defined in G.S. 115D-2(2).

c., d. Repealed by Session Laws 2011-145, s. 9.18(b), effective July 1, 2012.

(4) Matriculated status. - Being recognized as a student in a defined program of study leading to a degree, diploma, or certificate at an eligible postsecondary institution.

(5) Scholarship. - A scholarship for education awarded under this Article.

(6) Title IV. - Title IV of the Higher Education Act of 1965, as amended, 20 U.S.C. § 1070, et seq. (2005-344, s. 2; 2006-66, s. 9.19; 2006-221, s. 5B; 2006-259, s. 8(h); 2011-145, s. 9.18(b).)

§ 115C-499.2. Eligibility requirements for a scholarship.

In order to be eligible to receive a scholarship under this Article, a student seeking a degree, diploma, or certificate at an eligible postsecondary institution must meet all of the following requirements:

(1) Only needy North Carolina students are eligible to receive scholarships. For purposes of this subsection, "needy North Carolina students" are those eligible students whose expected family contribution under the federal methodology does not exceed five thousand dollars ($5,000).

(2) The student must meet all other eligibility requirements for the federal Pell Grant, with the exception of the expected family contribution.

(3) The student must qualify as a legal resident of North Carolina and as a resident for tuition purposes in accordance with definitions of residency that may from time to time be adopted by the Board of Governors and published in the residency manual of the Board of Governors.

(4) The student must meet enrollment standards by being admitted, enrolled, and classified as an undergraduate student in a matriculated status at an eligible postsecondary institution.

(5) In order to continue to be eligible for a scholarship for the student's second and subsequent academic years, the student must meet achievement standards by maintaining satisfactory academic progress in a course of study in accordance with the standards and practices used for federal Title IV programs by the eligible postsecondary institution in which the student is enrolled.

(6) (Repealed effective for 2014-2015 academic year and each subsequent academic year) A student may not receive a scholarship under this Article for more than four full academic years. (2005-344, s. 2; 2013-360, s. 11.15(a).)

§ 115C-499.2A. Semester limitation on eligibility for scholarship.

(a) Except as otherwise provided by subsection (c) of this section, a student with a matriculated status at a constituent institution of The University of North Carolina shall not receive a scholarship for more than 10 full-time academic semesters, or its equivalent if enrolled part-time, unless the student is enrolled in a program officially designated by the Board of Governors as a five-year degree program. If a student is enrolled in such a five-year degree program, then the student shall not receive a scholarship for more than 12 full-time academic semesters or the equivalent if enrolled part-time.

(b) Except as otherwise provided by subsection (c) of this section, a student with a matriculated status at a community college shall not receive a scholarship for more than six full-time academic semesters, or the equivalent if enrolled part-time.

(c) Upon application by a student, the appropriate postsecondary institution may grant a waiver to the student who may then receive a scholarship for the equivalent of one additional full-time academic semester if the student demonstrates that any of the following have substantially disrupted or interrupted the student's pursuit of a degree, diploma, or certificate: (i) a military service obligation, (ii) serious medical debilitation, (iii) a short-term or long-term disability, or (iv) other extraordinary hardship. The Board of Governors or the State Board of Community Colleges, as appropriate, shall establish policies and procedures to implement the waiver provided by this subsection. (2013-360, s. 11.15(b).)

§ 115C-499.3. Scholarship amounts; amounts dependent on net income available.

(a) Subject to the amount of net income available under G.S. 18C-164(b)(2), a scholarship awarded under this Article to a student at an eligible postsecondary institution shall be based upon the enrollment status and expected family contribution of the student and shall not exceed four thousand dollars ($4,000) per academic year, including any federal Pell Grant, to be used for the costs of attendance as defined for federal Title IV programs.

(b) Subject to the maximum amounts provided in this section, the Authority shall have the power to determine the actual scholarship amounts disbursed to students in any given year based on the amount of funds appropriated from the Education Lottery Fund. If the net income available is not sufficient to fully fund the scholarships to the maximum amount, all scholarships shall be reduced equally, to the extent practicable, so that every eligible applicant shall receive a proportionate scholarship amount.

(c) The minimum award of a scholarship under this Article shall be one hundred dollars ($100.00). (2005-344, s. 2; 2005-276, s. 31.1(v); 2006-226, s. 22; 2013-360, s. 6.11(d).)

§ 115C-499.4. Scholarship administration; reporting requirements.

(a) The scholarships provided for in this Article shall be administered by the Authority under rules adopted by the Authority in accordance with the provisions of this Article.

(b) The Authority shall report no later than June 1, 2008, and annually thereafter to the Joint Legislative Education Oversight Committee. The report shall contain, for the previous academic year, the amount of scholarship and grant money disbursed, the number of students eligible for the funds, the number of eligible students receiving the funds, and a breakdown of the eligible postsecondary institutions that received the funds.

(c) The Authority may use up to one and one-half percent (1.5%) of the funds transferred in accordance with Chapter 18C of the General Statutes for administrative purposes.

(d) Scholarship funds unexpended shall remain available for future scholarships to be awarded under this Article.

(e) The State Education Assistance Authority shall report annually to the Joint Legislative Commission on Governmental Operations regarding the use of the funds allocated to the Authority under S.L. 2005-344. (2005-344, s. 2; 2005-276, s. 31.1(v1); 2006-259, s. 8(k); 2006-264, s. 91(d).)

SUBCHAPTER VIII. LOCAL TAX ELECTIONS.

Article 36.

Voted Tax Supplements for School Purposes.

§ 115C-500. Superintendents must furnish boundaries of special taxing districts.

It shall be the duty of superintendents to furnish tax listers at tax listing time the boundaries of each taxing district as provided in G.S. 115C-276(m). (1981, c. 423, s. 1.)

§ 116-37.1. Center for public television.

(a) The Board of Governors is hereby authorized and directed to establish "the University of North Carolina Center for Public Television" (hereinafter called "the Center"). It shall be the functions of the Center, through itself or agencies with whom it may contract, to provide research, development, and production of noncommercial educational television programming and program materials; to provide distribution of noncommercial television programming through the broadcast facilities licensed to the University of North Carolina; and otherwise to enhance the uses of television for public purposes.

(b) The Center shall have a board of trustees, to be named "the Board of Trustees of the University of North Carolina Center for Public Television" (hereinafter called "the Board of Trustees"). The Board of Governors is hereby authorized and directed to establish the Board of Trustees of the Center and to delegate to the Board of Trustees such powers and duties as the Board of Governors deems necessary or appropriate for the effective discharge of the functions of the Center; provided, that the Board of Governors shall not be deemed by the provisions of this section to have the authority to delegate any responsibility it may have as licensee of the broadcast facilities of the University of North Carolina.

(1) The Board of Trustees of the University of North Carolina Center for Public Television shall be composed of the following membership: 11 persons appointed by the Board of Governors; four persons appointed by the Governor; two members appointed by the General Assembly, one upon the recommendation of the Speaker of the House of Representatives, and one upon the recommendation of the President Pro Tempore of the Senate in accordance with G.S. 120-121; and ex officio, the Secretary of the Department of Cultural Resources, the Secretary of the Department of Health and Human Services, the Superintendent of Public Instruction, the President of the Community College System, and the President of the University of North Carolina. In making initial appointments to the Board of Trustees, the Board of Governors shall designate six persons for two-year terms and five persons for four-year terms, and the Governor shall designate two persons for two-year terms and two persons for four-year terms. The initial members appointed to the Board of Trustees by the General Assembly shall serve for terms expiring June 30, 1983, and notwithstanding anything else in this section, their successors shall be appointed in 1983 and biennially thereafter for two-year terms. Thereafter, the term of office of appointed members of the Board of Trustees of the Center shall be four years. In making appointments to the Board of Trustees the appointing authorities shall give consideration to promoting diversity among the membership, to the end that, in meeting the responsibilities delegated to it, the Board of Trustees will reflect and be responsive to the diverse needs, interests, and concerns of the citizens of North Carolina.

(2) No person shall be appointed to the Board of Trustees who is an employee of the State or of any constituent institution; a public officer of the State as defined in G.S. 147-1, 147-2, and 147-3(c); a member of the Board of Governors; a trustee of a constituent institution; or the spouse of any of the foregoing. Any appointed member of the Board of Trustees who after appointment becomes any of the foregoing shall be deemed to have resigned from the Board of Trustees.

(3) Each ex officio member of the Board of Trustees shall personally serve on the Board of Trustees but may designate in writing a proxy for specified meetings which the ex officio member finds he or she is unable reasonably to attend.

(4) Each appointive member of the Board of Trustees shall personally serve on the Board of Trustees without benefit of proxy. Any appointive member who fails, for any reason other than ill health or service in the interest of the State or the nation, to attend three consecutive regular meetings of the Board of Trustees, shall be deemed to have resigned from the Board of Trustees.

(5) Vacancies in appointments made by the General Assembly shall be filled in accordance with G.S. 120-122. Other vacancies occurring during a term among the appointive membership of the Board of Trustees shall be filled for the remainder of the unexpired term by appointment of the original appointing authority for the vacant seat. The principal officer of the Board of Trustees shall promptly notify the Secretary of the University of North Carolina of the vacancy and the Secretary shall give written notice of the vacancy to the appropriate appointing authority.

(c) The chief administrative officer of the Center shall be a Director, who shall be elected by the Board of Governors upon recommendation of the President and who shall be responsible to the President. The Center shall have such other staff as the Board of Governors may authorize. (1979, c. 649, s. 1; 1981 (Reg. Sess., 1982), c. 1191, ss. 54, 55; 1987, c. 564, s. 33; 1995, c. 490, s. 61; 1997-443, s. 11A.118(a).)

§ 116-37.2. Regulation of University of North Carolina Hospitals at Chapel Hill Funds.

(a) As used in this section, "funds" means:

(1) Monies, or the proceeds of other forms of property, received by the University of North Carolina Hospitals at Chapel Hill as gifts or devises.

(2) Moneys received by the University of North Carolina Hospitals at Chapel Hill pursuant to grants from, or contracts with, the United States government or any agency or instrumentality thereof.

(3) Moneys received by the University of North Carolina Hospitals at Chapel Hill pursuant to grants from, or contracts with, any State agencies, any political subdivisions of the State, any other states or nations or political subdivisions thereof, or any private entities whereby the University of North Carolina Hospitals at Chapel Hill undertakes, subject to terms and conditions specified by the entity providing the moneys, to conduct research, training, or public service programs.

(4) Moneys received from or for the operation by the University of North Carolina Hospitals at Chapel Hill of any of its self-supporting auxiliary enterprises, including the Liability Insurance Trust Fund.

(5) Moneys received by the University of North Carolina Hospitals at Chapel Hill in respect to fees and other payments for services it renders in its hospital and/or clinical operations.

(5a) Moneys received by the University of North Carolina Hospitals at Chapel Hill in respect to borrowings for capital equipment or construction projects to further services it renders in either or both of its hospital or clinical operations.

(6) The net proceeds from the disposition effected pursuant to Article 7 of Chapter 146 of the General Statutes of any interest in real property owned by or under the supervision and control of the University of North Carolina Hospitals at Chapel Hill if the interest in real property had first been acquired by gift or devise or through expenditure of monies defined in this subsection, except the net proceeds from the disposition of an interest in real property first acquired by the University of North Hospitals at Chapel Hill through expenditure of monies received as a grant from a State agency.

(b) The Board of Directors of the University of North Carolina Health Care System, as established in G.S. 116-37(b), is responsible for the custody and management of the funds of the University of North Carolina Hospitals at Chapel Hill. The Board shall adopt uniform policies and procedures applicable to the deposit, investment, and administration of these funds, which shall assure that the receipt and expenditure of such funds is properly authorized and that the funds are appropriately accounted for. The Board may delegate authority, through the Chief Executive Officer of the University of North Carolina Health Care System to the President of the University of North Carolina Hospitals at Chapel Hill, when such delegation is necessary or prudent to enable the University of North Carolina Hospitals at Chapel Hill to function in a proper and expeditious manner.

(c) Funds under this section and investment earnings thereon are available for expenditure by the University of North Carolina Hospitals at Chapel Hill without further authorization from the General Assembly.

(d) Repealed by Session Laws 2011-145, s. 9.6E(c), effective July 1, 2011.

(e) Funds under this section are subject to the oversight of the State Auditor pursuant to Article 5A of Chapter 147 of the General Statutes but are not subject to the provisions of the State Budget Act except for capital improvements projects, which shall be authorized and executed in accordance with G.S. 143C-8-8 and G.S. 143C-8-9.

(f) The University of North Carolina Hospitals at Chapel Hill shall submit such reports or other information concerning its fund accounts under this section as may be required by the Board of Directors of the University of North Carolina Health Care System.

(g) Funds under this section, or the investment income therefrom, shall not take the place of State appropriations or any part thereof, but any portion of these funds available for general institutional purposes shall be used to supplement State appropriations to the end that the University of North Carolina Hospitals at Chapel Hill may improve and increase their functions, may enlarge their areas of service, and may become more useful to a greater number of people.

(h) The Board of Directors of the University of North Carolina Health Care System may deposit or invest the funds under this section in interest-bearing accounts and other investments in the exercise of its sound discretion, without regard to any statute or rule of law relating to the investment of funds by fiduciaries. (2005-417, s. 4; 2011-145, s. 9.6E(c); 2011-284, s. 85.)

§ 116-38. Child development research and demonstration center.

(a) The Chapel Hill City Board of Education is authorized to enter into long-term agreements and contracts with the University of North Carolina for the purpose of providing for the establishment and operation of a child development research and demonstration center. The Board is additionally authorized to lease or transfer title to real and personal property, including buildings and equipment, with or without compensation, to the University for this purpose.

(b) If an elementary school meeting the requirements for accreditation established by the State Board of Education is operated in conjunction with the center such school shall receive financial support through the Chapel Hill City Board of Education from State, county, and administrative unit sources on the same basis as the other elementary schools in the Chapel Hill city administrative unit.

(c) All personnel of the center whose salaries are paid in whole or part from funds administered by the State Board of Education or the Chapel Hill City Board of Education, from whatever sources derived, shall be employed only upon the mutual concurrence of the superintendent of the Chapel Hill city administrative unit and the director of the center. (1965, c. 690; 1971, c. 1244, s. 7.)

§ 116-39. Agricultural research stations.

The agricultural research stations shall be connected with North Carolina State University at Raleigh and shall be controlled by the Board of Governors of the University of North Carolina. (1907, c. 406, s. 12; C.S., s. 5825; 1963, c. 448, s. 9; 1965, c. 213; 1971, c. 1244, s. 8.)

§§ 116-39.1 through 116-39.2. Repealed by Session Laws 1971, c. 1244, s. 1.

§ 116-40. Board to accept gifts and congressional donations.

The Board of Governors shall use, as in its judgment may be proper, for the purposes of the University and for the benefit of education in agriculture and mechanic arts, as well as in furtherance of the powers and duties now or which may hereafter be conferred upon such Board by law, any funds, buildings, lands, laboratories, and other property which may be in its possession. The Board of Governors shall have power to accept and receive on the part of the State, property, personal, real or mixed, and any donations from the United States Congress to the several states and territories for the benefit of agricultural experiment stations or the agricultural and mechanical colleges in connection therewith, and shall expend the amount so received in accordance with the acts of the Congress in relation thereto. (1907, c. 406, s. 6; C.S., s. 5816; 1963, c. 448, s. 8; 1971, c. 1244, s. 9.)

§ 116-40.1. Land scrip fund.

The Board of Governors shall own and hold the certificates of indebtedness, amounting to one hundred and twenty-five thousand dollars ($125,000), issued for the principal of the land scrip fund, and the interest thereon shall be paid to them by the State Treasurer semiannually on the first day of July and January in each year for the purpose of aiding in the support of North Carolina State University at Raleigh in accordance with the act of the Congress approved July 2, 1862, entitled, "An act donating public lands to several states and territories which may provide colleges for the benefit of agriculture and mechanic arts." (1907, c. 406, s. 8; C.S., s. 5817; 1963, c. 448, s. 8; 1965, c. 213; 1971, c. 1244, s. 9.)

§ 116-40.2. Authorization to purchase insurance in connection with construction and operation of nuclear reactors.

In connection with the construction of, assembling of, use and operation of, any nuclear reactor now owned or hereafter acquired by it, North Carolina State University is hereby authorized and empowered to procure proper insurance against the hazards of explosion, implosion, radiation and any other special hazards unique to nuclear reactors, including nuclear fuel and all other components thereto. Further, North Carolina State University is authorized to enter into agreements with the United States Atomic Energy Commission prerequisite to licensing by that agency of nuclear reactors and to maintain as a part of such agreement or agreements appropriate insurance in amounts required by the Atomic Energy Commission of nuclear reactor licenses.

To the extent that North Carolina State University shall obtain insurance under the provisions of this section, it is hereby authorized and empowered to waive its governmental immunity from liability for damage to property or injury to or death to persons arising from the assembling, construction of, use and operation of nuclear reactors. Such immunity shall be deemed to have been waived by the act of obtaining such insurance, but only to the extent that North Carolina State University is indemnified by such insurance.

Any contract of insurance purchased pursuant to this section must be issued by a company or corporation duly licensed and authorized to do a business of insurance in this State except to the extent that such insurance may be furnished by or through a governmental agency created for the purpose of insuring against such hazards or through reinsurance pools or associations established to insure against such hazards.

Any person sustaining property damage or personal injury may sue North Carolina State University for damages for injury arising out of the construction, assembly, use or operation of a nuclear reactor on the campus of the University in the Superior Court of Wake County, and to the extent that the University is indemnified by insurance, it shall be no defense to any such action that the University was engaged in the performance of a governmental or discretionary function of the University. In the case of death alleged to have been caused by the assembly, construction, use or operation of such nuclear reactor, the personal representative of the deceased person may bring such action.

Nothing in this section shall in any way affect any other actions which have been or may hereafter be brought under the Tort Claims Act against North Carolina State University, nor shall the provisions of this section in any way abrogate or replace the provisions of the Workers' Compensation Act. (1969, c. 1023; 1971, c. 1244, s. 10; 1991, c. 636, s. 3; 1993, c. 553, s. 33.)

§ 116-40.3. Participation in sixth-year program of graduate instruction for superintendents, assistant superintendents, and principals of public schools.

Notwithstanding any other provision of law or the regulations of any administrative agency the educational institutions of East Carolina University, North Carolina Central University, North Carolina Agricultural and Technical State University, Appalachian State University, and Western Carolina University, are hereby authorized and shall be eligible colleges to participate in the sixth-year program adopted by the State Board of Education February 4, 1965, to provide a minimum of 60 semester hours of approved graduate, planned, nonduplicating instruction not beyond the master's degree for the education of superintendents, assistant superintendents, and principals of public schools. The satisfactory completion of such program and instruction shall qualify a person for the same certificate and stipend as now provided for other eligible educational institutions. (1965, c. 632; 1967, c. 1038; 1969, c. 114, s. 1; c. 608, s. 1; 1971, c. 1244, s. 10.)

§ 116-40.4. School of medicine authorized at East Carolina University; meeting requirements of accrediting agencies.

The Board of Trustees of East Carolina University is hereby authorized to create a school of medicine at East Carolina University, Greenville, North Carolina.

The school of medicine shall meet all requirements and regulations of the Council on Medical Education and Hospitals of the American Medical Association, the Association of American Medical Colleges, and other such accrediting agencies whose approval is normally required for the establishment and operation of a two-year medical school. (1965, c. 986, ss. 1, 2; 1967, c. 1038; 1971, c. 1244, s. 10.)

§ 116-40.5. Campus law enforcement agencies.

(a) The Board of Trustees of any constituent institution of The University of North Carolina, or of any teaching hospital affiliated with but not part of any constituent institution of The University of North Carolina, or the Board of Directors of the North Carolina Arboretum, may establish a campus law enforcement agency and employ campus police officers. Such officers shall meet the requirements of Chapter 17C of the General Statutes, shall take the oath of office prescribed by Article VI, Section 7 of the Constitution, and shall have all the powers of law enforcement officers generally. The territorial jurisdiction of a campus police officer shall include all property owned or leased to the institution employing the campus police officer and that portion of any public road or highway passing through such property or immediately adjoining it, wherever located.

(b) The Board of Trustees of any constituent institution of The University of North Carolina, or of any teaching hospital affiliated with but not part of any constituent institution of The University of North Carolina, or the Board of

Directors of the North Carolina Arboretum, having established a campus law enforcement agency pursuant to subsection (a) of this section, may enter into joint agreements with the governing board of any municipality to extend the law enforcement authority of campus police officers into any or all of the municipality's jurisdiction and to determine the circumstances in which this extension of authority may be granted.

(c) The Board of Trustees of any constituent institution of The University of North Carolina, or of any teaching hospital affiliated with but not part of any constituent institution of The University of North Carolina, or the Board of Directors of the North Carolina Arboretum, having established a campus law enforcement agency pursuant to subsection (a) of this section, may enter into joint agreements with the governing board of any county, and with the consent of the sheriff, to extend the law enforcement authority of campus police officers into any or all of the county's jurisdiction and to determine the circumstances in which this extension of authority may be granted.

(d) The Board of Trustees of any constituent institution of The University of North Carolina, or the Board of Directors of the North Carolina Arboretum, having established a campus law enforcement agency pursuant to subsection (a) of this section, may enter into joint agreements with the governing board of any other constituent institution of The University of North Carolina to extend the law enforcement authority of its campus police officers into any or all of the other institution's jurisdiction and to determine the circumstances in which this extension of authority may be granted. (1987, c. 671, s. 2; 1997-194, s. 1; 2001-397, s. 1; 2007-285, s. 1.)

§ 116-40.6. East Carolina University Medical Faculty Practice Plan.

(a) Medical Faculty Practice Plan. - The "Medical Faculty Practice Plan", a division of the School of Medicine of East Carolina University, operates clinical programs and facilities for the purpose of providing medical care to the general public and training physicians and other health care professionals.

(b) Personnel. - Employees of the Medical Faculty Practice Plan shall be deemed to be employees of the State and shall be subject to all provisions of State law relevant thereto; provided, however, that except as to the provisions of Articles 5, 6, 7, and 14 of Chapter 126 of the General Statutes, the provisions of Chapter 126 shall not apply to employees of the Medical Faculty Practice Plan, and the policies and procedures governing the terms and conditions of employment of such employees shall be adopted by the Board of Trustees of East Carolina University; provided, that with respect to such employees as may be members of the faculty of East Carolina University, no such policies and procedures may be inconsistent with policies established by, or adopted pursuant to delegation from, the Board of Governors of The University of North Carolina. Such policies and procedures shall be implemented on behalf of the Medical Faculty Practice Plan by a personnel office maintained by East Carolina University.

(1) The board of trustees shall fix or approve the schedules of pay, expense allowances, and other compensation, and adopt position classification plans for employees of the Medical Faculty Practice Plan.

(2) The board of trustees may adopt or provide for rules and regulations concerning, but not limited to, annual leave, sick leave, special leave with full pay, or with partial pay supplementing workers' compensation payments for employees injured in accidents arising out of and in the course of employment, working conditions, service awards, and incentive award programs, grounds for dismissal, demotion, or discipline, other personnel policies, and any other measures that promote the hiring and retention of capable, diligent, and effective career employees. However, an employee who has achieved career State employee status as defined by G.S. 126-1.1 by October 31, 1998, shall not have his or her compensation reduced as a result of this subdivision. Further, an employee who has achieved career State employee status as defined by G.S. 126-1.1 by October 31, 1998, shall be subject to the rules regarding discipline or discharge that were effective on October 31, 1998, and shall not be subject to the rules regarding discipline or discharge adopted after October 31, 1998.

(3) The board of trustees may prescribe the office hours, workdays, and holidays to be observed by the various offices and departments of the Medical Faculty Practice Plan.

(4) The board of trustees may establish boards, committees, or councils to conduct hearings upon the appeal of employees who have been suspended, demoted, otherwise disciplined, or discharged, to hear employee grievances, or to undertake any other duties relating to personnel administration that the board of trustees may direct.

The board of trustees shall submit all initial classification and pay plans, and other rules and regulations adopted pursuant to subdivisions (1) through (4) of this subsection to the Office of State Human Resources for review upon adoption by the board. Any subsequent changes to these plans, rules, and policies adopted by the board shall be submitted to the Office of State Human Resources for review. Any comments by the Office of State Human Resources shall be submitted to the Chancellor of East Carolina University and the President of The University of North Carolina.

(c) Purchases. - Notwithstanding the provisions of Articles 3, 3A, and 3C of Chapter 143 of the General Statutes to the contrary, the Board of Trustees of East Carolina University shall establish policies and regulations governing the purchasing requirements of the Medical Faculty Practice Plan. These policies and regulations shall provide for requests for proposals, competitive bidding, or purchasing by means other than competitive bidding, contract negotiations, and contract awards for purchasing supplies, materials, equipment, and services which are necessary and appropriate to fulfill the clinical and educational missions of the Medical Faculty Practice Plan. Pursuant to such policies and regulations, purchases for the Medical Faculty Practice Plan shall be effected by a purchasing office maintained by East Carolina University. The board of trustees shall submit all initial policies and regulations adopted under this subsection to the Division of Purchase and Contract for review upon adoption by the board. Any subsequent changes to these policies and regulations adopted by the board shall be submitted to the Division of Purchase and Contract for review. Any comments by the Division of Purchase and Contract shall be submitted to the Chancellor of East Carolina University and to the President of The University of North Carolina.

(d) Property. - The board of trustees shall establish rules and regulations for acquiring or disposing of any interest in real property for the use of the Medical Faculty Practice Plan. These rules and regulations shall include provisions for development of specifications, advertisement, and negotiations with owners for acquisition by purchase, gift, lease, or rental, but not by condemnation or exercise of eminent domain, on behalf of the Medical Faculty Practice Plan. This section does not authorize the board of trustees to encumber real property. Such rules and regulations shall be implemented by a property office maintained by East Carolina University. The board of trustees shall submit all initial rules and regulations adopted pursuant to this subsection to the State Property Office for review upon adoption. Any subsequent changes to these rules and regulations shall be submitted to the State Property Office for review. Any comments by the State Property Office shall be submitted to the Chancellor of East Carolina University and to the President of The University of North Carolina. After review by the Attorney General as to form and after the consummation of any such acquisition, East Carolina University shall promptly file, on behalf of the Medical Faculty Practice Plan, a report concerning the acquisition or disposition with the Governor and Council of State. Acquisitions and dispositions of any interest in real property pursuant to this section shall not be subject to the provisions of Article 36 of Chapter 143 of the General Statutes or the provisions of Chapter 146 of the General Statutes.

(e) Property - Construction. - Notwithstanding G.S. 143-341(3) and G.S. 143-135.1, the board of trustees shall adopt policies and procedures to be implemented by the administration of East Carolina University, with respect to the design, construction, and renovation of buildings, utilities, and other property developments for the use of the Medical Faculty Practice Plan, requiring the expenditure of public money for:

(1) Conducting the fee negotiations for all design contracts and supervising the letting of all construction and design contracts.

(2) Performing the duties of the Department of Administration, the Office of State Construction, and the State Building Commission under G.S. 133-1.1(d), Article 8 of Chapter 143 of the General Statutes, and G.S. 143-341(3).

(3) Using open-end design agreements.

(4) As appropriate, submitting construction documents for review and approval by the Department of Insurance and the Division of Health Service Regulation of the Department of Health and Human Services.

(5) Using the standard contracts for design and construction currently in use for State capital improvement projects by the Office of State Construction of the Department of Administration.

The board of trustees shall submit all initial policies and procedures adopted under this subsection to the Office of State Construction for review upon adoption by the board. Any subsequent changes to these policies and procedures adopted by the board shall be submitted to the Office of State Construction for review. Any comments by the Office of State Construction shall be submitted to the Chancellor of East Carolina University and to the President of The University of North Carolina. (1998-212, s. 11.8(f); 1999-252, s. 4(b); 2007-182, s. 1; 2013-382, s. 9.1(c).)

§ 116-40.7. Internal auditors.

(a) Internal auditors within The University of North Carolina and its constituent institutions shall provide independent reviews and analyses of various functions and programs within The University of North Carolina that will provide management information to promote accountability, integrity, and efficiency within The University of North Carolina.

(b) An internal auditor shall have access to any records, data, or other information of The University of North Carolina or the relevant constituent institution that the internal auditor believes necessary to carry out the internal auditor's duties.

(c) An internal auditor shall maintain, for 10 years, a complete file of all audit reports and reports of other examinations, investigations, surveys, and reviews issued under the internal auditor's authority. Audit work papers and other evidence and related supportive material directly pertaining to the work of that auditor's office shall be retained in accordance with Chapter 132 of the General Statutes. To promote cooperation and avoid unnecessary duplication of audit effort, audit work papers related to issued audit reports shall be, unless otherwise prohibited by law, made available for inspection by duly authorized representatives of the State and federal governments in connection with some matter officially before them. Except as otherwise provided in this subsection, or upon subpoena issued by a duly authorized court or court official, audit work papers shall be kept confidential and shall not be open to examination or inspection under G.S. 132-6 until completion of the audit report that is based on the working paper. Audit reports and the working papers on which they are based shall be public records subject to examination and inspection to the extent that they do not include information that, under State law, is confidential and exempt from Chapter 132 of the General Statutes or would compromise the security systems of The University of North Carolina. At the time that audit working papers are made available for public examination or inspection, the custodian of the audit working paper may redact the name and personally identifying information of a person who has initiated an allegation of (i) a violation of State or federal law or rule or regulation; (ii) fraud; (iii) misappropriation of State resources; (iv) substantial and specific danger to the public health and safety; or (v) gross mismanagement, gross waste of monies, or gross abuse of authority, if that person requests that the person's name and personally identifying information be kept confidential. (2004-203, s. 46; 2007-372, s. 3.)

§ 116-40.8. University of North Carolina at Pembroke designated as North Carolina's Historically American Indian University.

The University of North Carolina at Pembroke is officially designated as North Carolina's Historically American Indian University. (2005-153, s. 1.)

§ 116-40.9: Repealed by Session Laws 2011-74, s. 6(a), effective July 1, 2012.

§ 116-40.10: Repealed by Session Laws 2011-74, s. 5(a), effective July 1, 2012.

§ 116-40.11. Disciplinary proceedings; right to counsel for students and organizations.

(a) Any student enrolled at a constituent institution who is accused of a violation of the disciplinary or conduct rules of the constituent institution shall have the right to be represented, at the student's expense, by a licensed attorney or nonattorney advocate who may fully participate during any disciplinary procedure or other procedure adopted and used by the constituent institution regarding the alleged violation. However, a student shall not have the right to be represented by a licensed attorney or nonattorney advocate in either of the following circumstances:

(1) If the constituent institution has implemented a "Student Honor Court" which is fully staffed by students to address such violations.

(2) For any allegation of "academic dishonesty" as defined by the constituent institution.

(b) Any student organization officially recognized by a constituent institution that is accused of a violation of the disciplinary or conduct rules of the constituent institution shall have the right to be represented, at the organization's expense, by a licensed attorney or nonattorney advocate who may fully participate during any disciplinary procedure or other procedure adopted and used by the constituent institution regarding the alleged violation. However, a student organization shall not have the right to be represented by a licensed attorney or nonattorney advocate if the constituent institution has implemented a "Student Honor Court" which is fully staffed by students to address such violations.

(c) Nothing in this section shall be construed to create a right to be represented at a disciplinary proceeding at public expense. (2013-413, s. 6(c).)

§ 116-40.12. Reserved for future codification purposes.

§ 116-40.13. Reserved for future codification purposes.

§ 116-40.14. Reserved for future codification purposes.

§ 116-40.15. Reserved for future codification purposes.

§ 116-40.16. Reserved for future codification purposes.

§ 116-40.17. Reserved for future codification purposes.

§ 116-40.18. Reserved for future codification purposes.

§ 116-40.19. Reserved for future codification purposes.

Part 3A. Management Flexibility for Special Responsibility Constituent Institutions.

§ 116-40.20. Legislative findings.

(a) The General Assembly finds that The University of North Carolina and its constituent institutions is one of the State's most valuable assets. The General Assembly further finds that to provide the best benefit to North Carolina, the constituent institutions of The University of North Carolina need special budgeting flexibility in order to maximize resources, to enhance competitiveness with other peer institutions regionally, nationally, and internationally, and to provide the strongest educational and economic opportunity for the citizens of North Carolina.

(b) To ensure the continued preeminence of The University of North Carolina and its constituent institutions, it is the intent of the General Assembly to strengthen and improve these assets. The General Assembly commits to responsible stewardship and improvement of The University of North Carolina and its constituent institutions as provided by this Part. (2001-424, s. 31.11(a).)

§ 116-40.21. Board of governors may authorize management flexibility.

The Board of Governors of The University of North Carolina may authorize management flexibility for any special responsibility constituent institution as provided by this Part. The procedure for that authorization is the same as that to designate a constituent institution a special responsibility constituent institution under G.S. 116-30.1. (2001-424, s. 31.11(a).)

§ 116-40.22. Management flexibility.

(a) Definition. - For purposes of this section, the term "institution" means a special responsibility constituent institution that is granted management flexibility by the Board of Governors in compliance with this Part.

(b) Appoint and Fix Compensation of Senior Personnel. - Notwithstanding any provision in Chapter 116 of the General Statutes to the contrary, the Board of Trustees of an institution shall, on recommendation of the Chancellor, appoint and fix the compensation of all vice-chancellors, senior academic and administrative officers, and any person having permanent tenure at that institution. No later than January 1, 2002, the Board of Governors shall adopt policies, compensation structures, and pay ranges concerning the appointment and compensation of senior personnel appointed by the Board of Trustees pursuant to this section. Compensation for senior personnel fixed by the Board of Trustees pursuant to this section shall be consistent with the compensation structure, policies, and pay ranges set by the Board of Governors.

(c) Tuition and Fees. - Notwithstanding any provision in Chapter 116 of the General Statutes to the contrary, in addition to any tuition and fees set by the Board of Governors pursuant to G.S. 116-11(7), the Board of Trustees of the institution may recommend to the Board of Governors tuition and fees for program-specific and institution-specific needs at that institution without regard to whether an emergency situation exists and not inconsistent with the actions of the General Assembly. Any tuition and fees set pursuant to this subsection are appropriated for use by the institution. Notwithstanding this subsection, neither the Board of Governors of The University of North Carolina nor its Board of Trustees shall impose any tuition or mandatory fee at the North Carolina School of Science and Mathematics without the approval of the General Assembly, except as provided in subsection (f) of this section.

(d) Information Technology. - Notwithstanding any other provision of law, the Board of Trustees of an institution shall establish policies and rules governing the planning, acquisition, implementation, and delivery of information technology and telecommunications at the institution. These policies and rules shall provide for security and encryption standards; software standards; hardware standards; acquisition of information technology consulting and contract services; disaster recovery standards; and standards for desktop and server computing, telecommunications, networking, video services, personal digital assistants, and other wireless technologies; and other information technology matters that are necessary and appropriate to fulfill the teaching, educational, research, extension, and service missions of the institution. The Board of Trustees shall submit all initial policies and rules adopted pursuant to this subsection to the Office of Information Technology Services for review upon adoption by the Board of Trustees. Any subsequent changes to these policies and rules adopted by the Board of Trustees shall be submitted to the Office of Information Technology Services for review. Any comments by the Office of Information Technology Services shall be submitted to the Chancellor of that institution.

(e) Electronic Commerce. - The University is authorized to contract with service providers specializing in services offered to institutions of higher learning that offer systems or services under arrangements that provide for the receipt of funds electronically, provided the services are in compliance with the requirements of the payment industry security standards. For any funds collected and remitted to the University that are on deposit with the State Treasurer pursuant to G.S. 147-77, the funds shall be subject to the daily deposit requirements of the statute; provided that the State Treasurer may exempt the applicability of the daily deposit requirement for any standard business process resulting in a delay in the University receiving the funds from a service provider, when the exemption is based upon an acceptable business case that demonstrates an overall efficiency to the University and State. Such business case must first be endorsed by the University of North Carolina General Administration before submission to the State Treasurer for consideration.

(f) The Board of Governors of The University of North Carolina may approve, upon the recommendation of the Board of Trustees of the North Carolina School of Science and Mathematics, the imposition of fees not inconsistent with actions of the General Assembly for distance education services provided by the North Carolina School of Science and Mathematics to nonresidents and for students participating in extracurricular enrichment programs sponsored by the School. (2001-424, s. 31.11(a); 2006-66, s. 9.11(h); 2006-203, s. 4.1; 2013-360, s. 11.7(a); 2013-375, s. 2.)

§ 116-40.23. Reporting requirement; effective date of reported policies, procedures, and rules.

The Board of Trustees of a special responsibility constituent institution authorized to have management flexibility under this Part shall report to the Board of Governors and to the Joint Legislative Education Oversight Committee any policies, procedures, and rules adopted pursuant to G.S. 116-40.22 prior to implementation. The report shall be submitted to both at least 30 days before the next regularly scheduled meeting of the Board of Governors and shall become effective immediately following that same meeting unless otherwise provided for by the Board of Trustees. Any subsequent changes to the policies, procedures, or rules adopted by the Board of Trustees pursuant to G.S. 116-40.22 shall be reported to the Board of Governors and to the Joint Legislative Education Oversight Committee in the same manner. Failure of the Board of Governors to accept, review, or otherwise consider the report submitted by the Board of Trustees shall not affect in any manner the effective date of the policies, procedures, and rules contained in the report. (2001-424, s. 31.11(a).)

§ 116-41: Repealed by Session Laws 1963, c. 448, s. 15.

Part 4. Revenue Bonds for Service and Auxiliary Facilities.

§ 116-41.1. Definitions.

As used in this Part:

(1) "Board" means the Board of Governors of the University of North Carolina;

(2) "Construction" means acquisition, construction, provision, reconstruction, replacement, extension, improvement or betterment, or any combination thereof;

(3) "Cost," as applied to a project, shall include the cost of construction (as herein defined), the cost of all labor, materials and equipment, the cost of all lands, property, rights and easements acquired, financing charges, interest prior to and during construction and, if deemed advisable by the Board, for one year after completion of construction, cost of plans and specifications, surveys and estimates of cost and/or revenues, cost of engineering and legal services, and all other expenses necessary or incident to such construction, administrative expense and such other expenses, including reasonable provisions for initial operating expenses necessary or incident to the financing herein authorized and a reserve for debt service, and any expense incurred by the Board in the issuance of bonds under the provisions of this Part in connection with any of the foregoing items of cost;

(4) "Project" means any undertaking under this Part to acquire, construct or provide service and auxiliary facilities necessary or desirable for the proper and efficient operation of the University Enterprises, either as additions, extensions, improvements or betterments to the University Enterprises or otherwise, including one or more or any combination of any system, facility, plant, works, instrumentality or other property used or useful:

a. In obtaining, conserving, treating or distributing water for domestic, industrial, sanitation, fire protection or any other public or private use;

b. For the collection, treatment, purification or disposal of sewage, refuse or wastes;

c. For the production, generation, transmission or distribution of gas, electricity or heat;

d. In providing communication facilities including telephone facilities;

e. In providing storage, service, repair and duplicating facilities;

f. In improving, extending or adding to the University Enterprises as herein defined; and

g. In providing other service and auxiliary facilities serving the needs of the students, the staff or the physical plant of the University; and including all plants, works, appurtenances, machinery, equipment and properties, both personal and real, used or useful in connection therewith;

and in the case of the telephone, electric and water systems comprising a part of the University Enterprises such additions, extensions, improvements or betterments thereof as may be necessary or desirable, in the discretion of the Board, to provide service from such systems, where it may be reasonably made available, within the environs of the University, including, without limitation, areas presently served by the University Enterprises in Orange, Durham and Chatham Counties.

(5) "Revenue bonds" or "bonds" means bonds of the University issued by the Board to pay the cost, in whole or in part, of any project pursuant to this Part and the bond resolution or resolutions of the Board; provided, however, that bonds, issued as a separate series which are stated to mature not later than 20 years from their date may be designated "revenue notes" or "notes";

(6) "Revenues" means the income and receipts derived by or for the account of the University through the charging and collection of service charges;

(7) "Service charges" means rates, fees, rentals or other charges for, or for the right to, the use, occupancy, services or commodities of or furnished by any project, or by any other service or auxiliary facility of the University, including the University Enterprises, any part of the income of which is pledged to the payment of the bonds or the interest thereon;

(8) "University" means the body politic and corporate known and distinguished by the corporate name of the "University of North Carolina" under G.S. 116-3;

(9) "University Enterprises" means the following existing facilities, systems, properties, plants, works and instrumentalities located in or near the Town of Chapel Hill, North Carolina, presently in the jurisdiction of and operated by the University; the telephone, electric, heating and water systems, the laundry, Carolina Inn, service and repair shops, the duplicating shop, bookstores and student supply stores, and rental housing properties for faculty members. (1961, c. 1078, s. 1; 1963, c. 448, s. 16; c. 944, s. 1; 1965, c. 1033, s. 1; 1971, c. 636; c. 1244, s. 16.)

§ 116-41.2. Powers of Board of Governors generally.

In addition to the powers which the Board now has, the Board shall have the following powers subject to the provisions of this Part and subject to agreements with the holders of any revenue bonds issued hereunder:

(1) To acquire by gift, purchase or the exercise of the power of eminent domain or to construct, provide, improve, maintain and operate any project or projects;

(2) To borrow money for the construction of any project or projects, and to issue revenue bonds therefor in the name of the University;

(3) To establish, maintain, revise, charge and collect such service charges (free of any control or regulation by any State regulatory body until January 1, 1973, and thereafter only by the North Carolina Utilities Commission) as will produce sufficient revenues to pay the principal of and interest on the bonds and otherwise to meet the requirements of the resolution or resolutions of the Board authorizing the issuance of the revenue bonds;

(4) To pledge to the payment of any bonds of the University issued hereunder and the interest thereon the revenues of the project financed in whole or in part with the proceeds of such bonds, and to pledge to the payment of such bonds and interest any other revenues, subject to any prior pledge or encumbrance thereof;

(5) To appropriate, apply, or expend in payment of the cost of the project the proceeds of the revenue bonds issued for the project;

(6) To sell, furnish, distribute, rent, or permit, as the case may be, the use, occupancy, services, facilities and commodities of or furnished by any project or any system, facility, plant, works, instrumentalities or properties whose revenues are pledged in whole or in part for the payment of the bonds, and to sell, exchange, transfer, assign or otherwise dispose of any project or any of the University Enterprises or any other service or auxiliary facility or any part of any thereof or interest therein determined by resolution of the Board not to be required for any public purpose by the Board;

(7) To insure the payment of service charges with respect to the telephone, electric and water systems of the University Enterprises, as the same shall become due and payable, the Board may, in addition to any other remedies which it may have:

a. Require reasonable advance deposits to be made with it to be subject to application to the payment of delinquent service charges, and

b. At the expiration of 30 days after any such service charges become delinquent, discontinue supplying the services and facilities of such telephone, electric and water systems.

(8) To retain and employ consultants and other persons on a contract basis for rendering professional, technical or financial assistance and advice in undertaking and carrying out any project and in operating, repairing or maintaining any project or any system, facility, plant, works, instrumentalities or properties whose revenues are pledged in whole or in part for the payment of the bonds; and

(9) To enter into and carry out contracts with the United States of America or this State or any municipality, county or other public corporation and to lease property to or from any person, firm or corporation, private or public, in connection with exercising the powers vested under this Part. (1961, c. 1078, s. 2; 1971, c. 634, s. 2; c. 636; c. 1244, s. 15.)

§ 116-41.3. University authorized to pay service charges; payments deemed revenues.

The University is hereby authorized to pay service charges for, or for the right to, the use, occupancy, services or commodities of or furnished by any project or by any other service or auxiliary facility of the University, including the University Enterprises, and the income and receipts derive from such service charges paid by the University shall be deemed to be revenues under the provisions of this Part and shall be applied and accounted for in the same manner as other revenues. (1961, c. 1078, s. 3.)

§ 116-41.4. Bonds authorized; amount limited; form, execution and sale; terms and conditions; use of proceeds; additional bonds; interim receipts or temporary bonds; replacement of lost, etc., bonds; approval or consent for issuance; bonds not debt of State; bond anticipation notes.

The Board is hereby authorized to issue, subject to the approval of the Director of the Budget, at one time or from time to time, revenue bonds of the University for the purpose of undertaking and carrying out any project or projects hereunder; provided, however, that the aggregate principal amount of revenue bonds which the Board is authorized to issue under this section during the biennium ending June 30, 1969, shall not exceed three million five hundred thousand dollars ($3,500,000); provided, further, the Board shall have authority to issue revenue bonds under this section in an additional aggregate principal amount not to exceed three million five hundred thousand dollars ($3,500,000) during the biennium ending June 30, 1971; provided, however, that the aggregate principal amount of revenue bonds which the Board is authorized to issue under this section during the biennium ending June 30, 1973, shall not exceed thirteen million dollars ($13,000,000); provided, further, that the aggregate principal amount of revenue bonds which the Board is authorized to issue under this section during the biennium ending June 30, 1975, shall not exceed thirteen million dollars ($13,000,000). The bonds shall be dated, shall mature at such time or times not exceeding 30 years from their date or dates, and shall bear interest at such rate or rates as may be determined by the Board, and may be made redeemable before maturity at the option of the Board at such price or prices and under such terms and conditions as may be fixed by the Board prior to the issuance of the bonds. The Board shall determine the form and manner of execution of the bonds, and any interest coupons to be attached thereto, and shall fix the denomination or denominations of the bonds and the place or places of payment of principal and interest, which may be at any bank or trust company within or without the State. In case any officer whose signature or a facsimile of whose signature appears on any bonds or coupons shall cease to be such officer before the delivery of such bonds, such signature or such facsimile shall nevertheless be valid and sufficient for all purposes the same as if he had remained in office until such delivery. Notwithstanding any of the other provisions of this Part or any recitals in any bonds issued under the provisions of this Part, all such bonds shall be deemed to be negotiable instruments under the laws of this State. The bonds may be issued in coupon or registered form or both, as the Board may determine, and provision may be made for the registration of any coupon bonds as to principal alone and also as to both principal and interest, and for the reconversion into coupon bonds of any bonds registered as to both principal and interest. The Board may sell such bonds in such manner, at public or private sale, and for such price, as it may determine to be for the best interests of the University.

The proceeds of the bonds of each issue shall be used solely for the purpose for which such bonds shall have been authorized and shall be disbursed in such manner and under such restrictions, if any, as the Board may provide in the resolution authorizing the issuance of such bonds. Unless otherwise provided in the authorizing resolution, if the proceeds of such bonds, by error of estimates or otherwise, shall be less than such costs, additional bonds may in like manner be issued to provide the amount of such deficit and shall be deemed to be of the same issue and shall be entitled to payment from the same fund without preference or priority of the bonds first issued for the same purpose.

The resolution providing for the issuance of revenue bonds may also contain such limitations upon the issuance of additional revenue bonds as the Board may deem proper, and such additional bonds shall be issued under such restrictions and limitations as may be prescribed by such resolution.

Prior to the preparation of definitive bonds, the Board may, under like restrictions, issue interim receipts or temporary bonds, with or without coupons, exchangeable for definitive bonds when such bonds shall have been executed and are available for delivery. The Board may also provide for the replacement of any bonds which shall become mutilated or be destroyed or lost.

Bonds may be issued by the Board under the provisions of this Part, subject to the approval of the Director of the Budget, but without obtaining the consent of any other commission, board, bureau or agency of the State, and without any other proceedings or the happening of any other conditions or things than those consents, proceedings, conditions or things which are specifically required by this Part.

Revenue bonds issued under the provisions of this Part shall not be deemed to constitute a debt of the State of North Carolina or a pledge of the faith and credit of the State, but such bonds shall be payable solely from the funds herein provided therefor and a statement to that effect shall be recited on the face of the bonds.

The Board is hereby authorized to issue, subject to the approval of the Director of the Budget, at one time or from time to time, revenue bond anticipation notes of the Board in anticipation of the issuance of bonds authorized pursuant to the provisions of this Part. The principal of and the interest on such notes shall be payable solely from the proceeds of bonds or renewal notes or, in the event bond or renewal note proceeds are not available, any available revenues of the project or projects for which such bonds shall have been authorized. The notes of each issue shall be dated, shall mature at such time or times not exceeding two years from their date or dates, shall bear interest at such rate or rates as may be determined by the Board, and may be made redeemable before maturity, at the option of the Board, at such price or prices and under such terms and conditions as may be fixed by the Board, and may be made redeemable before maturity, at the option of the Board, at such price or prices and under such terms and conditions as may be fixed by the Board prior to the issuance of the notes. The Board shall determine the form and manner of execution of the notes, including any interest coupons to be attached thereto, and shall fix the denomination or denominations of the notes and the place or places of payment of principal and interest, which may be at any bank or trust company within or without the State. In case any officer, whose signature or a facsimile of whose signature shall appear on any notes or coupons, shall cease to be such officer before the delivery of such notes, such signature or such facsimile shall nevertheless be valid and sufficient for all purposes the same as if he had remained in office until such delivery. Notwithstanding any of the other provisions of this Part or any recitals in any notes issued under the provisions of this Part, all such notes shall be deemed to be negotiable instruments under the laws of this State. The notes may be issued in coupon or registered form or both, as the Board may determine, and provision may be made for the registration of any coupon notes as to principal alone and also as to both principal and interest, and for the reconversion into coupon notes of any notes registered as to both principal and interest. The Board may sell such notes in such manner, at public or private sale, and for such price, as it may determine to be for the best interests of the University.

The proceeds of the notes of each issue shall be used solely for the purpose for which the bonds in anticipation of which such notes are being issued shall have been authorized, and such note proceeds shall be disbursed in such manner and under such restrictions, if any, as the Board may provide in the resolution authorizing the issuance of such notes or bonds.

The resolution providing for the issuance of notes or bonds may also contain such limitations upon the issuance of additional notes as the Board may deem proper, and such additional notes shall be issued under such restrictions and limitations as may be prescribed by such resolution.

Notes may be issued by the Board under the provisions of this Part, subject to the approval of the Director of the Budget, but without obtaining the consent of any other commission, board, bureau or agency of the State, and without any other proceedings or the happening of any other conditions or things than those consents, proceedings, conditions or things which are specifically required by this Part.

Revenue bond anticipation notes issued under the provisions of this Part shall not be deemed to constitute a debt of the State of North Carolina or a pledge of the faith and credit of the State, but such notes shall be payable solely from the funds herein provided therefor and a statement to that effect shall be recited on the face of the notes.

Unless the context shall otherwise indicate, the word "bonds," wherever used in this Part, shall be deemed and construed to include the words "bond anticipation notes." (1961, c. 1078, s. 4; 1963, c. 944, s. 2; 1965, c. 1033, s. 2; 1967, c. 724; 1969, c. 1236; 1971, c. 636; c. 1244, s. 15; 1973, c. 663; 1983, c. 577, s. 3; 1985 (Reg. Sess., 1986), c. 955, ss. 32, 33; 2006-203, s. 48.)

§ 116-41.5. Contents of resolution authorizing issuance; powers liberally construed; deposit and use of revenues; rights and remedies of bondholders; service charges; insurance of projects; depositaries.

The Board in the resolution authorizing the issuance of bonds under this Part may provide for a pledge to the payment of such revenue bonds and the interest thereon of the revenue derived from the project and also for a pledge of the revenues derived from any system, facility, plant, works, instrumentalities or properties improved, bettered, or extended by the project or otherwise within the jurisdiction of or operated by the University in connection with the University of North Carolina at Chapel Hill, North Carolina, the revenues derived from any future improvements, betterments or extensions of the project, the revenues derived from the University Enterprises, or any part thereof, or the revenues from the project and any or all of the revenues mentioned in this sentence, without regard to whether the operations involved are deemed governmental or proprietary, it being the purpose hereof to vest in the Board broad powers which shall be liberally construed. So long as any revenues of the University mentioned in this paragraph are pledged for the payment of the principal of or interest on any bonds issued hereunder, such revenues shall be deposited in a special fund and shall be applied and used only as provided in the resolution authorizing such bonds, subject, however, to any prior pledge or encumbrance thereof.

The resolution authorizing the issuance of the bonds may contain provisions for protecting and enforcing the rights and remedies of the holders of the bonds, including covenants setting forth the duties of the University in relation to the construction of any project to be financed with the proceeds of said bonds, and to the maintenance, repair, operation and insurance of such project or any other project, systems, facilities, plants, works, instrumentalities, properties, the University Enterprises or any part thereof, if the revenues thereof are in any way pledged as security for the bonds; the fixing and revising of service charges and the collection thereof; and the custody, safeguarding and application of all moneys of the University pertaining to the project and the bonds, and all revenues pledged therefor. Notwithstanding the provisions of any other law, the Board may carry insurance on any such project in such amounts and covering such risks as it may deem advisable. It shall be lawful for any bank or trust company incorporated under the laws of the State of North Carolina which may act as depositary of the proceeds of bonds or of revenues to furnish such indemnifying bonds or to pledge such securities as may be required by the Board. Such resolution may set forth the rights and remedies of the bondholders and may restrict the individual right of action by bondholders. Such resolution may contain such other provisions in addition to the foregoing as the Board may deem reasonable and proper for the security of the bondholders.

The Board may provide for the payment of the proceeds of the bonds and any revenues pledged therefor to such officer, board or depositary as it may designate for the custody thereof, and for the method of disbursement thereof, with such safeguards and restrictions as it may determine. All expenses incurred in carrying out the provisions of such resolution may be treated as a part of the cost of operation. (1961, c. 1078, s. 5; 1971, c. 1244, s. 15.)

§ 116-41.6. Pledge of revenues; lien.

All pledges of revenues under the provisions of this Part shall be valid and binding from the time such pledges are made. All such revenues so pledged shall immediately upon receipt thereof be subject to the lien of such pledge without any physical delivery thereof or further action, and the lien of such pledge shall be valid and binding as against all parties having claims of any kind in tort, contract or otherwise against the University, irrespective of whether such parties have notice thereof. (1961, c. 1078, s. 6.)

§ 116-41.7. Proceeds of bonds, revenues, etc., deemed trust funds.

The proceeds of all bonds issued and all revenues and other moneys received pursuant to the authority of this Part shall be deemed to be trust funds, to be held and applied solely as provided in this Part. The resolution authorizing the issuance of bonds shall provide that any officer to whom, or bank, trust company or fiscal agent to which, such moneys shall be paid shall act as trustee of such moneys and shall hold and apply the same for the purposes hereof, subject to such regulations as such resolution may provide. (1961, c. 1078, s. 7.)

§ 116-41.8. Rights and remedies of bondholders

Any holder of revenue bonds issued under the provisions of this Part or of any of the coupons appertaining thereto, except to the extent that the rights herein given may be restricted by the resolution authorizing the issuance of such bonds, may, either at law or in equity, by suit, action, mandamus or other proceeding, protect and enforce any and all rights under the laws of the State of North Carolina, including this Part, or under such resolution, and may enforce and compel the performance of all duties required by this Part or by such resolution to be performed by the University or by any officer thereof or the Board, including the fixing, charging and collecting of service charges. (1961, c. 1078, s. 8; 1971, c. 1244, s. 15.)

§ 116-41.9. Refunding revenue bonds.

The University is hereby authorized, subject to the approval of the Director of the Budget, to issue from time to time refunding revenue bonds for the purpose of refunding any revenue bonds issued by the University under this Part in connection with any project or projects, including the payment of any redemption premium thereon and any interest accrued or to accrue to the date of redemption of such bonds. The University is further authorized, subject to the approval of the Director of the Budget, to issue from time to time refunding revenue bonds for the combined purpose of

(1)   Refunding any revenue bonds or refunding revenue bonds issued by the University in connection with any project or projects including the payment of any redemption premium thereon and any interest accrued or to accrue to the date of redemption of such bonds, and

(2)   Paying all or any part of the cost of any project or projects.

The issuance of such refunding revenue bonds, the maturities and other details thereof, the rights and remedies of the holders thereof, and the rights, powers, privileges, duties and obligations of the University with respect to the same, shall be governed by the foregoing provisions of this Part insofar as the same may be applicable. (1961, c. 1078, s. 9; 1983, c. 577, s. 4; 1985 (Reg. Sess.,1986), c. 955, ss. 34, 35; 2006-203, s. 49.)

§ 116-41.10. Exemption from taxation.

The bonds issued under the provisions of this Part and the income therefrom shall at all times be free from taxation within the State. (1961, c. 1078, s. 10.)

§ 116-41.11. Executive committee may be authorized to exercise powers and functions of Board.

The Board by resolution may authorize its executive committee to exercise or perform any of the powers or functions vested in the Board under this Part. (1961, c. 1078, s. 11; 1971, c. 1244, s. 15.)

§ 116-41.12. Part provides supplemental and additional powers; compliance with other laws not required.

This Part shall be deemed to provide an additional and alternative method for the doing of the things authorized hereby and shall be regarded as supplemental and additional to powers conferred by other laws, and shall not be regarded as in derogation of or as repealing any powers now existing under any other law, either general, special or local; provided, however, that the issuance of revenue bonds or refunding revenue bonds under the provisions of this Part need not comply with the requirements of any other law applicable to the issuance of bonds and provided, further, that all general, special or local laws, or parts thereof, inconsistent herewith are hereby declared to be inapplicable to the provisions of this Part. (1961, c. 1078, s. 12.)

§ 116-41.13. Distinguished Professors Endowment Trust Fund; purpose.

The General Assembly of North Carolina recognizes that the public university system would be greatly strengthened by the addition of distinguished scholars. It further recognizes that private as well as State support is preferred in helping to obtain distinguished scholars for the State universities and that private support will help strengthen the commitment of citizens and organizations in promoting excellence throughout all State universities. It is the intent of the General Assembly to establish a trust fund to provide the opportunity to each

State university to receive and match challenge grants to create endowments for selected distinguished professors to occupy chairs within the university. The associated foundations that serve the universities shall solicit and receive gifts from private sources to provide for matching funds to the trust fund challenge grants for the establishment of endowments for chairs within universities. (1985, c. 757, s. 202.)

§ 116-41.13A. Distinguished Professors Endowment Trust Fund; definitions.

The following definitions apply in this Part:

(1) "Focused growth institution" means Elizabeth City State University, Fayetteville State University, North Carolina Agricultural and Technical University, North Carolina Central University, The University of North Carolina at Pembroke, Western Carolina University, and Winston-Salem State University.

(2) "Special needs institution" means the North Carolina School of the Arts, redesignated effective August 1, 2008, as the "University of North Carolina School of the Arts," and The University of North Carolina at Asheville. (2003-293, s. 1; 2008-192, s. 6.)

§ 116-41.14. Distinguished Professors Endowment Trust Fund; establishment; maintenance.

There is established a Distinguished Professors Endowment Trust Fund to be maintained by the Board to provide challenge grants to the constituent institutions. All appropriated funds deposited into the trust fund shall be invested pursuant to G.S. 116-36. Interest income accruing to that portion of the trust fund not matched shall increase the total funds available for challenge grants. (1985, c. 757, s. 202.)

§ 116-41.15. Distinguished Professors Endowment Trust Fund; allocation; administration.

(a) For constituent institutions other than focused growth institutions and special needs institutions, the amount appropriated to the trust shall be allocated by the Board as follows:

(1) On the basis of one three hundred thirty-four thousand dollar ($334,000) challenge grant for each six hundred sixty-six thousand dollars ($666,000) raised from private sources; or

(2) On the basis of one one hundred sixty-seven thousand dollar ($167,000) challenge grant for each three hundred thirty-three thousand dollars ($333,000) raised from private sources; or

(3) On the basis of one challenge grant of up to six hundred sixty-seven thousand dollars ($667,000) for funds raised from private sources in twice the amount of the challenge grant.

If an institution chooses to pursue the use of the allocated challenge grant funds described in either subdivision (1), subdivision (2), or subdivision (3) of this subsection, the challenge grant funds shall be matched by funds from private sources on the basis of two dollars of private funds for every one dollar of State funds.

(b) For focused growth institutions and special needs institutions, the amount appropriated to the trust shall be allocated by the Board as follows:

(1) On the basis of one five hundred thousand dollar ($500,000) challenge grant for each five hundred thousand dollars ($500,000) raised from private sources; or

(2) On the basis of one two hundred fifty thousand dollar ($250,000) challenge grant for each two hundred fifty thousand dollars ($250,000) raised from private sources; or

(3) On the basis of one challenge grant of up to one million dollars ($1,000,000) for funds raised from private sources in the same amount as the challenge grant.

If an institution chooses to pursue the use of the allocated challenge grant funds described in either subdivision (1), subdivision (2), or subdivision (3) of this subsection, the challenge grant funds shall be matched by funds from private sources on the basis of one dollar of private funds for every dollar of State funds.

(c) Matching funds shall come from contributions made after July 1, 1985, and pledged for the purposes specified by G.S. 116-41.14. Each participating constituent institution's board of trustees shall establish its own Distinguished Professors Endowment Trust Fund, and shall maintain it pursuant to the provision of G.S. 116-36 to function as a depository for private contributions and for the State matching funds for the challenge grants. The State matching funds shall be transferred to the constituent institution's Endowment Fund upon notification that the institution has received and deposited the appropriate amount required by this section in its own Distinguished Professors Endowment Trust Fund. Only the net income from that account shall be expended in support of the distinguished professorship thereby created. (1985, c. 757, s. 202; 2003-293, s. 2; 2005-276, s. 9.21(a).)

§ 116-41.16. Distinguished Professors Endowment Trust Fund; contribution commitments.

(a) For constituent institutions other than focused growth institutions and special needs institutions, contributions may also be eligible for matching if there is:

(1) A commitment to make a donation of at least six hundred sixty-six thousand dollars ($666,000), as prescribed by G.S. 143C-4-5, and an initial payment of one hundred eleven thousand dollars ($111,000) to receive a grant described in G.S. 116-41.15(a)(1); or

(2) A commitment to make a donation of at least three hundred thirty-three thousand dollars ($333,000), as prescribed by G.S. 143C-4-5, and an initial payment of fifty-five thousand five hundred dollars ($55,500) to receive a grant described in G.S. 116-41.15(a)(2); or

(3) A commitment to make a donation in excess of six hundred sixty-six thousand dollars ($666,000), as prescribed by G.S. 143-31.4 [G.S. 143C-4-5], and an initial payment of one-sixth of the committed amount to receive a grant described in G.S. 116-41.15(a)(3); and if the initial payment is accompanied by a written pledge to provide the balance within five years after the date of the initial payment. Each payment on the balance shall be no less than the amount of the initial payment and shall be made on or before the anniversary date of the initial payment. Pledged contributions may not be matched prior to the actual collection of the total funds. Once the income from the institution's Distinguished Professors Endowment Trust Fund can be effectively used pursuant to G.S. 116-41.17, the institution shall proceed to implement plans for establishing an endowed chair.

(b) For focused growth institutions and special needs institutions, contributions may also be eligible for matching if there is:

(1) A commitment to make a donation of at least five hundred thousand dollars ($500,000), as prescribed by G.S. 143C-4-5, and an initial payment of eighty-three thousand three hundred dollars ($83,300) to receive a grant described in G.S. 116-41.5(b)(1); or

(2) A commitment to make a donation of at least two hundred fifty thousand dollars ($250,000), as prescribed by G.S. 143C-4-5, and an initial payment of forty-one thousand six hundred dollars ($41,600) to receive a grant described in G.S. 116-41.15(b)(2); or

(3) A commitment to make a donation in excess of five hundred thousand dollars ($500,000), as prescribed by G.S. 143-31.4 [G.S. 143C-4-5], and an initial payment of one-sixth of the committed amount to receive a grant described in G.S. 116-41.15(b)(3);

and if the initial payment is accompanied by a written pledge to provide the balance within five years after the date of the initial payment. Each payment on the balance shall be no less than the amount of the initial payment. Pledged contributions may not be matched prior to the actual collection of the total funds. Once the income from the institution's Distinguished Professors Endowment Trust Fund can be effectively used pursuant to G.S. 116-41.17, the institution shall proceed to implement plans for establishing an endowed chair. (1985, c. 757, s. 202; 2003-293, s. 3; 2005-276, s. 9.21(b); 2006-203, s. 50.)

§ 116-41.17. Distinguished Professors Endowment Trust Fund; establishment of chairs.

When the sum of the challenge grant and matching funds in the Distinguished Professors Endowment Trust Fund reaches:

(1) One million dollars ($1,000,000), if the sum of funds described in G.S. 116-41.15(a)(1) or G.S. 116-41.15(b)(1); or

(2) Five hundred thousand dollars ($500,000), if the sum of funds described in G.S. 116-41.15(a)(2) or G.S. 116-41.15(b)(2); or

(3) An amount up to two million dollars ($2,000,000), if the sum of funds described in G.S. 116-41.15(a)(3) or G.S. 116-41.15(b)(3);

the board of trustees may recommend to the Board, for its approval, the establishment of an endowed chair or chairs. The Board, in considering whether to approve the recommendation, shall include in its consideration the programs already existing in The University of North Carolina. If the Board approves the recommendation, the chair or chairs shall be established. The chair or chairs, the property of the constituent institution, may be named in honor of a donor, benefactor, or honoree of the institution, at the option of the board of trustees. (1985, c. 757, s. 202; 2005-276, s. 9.21(c).)

§ 116-41.18. Distinguished Professors Endowment Trust Fund; selection of Distinguished Professors.

(a) Each constituent institution that receives, through private gifts and an allocation by the Board of Governors, funds for the purpose shall, under procedures established by rules of the Board of Governors and the board of trustees of the constituent institution, select a holder of the Distinguished Professorship. Once given, that designation shall be retained by the distinguished professor as long as he remains in the full-time service of the institution as a faculty member, or for more limited lengths of time when authorized by the Board of Governors and the board of trustees at the institution when the Distinguished Professorship is originally established or vacated. When a distinguished professorship becomes vacant, it shall remain assigned to the institution and another distinguished professor shall be selected under procedures established by rules of the Board of Governors and the board of trustees of the constituent institution.

(a1) No rule shall prevent the constituent institutions of The University of North Carolina from selecting holders of Distinguished Professorships from among existing faculty members or newly hired faculty members.

(b) The Board of Governors of The University of North Carolina shall promulgate rules to implement this section.

(c) There is appropriated from the General Fund to the Board of Governors of The University of North Carolina the sum of two million dollars ($2,000,000) for fiscal year 1985-86, and the sum of two million dollars ($2,000,000) for fiscal year 1986-87, to implement this section. (1985, c. 757, s. 202; 1991 (Reg. Sess., 1992), c. 1030, s. 31; 1995, c. 507, s. 15.12; 1997-443, s. 10.6.)

§ 116-41.19. Distinguished Professors Endowment Trust Fund; promulgation of rules.

The Board of Governors of The University of North Carolina shall promulgate rules to implement this Part. (1985, c. 757, s. 202.)

Part 5. Miscellaneous Provisions.

§§ 116-42 through 116-42.4: Repealed by Session Laws 1973, c. 495, s. 2.

§ 116-43. Escheat receipts prior to July 1, 1971.

All property that has heretofore escheated to the University of North Carolina, and all interest and earnings thereon, shall be set apart by the Board of Governors of the University for the six member campuses of the University of North Carolina as constituted on June 30, 1971, so that the interest and earnings from said fund shall be used for maintenance and/or for scholarships and loan funds for worthy and needy students, residents of the State, attending the member campuses of the University of North Carolina as constituted on June 30, 1971, under such rules and regulations as shall be adopted by the Board of Governors. (1874-5, c. 236, s. 2; Code, s. 2630; Rev., s. 4285; C.S., s. 5787; 1947, c. 614, s. 4; 1953, c. 1202, s. 3; 1971, c. 1244, s. 17.)

§ 116-43.1. Institute for Transportation Research and Education.

The Board of Governors of the University of North Carolina is authorized to establish an Institute for Transportation Research and Education to facilitate the development of a broad program of transportation research and education involving other organizations and institutions which have related programs. The immediate purpose of the Institute shall be to create a management structure to coordinate and eventually merge the Highway Safety Programs of the National Driving Center and the North Carolina Highway Safety Research Center. The

Board of Governors of the University of North Carolina is further authorized to establish a Council for Transportation Research and Education to represent all interests in transportation research and education, including but not limited to transportation safety. (1975, 2nd Sess., c. 983, s. 57.)

§ 116-43.5: Repealed by Session Laws 2011-145, s. 9.18(c), as amended by Session Laws 2012-142, s. 9.2(c), effective July 1, 2012.

§ 116-43.10. Academic Common Market program.

(a) The Southern Regional Education Board operates an Academic Common Market program. Under this program, qualified students from participating states may apply to attend programs at public universities in participating states that are not available in their home state's university system. North Carolina's participation for graduate programs provides a cost-effective means of offering educational access for North Carolina residents. North Carolinians are able to attend graduate programs that are not available at The University of North Carolina at reduced rates, and the State avoids the cost associated with the development of new academic programs.

(b) The Board of Governors of The University of North Carolina may continue participation in the Southern Regional Education Board's Academic Common Market at the graduate program level. The Board of Governors shall examine the graduate programs offered in The University of North Carolina System and select for participation only those graduate programs that are likely to be unique or are not commonly available in other Southern Regional Education Board states. Out-of-state tuition shall be waived for students who are residents of other Southern Regional Education Board states and who are participating in the Academic Common Market program. If accepted into The University of North Carolina graduate programs that are part of the Academic Common Market, these students shall pay in-State tuition and shall be treated for all purposes of The University of North Carolina as residents of North Carolina.

(c) Once a student is enrolled in The University of North Carolina System under the Academic Common Market program, the student shall be entitled to pay in-State tuition as long as the student is enrolled in that graduate program. (2005-276, s. 9.24; 2013-410, s. 36.5.)

§ 116-43.15. Use of college or university facilities by public school students pursuant to cooperative programs.

The existing facilities of any constituent institution of The University of North Carolina and the existing facilities of any private college or university licensed in accordance with G.S. 116-15 that comply with the North Carolina State Building Code and applicable local ordinances for those facilities may be used without modification for public school students in joint or cooperative programs such as middle or early college programs and dual enrollment programs. Designs for new facilities of any constituent institution of The University of North Carolina and new facilities of any private college or university licensed in accordance with G.S. 116-15 that comply with the North Carolina State Building Code and applicable local ordinances for those facilities may be used without modification for public school students in joint or cooperative programs such as middle or early college programs and dual enrollment programs.

For the purpose of establishing Use and Occupancy Classifications, these programs shall be considered "Business - Group B" in the same manner as other college and university uses. (2006-66, s. 8.11(b); 2006-221, s. 5; 2009-305, s. 5.)

§ 116-43.16. Small business counseling information.

Documents submitted to The University of North Carolina's Small Business and Technology Development Centers by an individual seeking business counseling or technical assistance and documents created by a Center to provide the individual with counseling and technical assistance are not public records as defined by G.S. 132-1. (2011-297, s. 2.)

§ 116-44. Repealed by Session Laws 1971, c. 1244, s. 1.

§ 116-44.1. Transferred to § 116-42 by Session Laws 1971, c. 1244, s. 11.

§ 116-44.2. Transferred to § 116-38 by Session Laws 1971, c. 1244, s. 7.

Part 6. Traffic and Parking.

§ 116-44.3. Definitions.

Unless the context clearly requires another meaning, the following words and phrases have the meanings indicated when used in this Part:

(1) "Board of trustees" and "constituent institution" have the meanings assigned in G.S. 116-2.

(2) "Campus" means that University property, without regard to location, which is used wholly or partly for the purposes of a particular constituent institution of the University of North Carolina.

(3) "University" means a constituent institution as defined in G.S. 116-2.

(4) "University property" means property that is owned or leased in whole or in part by the State of North Carolina and which is subject to the general management and control of the Board of Governors of the University of North Carolina. (1973, c. 495, s. 1.)

§ 116-44.4. Regulation of traffic and parking and registration of motor vehicles.

(a) Except as otherwise provided in this Part, all of the provisions of Chapter 20 of the General Statutes relating to the use of highways of the State and the operation of motor vehicles thereon are applicable to all streets, alleys, driveways, parking lots, and parking structures on University property. Nothing in this section modifies any rights of ownership or control of University property, now or hereafter vested in the Board of Governors of the University of North Carolina or the State of North Carolina.

(b) Each board of trustees may by ordinance prohibit, regulate, divert, control, and limit pedestrian or vehicular traffic and the parking of motor vehicles and other modes of conveyance on the campus. In fixing speed limits, the board of trustees is not subject to G.S. 20-141(f1) or (g2), but may fix any speed limit reasonable and safe under the circumstances as conclusively determined by the board of trustees. The board of trustees may not regulate traffic on streets open to the public as of right, except as specifically provided in this Part.

(c) Each board of trustees may by ordinance provide for the registration of motor vehicles maintained or operated on the campus by any student, faculty member, or employee of the University, and may fix fees for such registration. The ordinance may make it unlawful for any person to operate an unregistered motor vehicle on the campus when the vehicle is required by the ordinance to be registered.

(d)   Each board of trustees may by ordinance set aside parking lots and other parking facilities on the campus for use by students, faculty, and employees of the University and members of the general public attending schools, conferences, or meetings at the University, visiting or making use of any University facilities, or attending to official business with the University. The board of trustees may issue permits to park in these lots and garages and may charge a fee therefor. The board of trustees may also by ordinance make it unlawful for any person to park a motor vehicle in any lot or other parking facility without procuring the requisite permit and displaying it on the vehicle. No permit to park shall be issued until the student requesting the permit provides the name of the insurer, the policy number under which the student has financial responsibility, and the student certifies that the motor vehicle is insured at the levels set in G.S. 20-279.1(11) or higher. This subsection applies to motor vehicles that are registered in other states as well as motor vehicles that are registered in this State pursuant to Chapter 20 of the General Statutes.

(e)   Each board of trustees may by ordinance set aside spaces in designated parking areas or facilities in which motor vehicles may be parked for specified periods of time. To regulate parking in such spaces, the board of trustees may install a system of parking meters and make it unlawful for any person to park a motor vehicle in a metered space without activating the meter for the entire time that the vehicle is parked, up to the maximum length of time allowed for that space. The meters may be activated by coins of the United States. The board of trustees may also install automatic gates, employ attendants, and use any other device or procedure to control access to and collect the fees for using its parking areas and facilities.

(f)   The board of trustees may by ordinance provide for the issuance of stickers, decals, permits, or other indicia representing the registration status of vehicles or the eligibility of vehicles to park on the campus and may by ordinance prohibit the forgery, counterfeiting, unauthorized transfer, or unauthorized use of them.

(g)   Violation of an ordinance adopted under any portion of this Part is an infraction as defined in G.S. 14-3.1 and is punishable by a penalty of not more than fifty dollars ($50.00). An ordinance may provide that certain prohibited acts shall not be infractions and in such cases the provisions of subsection (h) may be used to enforce the ordinance.

(h) An ordinance adopted under any portion of this Part may provide that violation subjects the offender to a civil penalty. Penalties may be graduated according to the seriousness of the offense or the number of prior offenses by the person charged. Each board of trustees may establish procedures for the collection of these penalties and they may be enforced by civil action in the nature of debt. The board of trustees may also provide for appropriate administrative sanctions if an offender does not pay a validly due penalty or upon repeated offenses. Appropriate administrative sanctions include, but are not limited to, revocation of parking permits, termination of vehicle registration, and termination or suspension of enrollment in or employment by the University.

(i) An ordinance adopted under any portion of this Part may provide that any vehicle illegally parked may be removed to a storage area. Regardless of whether a constituent institution does its own removal and disposal of motor vehicles or contracts with another person to do so, the institution shall provide a hearing procedure for the owner. For purposes of this subsection, the definitions in G.S. 20-219.9 apply.

(1) If the institution operates in such a way that the person who tows the vehicle is responsible for collecting towing fees, all provisions of Article 7A, Chapter 20, apply.

(2) If the institution operates in such a way that it is responsible for collecting towing fees, it shall:

a. Provide by contract or ordinance for a schedule of reasonable towing fees,

b. Provide a procedure for a prompt fair hearing to contest the towing,

c. Provide for an appeal to district court from that hearing,

d. Authorize release of the vehicle at any time after towing by the posting of a bond or paying of the fees due, and

e. If the institution chooses to enforce its authority by sale of the vehicle, provide a sale procedure similar to that provided in G.S. 44A-4, 44A-5, and 44A-6, except that no hearing in addition to the probable cause hearing is required. If no one purchases the vehicle at the sale and if the value of the vehicle is less than the amount of the lien, the institution may destroy it.

(j) Evidence that a motor vehicle was found parked or unattended in violation of an ordinance of the board of trustees is prima facie evidence that the vehicle was parked by:

(1) The person holding a University parking permit for the vehicle, or

(2) If no University parking permit has been issued for the vehicle, the person in whose name the vehicle is registered with the University pursuant to subsection (c), or

(3) If no University parking permit has been issued for the vehicle and the vehicle is not registered with the University, the person in whose name it is registered with the North Carolina Division of Motor Vehicles or the corresponding agency of another state or nation.

The rule of evidence established by this subsection applies only in civil, criminal, or administrative actions or proceedings concerning violations of ordinances of the board of trustees. G.S. 20-162.1 does not apply to such actions or proceedings.

(k) Each board of trustees shall cause to be posted appropriate notice to the public of applicable traffic and parking restrictions.

(l) All ordinances adopted under this Part shall be recorded in the minutes of the board of trustees and copies thereof shall be filed in the offices of the President of the University of North Carolina and the Secretary of State. Each board of trustees shall provide for printing and distributing copies of its traffic and parking ordinances.

(m) All moneys received pursuant to this Part, except for the clear proceeds of all civil penalties collected pursuant to subsection (h) of this section, shall be placed in a trust account in each constituent institution, are appropriated, and may be used for any of the following purposes:

(1) To defray the cost of administering and enforcing ordinances adopted under this Part;

(2) To develop, maintain, and supervise parking areas and facilities;

(3) To provide bus service or other transportation systems and facilities, including payments to any public or private transportation system serving University students, faculty, or employees;

(4) As a pledge to secure revenue bonds for parking facilities issued under Article 21 of this Chapter;

(5) Other purposes related to parking, traffic, and transportation on the campus.

The clear proceeds of all civil penalties collected pursuant to subsection (h) of this section shall be remitted to the Civil Penalty and Forfeiture Fund in accordance with G.S. 115C-457.2. (1973, c. 495, s. 1; 1975, c. 716, s. 5; 1981 (Reg. Sess., 1982), c. 1239, s. 3; 1983, c. 420, s. 5; 1985, c. 764, s. 36; 2001-336, s. 1; 2005-276, s. 6.37(r); 2006-203, s. 51.)

Vision Books Order Form

Fax Orders:	1-980-299-5965
Phone Orders:	1-704-898-0770
E-mail Orders:	www.visionbooks.org
Mail Orders:	Vision Books, LLC P.O. Box 42406 Charlotte, NC 28215

Shipp To:
Name_____
Address_____
City_____State_____Zip_____
Phone_____Fax_____
Email_____@_____

Bill To: We can bill a third party on your behalf.
Name_____
Address_____
City_____State_____Zip_____
Phone____(_____)_____Fax_____
Email_____@_____

Pamphlet Number ($15.00 Each)	Qty	Total Cost
_____	_____	_____
_____	_____	_____
_____	_____	_____
_____	_____	_____
_____	_____	_____
_____	_____	_____
_____	_____	_____
Full Volume Set 1-92	92 Pamphlets	1,380.00

Free Shipping Shipping & Handling on Full Volume Orders
Add $1.00 Shipping & Handling per pamphlet $_____

Total Cost $_____

Thank you for your support. Management!

DID YOU ENJOY THIS BOOK?

Vision Books, LLC would like to hear from you! If you or someone you know has been fasely imprisoned, we would like to hear your story. If the 'North Carolina Criminal Law and Procedure' has had an effect in your life or if you have suggestions, we would like to hear from you. Send your letters to:

Vision Books, LLC
Attn: Staff Writers
P.O. Box 42406
Charlotte, NC 28215
Email: staff@visionbooks.org

Order Additional Copies:

Fax Orders:	1-980-299-5965
Phone Orders:	1-704-898-0770
E-mail Orders:	www.visionbooks.org
Mail Orders:	Vision Books, LLC P.O. Box 42406 Charlotte, NC 28215

www.ingramcontent.com/pod-product-compliance
Lightning Source LLC
Chambersburg PA
CBHW051624170526
45167CB00001B/56